Motherhood In and After Prison

The Impact of Maternal Incarceration

Lucy Baldwin

With a Foreword by Lady Edwina Grosvenor

≋ WATERSIDE PRESS

Motherhood In and After Prison
The Impact of Maternal Incarceration
Lucy Baldwin

ISBN 978-1-914603-20-4 (Paperback)
ISBN 978-1-914603-21-1 (Epub ebook)
ISBN 978-1-914603-22-8 (Adobe ebook)

Cover design © 2022 Waterside Press.

Main UK distributor Gardners Books, 1 Whittle Drive, Eastbourne, East Sussex, BN23 6QH. Tel: +44 (0)1323 521777; sales@gardners.com; www.gardners.com

North American distribution Ingram Book Company, One Ingram Blvd, La Vergne, TN 37086, USA. Tel: (+1) 615 793 5000; inquiry@ingramcontent.com

Cataloguing-In-Publication Data A catalogue record for this book can be obtained from the British Library.

Printed by Severn, Gloucestershire.

Ebook *Motherhood In and After Prison* is available as an ebook and also to subscribers via library models.

Published 2022 by
Waterside Press
Sherfield Gables
Sherfield-on-Loddon
Hook, Hampshire
United Kingdom RG27 0JG

Telephone +44(0)1256 882250
E-mail enquiries@watersidepress.co.uk
Online catalogue WatersidePress.co.uk

Contents

About the Author

Dr Lucy Baldwin is a Senior Lecturer in Criminology at De Montfort University. She is also a qualified social worker and probation officer with over 35 years' experience in social and criminal justice. Her work led her to research the entire spectrum of maternal imprisonment, and become a campaigner for the better treatment of women by the justice system. She is the author of the acclaimed *Mothering Justice: Working With Mothers in Criminal and Social Justice Settings* (Waterside Press, 2015), the first whole book in the UK to take motherhood and criminal justice as its focus.

Acknowledgements

First and foremost I would like to thank the mothers whose bravery and resilience led them to share the lived experiences described in this book. I carry every one of you in my heart. It felt a huge responsibility to host your narratives, but I hope to have done you proud. Equally, I hope *you* are proud of the positive changes that are already occurring in policy and practice surrounding maternal imprisonment, changes that are informed by my research for this book, but most importantly by your voices.

I would also like to thank my family and friends for their unending support of my all-encompassing passion for all things maternal imprisonment — your tolerance is appreciated. I include here Lady Edwina Grosvenor who kindly contributed the Foreword and who is a wonderful champion of and advocate for positive change concerning women.

Thank you also to Alex Gibson for the beautiful cover, and to Bryan Gibson at Waterside Press for his patience, uniqueness and unfailing ability to surprise.

Lucy Baldwin
May 2022

This book is dedicated to Beth and Emma, two mums who tragically died whilst I was writing it. They are not forgotten, and I would like this work to serve as a tribute not just to their memory but to that of all those who have lost their lives in or soon after prison.

The author of the Foreword

Lady Edwina Grosvenor is the Founder and Chair of One Small Thing, an organization which aims to redesign the justice system for women and their children through building Hope Street, a residential community and blueprint for change.

Foreword by Lady Edwina Grosvenor

Until the moment that the umbilical cord is cut, the unborn baby and the mother are one. They feed as one, they move as one, what the mother feels and experiences the unborn baby feels and experiences. Once the baby is born this pattern carries on. The baby and mother remain hugely dependent on one another, not just for joy and happiness but for their very survival. The feeling of being one remains long after that cord is cut.

The separation of a baby from its mother is the severance of this profound and powerful bond which equates to torture for both mother and baby. It should only be done in the most extreme of circumstances. The traumatic, predictable, lifelong consequences of such actions should not be underestimated. However, it is not only mothers of young babies who are criminalised and imprisoned. Mothers and grandmothers of children of all ages are impacted by maternal imprisonment.

The mothers in this contemporary and profoundly moving book powerfully and painfully describe the impact this 'profound hurt' has on them and their dependants, again a hurt that persists for many decades post-release. It puts the voice of the mother—and the role of mothering—and grandmothering—centre stage. A gift to practitioners it powerfully highlights the complexities of mothering, the different types and contexts of mothering, and the difficulties of mothering for some when they may have not been mothered well themselves. It provides an empathetic and humane framework within which policy and practice change can grow.

Lucy Baldwin illustrates why it is imperative that we action new policies to tackle the issue of separating mothers from their babies due to short prison sentences. Such actions have an astoundingly deleterious effect on not just the mother and her child, but it also wreaks havoc on family members and society as a whole for generations. The book powerfully argues that in order for the Criminal Justice System to be fully 'trauma-informed,' then our justice and practice responses to criminalised women must 'factor in' motherhood and maternal trauma. Policymakers must take heed. If they do not, then tragedies such as Beth's story highlighted in *Chapter 4* will continue to occur. Mothers will die and children will grow up motherless and be absorbed into the care system.

Fortuitously, it doesn't need to be this way. It is possible to think differently, to build differently, to act differently. The concept of the women's centre has proven what can be achieved. We must build on their model; we must sustain their success and the trail they have blazed. There has to be ways to capture what Lucy calls in the book the 'missed and lost opportunities' to support women, often in ways that could help them avoid criminalisation altogether — but most certainly to avoid imprisonment. A philosophical and architectural redesign of community justice for women is essential.

Mothers should be able to pay their dues to society, make amends without us having to penalise innocent babies which only serves to perpetuate multi-generational trauma. A redesigned, trauma-informed, gender specific, sustainable community justice system built at the local level is what is needed. One which is robust and effective, that invites confidence from the judiciary, social services and justice agencies. A system which addresses need, promotes recovery, which strengthens family relations, and allows humanity to flourish for the sake of the whole family and for the health of our local communities.

This timely book beautifully educates without judgement and is a must read for policymakers and practitioners alike, driving home a most critical message about the colossal and devastating impact of imprisoning mothers.

Preface

My purpose in writing this book is to offer fresh insights, knowledge and understanding concerning the profound, traumatic, and enduring impact of maternal imprisonment. The persistent pains of such imprisonment, especially beyond five years post-release from prison, is underexplored and to a large extent shielded from view. This is particularly so in so far as imprisonment affects mothers' identity and role, and the view others in society may adopt of such women. I hope this book will go some way towards rectifying this. It centres on the voices of 43 criminalised mothers through one-to-one interviews and letters concerning their experiences of prison and also pre and post-release.

Throughout the Mothers who took part will henceforth be designated using an upper-case M on the word 'Mother' to distinguish them from mothers in general or references to mothers in works by other authors or commentators. Their accounts were gathered as part of my own first-hand research undertaken from 2020 onwards.[1]

The Mothers described criminalised motherhood as a paradox; they experienced judgement, discrimination, and oppression alongside joy and hope. When motherhood was combined with criminalisation, the judgement and gaze that they experienced in a patriarchally constructed and influenced society were magnified. Navigating through the criminal justice system and especially through imprisonment was a painful experience for them, not least because of physical separation from their children, but additionally due to institutional thoughtlessness and lack of recognition concerning their maternal identity, maternal emotions, and maternal role. This occurred at every stage of the criminal justice process.

The impact was intergenerational and had implications for the Mothers' wellbeing, engagement in rehabilitation and desistance from crime. New knowledge is also demonstrated about the experiences of criminalised *grandmothers*, again especially in relation to their maternal identity and role.

---

1.   See Baldwin, L. (2021) in the *References and Bibliography*.

The scheme of the book

Part I: 'Overview' sets the scene by providing a whistle stop tour of the history of criminal justice for women and mothers. *Chapter 1* tells readers about the challenges I myself faced as a mother, how my interest in the subject of the book developed and more about my motivation for writing it. Next, in *Chapter 2*, 'Gendered Criminal Justice' I examine the historical context and legacy of maternal imprisonment within the broader context in which women are imprisoned today. *Chapter 3* highlights the significance of the ideals and ideas surrounding motherhood and the impact this continues to have on maternal identity and role. These chapters are key to understanding the context in which the Mothers in this book were imprisoned. This part then dedicates itself to the Mothers themselves, introducing them and their circumstances in *Chapter 4*.

Part II: 'Findings' hosts the Mothers' voices as they describe their criminalisation and imprisonment. These are represented in three sets of findings; separate chapters cover the Mothers' lives pre-prison (*Chapter 5*), revealing how long before entering prison they were disadvantaged and how multiple opportunities for support were missed and lost. Opportunities that had they been seized may have prevented the Mothers entering prison, or indeed becoming criminalised at all.

Chapters 6, 7 and *8* describe the Mothers' experiences whilst incarcerated. It reveals how the 'institutional thoughtlessness' of the prison interacted with the Mothers' pain to provide a hostile, frightening and sometimes life-threatening space where their maternal identities were disrupted and impacted.

Chapters 9, 10 and *11* reveal how the impact of maternal imprisonment endures long after mothers are released, sometimes for decades, sometimes forever. These chapters describe how the now 'tainted' mothers struggled to renegotiate their place in their families and children's lives. It reveals the enduring sense of trauma that haunted Mothers through their post-prison mothering, and sometimes grandmothering.

Finally *Part III*: 'Conclusions and Recommendations' reviews the evidence and describes the impact of my findings. It then sets out recommendations for policy and practice which if implemented would, I believe, significantly improve outcomes for imprisoned mothers, their children, and in the case of imprisoned grandmothers their grandchildren as well.

As with *Mothering Justice*, the book is interspersed using the same 'Pause for Thought' device of that book, where you the reader are asked to reflect on what I have written, examine your own thoughts and feelings, and perhaps think about what you may have learned that can inform your professional practice or personal understanding.

The book concludes with recommendations for research, policy and practice that would contribute to understanding and challenging the social, political and criminal justice context of mothers who break the law.

If implemented, the matricentric-feminist criminological ideas that I set out in *Part III* would I believe lead to fewer mothers being imprisoned and better outcomes for criminalised mothers, which in turn would facilitate better outcomes for children and society.

Lucy Baldwin

June 2022

List of abbreviations

BAME — Black and minority ethnic
CJS — Criminal justice system
CRL — Childcare resettlement leave
FEW — Family engagement worker
GM — Grandmother
HMIP — Her Majesty's Inspectorate of Prisons
HMIPP — Her Majesty's Inspectorate of Prisons and Probation
HMPS — Her Majesty's Prison Service
LA — Local authority
MBU — Mother and baby unit
MF — Matricentric feminism
MoJ — Ministry of Justice
NOMS — National Offender Management Service
PACT — Prison Advice and Care Trust
PRT — Prison Reform Trust
PSI — Prison Service Instruction
PSO — Prison Service Order
PSR — Pre-sentence report
ROTL — Release on temporary license
TR — Transforming Rehabilitation
UNCRC — United Nations Convention on the Rights of the Child

PART I
OVERVIEW

CHAPTER 1

Introduction

'In there [prison] I was not a mother, they stripped that from
me, I was just a prisoner, not someone's mum, now I'm out I
don't really know what I am, half a mother, half a failure. I don't
think I'll ever feel like a good mum again.' (Queenie)

When I edited *Mothering Justice*[1] it was I believe the first whole book in
the UK to take *motherhood and criminal justice* as its focus. Since then,
thankfully, the landscape has changed somewhat and there is much more
interests in maternal and female imprisonment. Tragically, not least
because in the last two years two babies have been born dead in prison
cells. Perhaps even more tragically the babies were born to mothers whose
needs would have been far more effectively met in the community.

This book is based on my own direct research with 43 Mothers[2] who
were living in and/or surviving after prison.[3] My aims were to explore
the experiences of criminalised mothers and to facilitate mothers in
revealing the enduring impact maternal imprisonment had on their
maternal identity and maternal role. My motivation for wanting to do
this was rooted in my own life experiences and my previous practice as a
social worker and as a probation officer. The following poem[4] was given
to me by a mother in prison when I was in the latter role. It powerfully
reveals the pain of incarcerated motherhood—on both sides of the bars.

---

1. Baldwin, L. (2015).
2. See the explanation concerning Mothers (upper case M) in the *Preface*.
3. See Baldwin, L. (2021).
4. One of a collection in Baldwin, L., Raikes, B. (2019), *Seen & Heard: 100 Poems by Parents and Children Affected by Imprisonment*, Waterside Press.

Drifting Away

I was taken without warning, no time to prepare me, to prepare you.
Wrenched screaming from court, you not yet knowing, blissfully unaware.
You're staying with friends, taken in, in pity, the outsider.
We connect after days of mutual torture, fast
words, anger, recrimination, loss,
Pain
You hate me, I love you. A few short months,
I'm sorry, driven by desperation.
Every day I heard your pain, you were adrift,
untethered, a boat with no anchor.
Drifting further away
The day came and went, no call, no you, where were
you, then the late-night knock on my door
You were 'missing,' they didn't want to worry me, they found you.
In the woods. You left a note, it was too much, you are sorry. You felt lost.
You drifted away.
I'm still here. Now I'm lost, I'm drifting too. I never want to leave.
I don't want to live in the world outside, not without you.
But I will, I owe you … to live my life and yours — and to live it well.
No more drifting, but anchors, a mooring, a safe crossing
In your Honour

Written by Danielle (a mother in prison)

Danielle gave me the poem and asked me to share it with those in power, 'to make them see the harm it causes.' She was in prison for a first and minor offence committed in poverty, and after a lifetime of abuse. Her 13-year-old son, left outside with Danielle's abusive partner, could not cope without her. To him, the 'few short months' his mother was to be imprisoned felt like a lifetime, an expanse in front of him that seemed unsurvivable without her. So he took his own life, alone in the woods still only 13. Imagine having to deal with that as a child. Imagine having to deal with that as his mother — still in prison, alone with her thoughts and her self-blame, trying to navigate through the unbearable grief that the loss of a child brings. It is a miracle that Danielle survived. But survive she did. Danielle did go on to have another child, a girl and she has never returned to prison. Not because prison 'worked' for her but because she did what she promised her son, she lived her life well. After gaining support from a women's centre, leaving her abusive ex-partner and accessing therapy, she lived her life for the both of them and wanted to make it the best life possible.

Danielle's story is important on so many levels, not least because it reveals the harm of maternal imprisonment alongside the pain of separation from children and just how deeply that experience is felt by both. Her lived experience illustrates the broader, societal challenges many criminalised women face, such as experiences of abuse, and poverty—and importantly, how they intertwine to impact on women and their children. Understanding her poem provides a context in which women's 'offending' occurs (and can cease). Additionally and importantly, it also reveals the strength and resilience of women, of mothers; who against all odds survive and continue to mother through adversity.

This book, like others (see, e.g. Lockwood, 2020; Minson, 2020; Masson, 2019; Booth 2020), highlights women's 'vulnerabilities' and the challenges women face, alongside exploring challenges women have often lived through before they become criminalised. However, it is equally important to show that the women, the Mothers in this book are *more* than their vulnerabilities. The reality is that most women survive prison (though not all), equally most women have already survived so much before prison and will survive after prison. However, all too often women's survival is testament to their *own* determination, resilience and hope, rather than a reflection on the structures and systems designed to 'support' women—but which instead, and all too often, fail them.

Reflecting Motherhood

As I outlined in *Mothering Justice*, like many women I hold motherhood dear to my heart. I was lucky that, even at 16 years of age, it was the making of me. I have said before that becoming a mother saved my life.

I was a young teenage mother mothering in a society that was quick to judge me, a society where my lived experiences of abuse, trauma and poverty rendered me 'risky.' Despite none of those circumstances being of my own making. Nonetheless, I was lucky enough to be supported by *some* professionals rather than mistrusted by them all. I was given support and encouraged in a belief I could make my life better (and that of my children), as opposed to having my choices and opportunities taken from me. Yet I have always had a 'there but the grace of god' attitude about how my life turned-out the way it did.

With my life history I was perhaps more 'likely' to be the subject of this book than its author. I see myself in some of the Mothers I have worked and researched with, and I want to 'pay it forward' in terms of giving something back, but I am also hoping that I can help motivate other mothers to challenge negative beliefs and the external limits placed on them (and internal ones too). Thus, I hope, in writing this book, that I can somehow, in some small way, encourage researchers, activists and practitioners to always centre the voices of women and mothers, to facilitate empowerment in a way that supports and encourages women/ mothers to be their best self.

Sometimes if others fight for and believe in us it gives us the message that we are worth it, and so then we will be more willing and able to fight for ourselves. But if all a person encounters is judgement, apathy and neglect, then they may never 'receive' the message that they have any worth or hope or contribution to make to society.

My own maternal identity
From the second I knew I was pregnant (at 16), I felt like I had a purpose and a use (other than being someone's punching bag or object of sexual abuse, which I had previously felt was my role in life). I knew without question I would love my child devotedly. Although not planned for, I was desperate to have my baby. I felt a baby would know no better than to love me warts and all. It is not dramatic to say that, without question, becoming pregnant at that point saved my life. I have no doubt that, without my baby, I would have taken the learning from my previous suicide attempt and successfully taken my life at a not-too-distant point.

Before him, Christopher, my life felt nothing, was nothing; with him I was someone's mum, I was not worthless—well at least not to him. Without realising it then, I saw motherhood as a source of power, freedom and agency, rather than a site of oppression as purported by some areas of radical feminism (see, e.g. Rich, 1995). Rooted in my childhood experiences and despite my own experience of being mothered, I had a clear mothering script or narrative regarding good and bad mothering. I was determined to mother well, which to me at that time meant, above all else, to love my children devotedly and to put them first, always.

Early in my research I realised that I was perhaps empathising with the Mothers who felt the pain of separation from their children more than I did with Mothers who seemed to take the separation 'in their stride.' I was aware that I was, whether I liked it or not, experiencing feelings of judgement. Reflecting on this took up a considerable amount of time and emotional energy and triggered feelings of guilt. However, not only did my reaction trouble me for my own self-assessment, but it also reiterated to me just how susceptible all mothers are to scrutiny and judgement from the wider world, especially mothers who are deemed not be living up to or conforming to the ideals of 'good motherhood.' If I, as a huge advocate for mothers, a social worker trained in anti-oppressive practice, educated and feminist, could judge mothers this way, then what hope was there that others would not? Thus, the interviews with the Mothers reiterated to me that not only did they accept traditional models of motherhood, but that so did I, and arguably so do most of us.

It seems most mothers, to a greater or lesser extent absorb traditional motherhood values, emotions, and roles, and the subsequent pressure this exerts. I am 'educated' I resist patriarchal-based assumptions and restrictions about mothers and mothering, I consider myself a feminist. Yet I, too, on many levels have accepted these norms, striving to be a good mother and to mother well within a culturally and socially constructed norm. I call it the invisible 'Mothers' Code of Conduct.' I personally see motherhood as a source of power, liberation, and unity, but I appreciate that others see motherhood as oppressed and oppressive.

Undoubtedly influenced by patriarchal and motherhood ideology, I have huge guilt that I have not always been able to provide the stable family life I would have wished for my children, at least in the traditional sense. I have spent most of their childhoods as a single parent and we have, as a family, experienced significant trauma and upheaval, including the suicide of my two sons' father.

Essentially, at 18, I was a single parent of a very young baby and an 18-month-old toddler. I was desperate, as a mother, to ensure that my children would leave the poverty and benefits-reliant existence we found ourselves in, so I made the decision that I needed an education so that I could have a *career* and not *just a job*. I felt that as a 'good mother' I needed to be my children's provider and role model. This was important to me as even though my boys were tiny I wanted to be the best I could be to maximise the chances of them being proud of me. I remember feeling that was desperately important.

Another hugely motivating factor was that I wanted to challenge the perceptions of others that I would inevitably fail — not just people in my small world, but also more generally. In the mid-1980s and early-1990s, Tory Britain was very much against the 'scourge of the single mother'; whom at that time Margaret Thatcher labelled the cause of teen criminality, evidence of loose morals, and as being responsible for the breakdown of traditional family values (see e.g. Atkinson et al, 1998).[5] This broad-based societal and media attack on young single mothers had a profound impact on me and my self-worth. I felt then, and to some extent still feel, the need to justify and prove myself, perhaps especially in relation to motherhood. However, importantly, my cumulative experiences, the seeds of what would later become my commitment to the pursuit of social justice, and a realisation that when mothers are disadvantaged and judged there are deep implications for her and her children, took root. Such are the roots of my feminist and matricentric principles and beliefs and as such they contribute to and underpin this book.

With the benefit of education and hindsight, I recognise the influence of patriarchal and Victorian values which have long influenced perceptions of how women and girls, particularly mothers, should and should not behave or 'be.' I now recognise this as being *stigmatised*. At

---

5.   'Discussion of Perceptions of Single Mothers': http://eprints.whiterose.ac.uk/88198/1/ Happy%20Families.pdf

the time I just felt exposed, self-conscious and judged. Similarities can be drawn with criminalised mothers who also describe such feelings, who are labelled, and who experience the judgemental attitudes accompanying stigma and negative media portrayal of mothers who break the law.

'Good motherhood' and positive role models

Thus, motherhood was my motivation to succeed, but it was education that gave me the passport. I became educated by luck. As previously described in my book *Mothering Justice,* a vicar and a health visitor saw potential in me and encouraged me to register for A-Levels, also paying for a year of childcare. I completed those qualifications within a year (as opposed to the normal two-year syllabus) so I did not get wonderful grades but achieved enough to access university. I was lucky. Many if not most of the mothers who enter prison are not so lucky. They did not have that different pathway presented to or available to them. For me it was different and although the demons of my past experiences followed me into adulthood, affecting my choices and relationships both negatively and positively, I have mostly lived a relatively stable and mostly safe life. Certainly I have been able to use my resilience to move forwards — but purely because I had options, positive, healthy friends and some professional support.

In relation to women I have worked with over the years, and certainly the Mothers in this book, I have always felt it is only due to good luck, sometimes good judgement, and other times sheer determination, that I ended up on a different trajectory from the women in my research. Addiction is a feature in many of the lives of women in the criminal justice system and I genuinely consider myself fortunate that my only addiction was not illegal (cake!) and that my coping strategies were essentially private and inward facing; facilitating secrecy and — to some extent — deception and ill-health, but not criminality. My past is part of what drives me, and definitely why I became a social worker and a probation officer before becoming an 'academic' in 2004.

In addition to the commonalities and relevance of my lived experience I became a grandmother and a step-grandmother whilst preparing this book. This new role has had a significant impact on me and on what I was finding out. My newfound grandmotherly duties and role in supporting my daughter and son via childcare, and in supporting my sons and daughter through their journeys into parenthood, contributed to my understanding of the significant role grandmothers play in the role of the Mothers. For example, my specific inclusion of/appreciation for the grandmother perspective (either as carers when their own adult offspring are imprisoned, or as criminalised grandmothers) was probably triggered by my new grandmother status. I also asked questions about maternal relationships with grandparents that I might not otherwise have thought to ask. I am not certain I would have explored this as fully had I not become a grandmother right at the start of my research — and for that I am thankful as grandmothers' voices are also represented in this book when elsewhere grandmothers in prison have often remained invisible and unheard. Becoming a grandmother also reiterated to me that motherhood never ends — whether our children are young, teenagers, adults, no longer in our care, or in fact no longer living, we still regard ourselves as mothers. We feel emotions *as mothers* and view the world through *the lens of a mother.*

The researcher/researched relationship

Letherby (2004) and Oakley (2016) argue that the presence of the 'personal' story of any researcher is essential to accurately viewing, and ergo understanding, the research itself. Feminist research, particularly research with women, values the presence and transparency of the researcher and the acknowledgment that the research relationship, i.e. researcher/participant, is relevant to the content of that research in terms of purpose, method, value, results. As an academic and a researcher, I appreciate the significance of what Olsen describes as an 'acute awareness' (2011: 135) of how my own background can shape the research experience, and affect research relationships with participants, a critical component of feminist research. My awareness of the similarity between myself and the Mothers who underpin this book is acute. Not only because of my abusive past, my working-class background, but also, and significantly because I once stole food (bread and baked beans) to feed my children when I had lost my last five pound note the day before I was due to receive my child benefit the following day. I am painfully aware of the potential consequences had I been caught and am forever grateful that I was not, but I still remember deep feelings of failure and shame that I 'had to resort' to theft to feed my children.

Although in this book I do not go as far as Letherby (1997) and involve or 'weave' my own autobiographical account directly into my interviews or analysis, I do acknowledge that my representation of the Mothers' stories is filtered through my own biographical lens. As Cotterill and Letherby suggest

> 'As feminist researchers studying women's lives, we take their autobiographies and become their biographers [...] Thus, their lives are filtered through us and the filtered stories of our lives are present, (whether we admit it or not) in our written accounts.' (Letherby, 2003: 142)

Burgess Procter (2014: 125) identifies the importance of a non-hierarchical relationship with participants in feminist research, endorsing a compassionate stance which emphasises care, connectedness and collaboration. She states that this is '*especially* true of feminist research involving abused women and survivors of other forms of victimisation,' which many of the Mothers were. I believe, to an extent, my background and motherhood provided me with knowledge that assisted me in establishing good relationships with the Mothers, and in understanding their experiences. It also influenced how the Mothers related to me; enabling them to feel comfortable, facilitating open, honest and deep conversations.

All the Mothers asked me if I was a mother if I had not already revealed it, mostly during our informal 'warming-up' conversations prior to the interviews and before the recorder was switched on. Although always mindful of not oversharing and shifting the focus to myself, I did not shy away from speaking about my children. This often led to Mothers drawing attention to our shared role as mothers when speaking about their experiences: 'Well you know what I mean don't you? As a mother I mean ... you can imagine, can't you?' (Dee); '... Can you imagine not seeing your granddaughter straightaway ... well I know you can put yourself in my shoes, can't you?' (Ursula); or 'A man wouldn't get the pain, but

I bet you know what I mean … its different for us Mothers isn't it? We feel it different, don't we? (Cynthia). This synergy was important to the Mothers and to my writing. Cooper and Rogers argue that mothering as an 'insider role' during research is a 'powerful and reflexive position' and as such is especially valuable in qualitative research such as this (2014: 2).

The similarity in our background, but specifically our shared mothering identity, made me more relatable, ergo trustworthy and safe, which ensured the Mothers were comfortable and open in our interviews. In short, me being a mother was something that 'mattered' to this research, and indeed to the Mothers themselves.

Echoing previous research (Cooper and Rogers, 2015), the interviews themselves often became an 'interactive process,' where both me and the Mothers 'gained' something. Mothers often stated that the interview had a profound effect on them and, despite being only one meeting, they often said they felt they 'knew' me, 'trusted' me and, importantly, that I could relate to them, and them to me. Some described the interview as 'cathartic,' and it was the 'first' time they had been asked about their criminal justice experiences *as mothers,* which for some meant it was the first time they were able to acknowledge and appreciate their maternal pain.

I am not suggesting that having a shared background, especially related to past abuse, is essential to feminist research. I do feel that my own background assisted me to be not only an effective feminist researcher but, importantly, to be 'trauma-informed'[6] in my approach. However, equally as relevant and important to recognise and acknowledge was the fact that I am no longer in my original circumstances. Whatever similarities I may have shared with my participants in my past, many aspects of my present are very different from most of my participants. I no longer live in poverty. I have a relatively professional, apparently successful career. Although not affluent, I am relatively comfortable and very grateful for

---

6. Trauma-informed is a way of working sensitively with people who have experienced abuse being mindful of words, phrases and ways of being that may trigger harms related to experiences in someone's past and, e.g. re-awaken anxiety, fear, worries, oppression, even if unintentionally. The need for practitioners, volunteers, etc. to be fully trauma-informed has a growing number of adherents committed to this cause. See, e.g. the networking 'hub' established by Lisa Cherry: www.lisacherry.co.uk/the-trauma-informed-community-hub

that. I am finally in a safe and loving relationship and enjoy good relationships with all my children and grandchildren. That is not to say I do not bear the scars physically and mentally of a damaged past. I consider myself to be a hugely imperfect person and remain haunted by many ghosts of my past.

As do all researchers, I brought my experiences and their consequences with me into this book, and I have had to engage with those experiences (previously put to the back of my mind) to be fully reflexive. In turn, it was important to ensure that, as far as possible, my own experiences and beliefs did not unconsciously influence or shape my interviews, attitudes or analysis (understanding) — and that, if it did, I would be able to recognise and acknowledge this.

I felt my 'new' position and increased agency fuelled my sense of responsibility and activism, leading to me becoming very involved in the active pursuit of positive change and publication — not borne out of self-gain or a feeling of superiority but a genuine passion and desire for positive change. Importantly to me, my activism is in keeping with feminist research methodology and reflects my matricentric and feminist stance. The empowerment of others is an important part of all feminist research. Again, in line with feminist action research principles although perhaps not as common as it ought to be.

Being 'there' as a mother

For so many women motherhood intersects with, and sometimes competes with, our working lives. Whilst 'progress,' and feminism though absolutely necessary and invaluable, have in some ways resulted in mothers feeling like they have simply 'more to do.' The pressures of motherhood are vast, we are expected to be good mothers, good role models — basically good everything! Many mothers are mothering full-time and working full-time — which of course means they consider themselves jugglers and plate spinners! This was never more apparent to me than when writing, working full-time, mothering, and grandmothering full-time, and trying to be an activist and champion of change part-time. The long held and widely accepted beliefs around 'good' motherhood collided with the demands of, and desire, to do well in my other life roles. The demands of work, family, childcare and studying often created conflicting feelings regarding my motherhood. I was sometimes consumed with guilt and regret that I was not making enough time for my children and grandchildren yet remained committed to my task. Having to tell my (adult) children and grandchildren I was 'busy' triggered these feelings of maternal guilt, which were compounded by the empathic guilt I felt because I 'could' see/speak to my children if I 'wanted' to — but mothers in prison do not always have that luxury. This reinforced to me Enos' (2001) concept of 'doing' mothering as opposed to simply 'being' a mother. Again, this reflection powerfully interacted with my writing by me recognising that *availability* is key to *my* mothering, leading me to question whether availability is key to mothering in general and ultimately to the question 'How available are/can mothers be in prison?' This made me very aware, not only of the importance of 'being there' for children, but also that it is not just dependent children (usually the focus of policy and practice developments) who need their prison mothers. Older children and ergo older mothers need that connection too.

The widely held ideals and ideas around motherhood, particularly around 'good' motherhood also made me think about how challenging it is to mother in circumstances that are not fully conducive to positive mothering. For example, how easy is it to mother in poverty, in a violent relationship, through addiction, following trauma? — or indeed and like many mothers in prison are doing/have done, *through all of this.* The answer is it isn't easy at all, it is incredibly challenging and yet there is an expectation that despite the challenges or circle of circumstances mothers are mothering in, they will survive, they will mother well and their children will thrive, because that's what mothers do!

Yet all too often mothers are mothering through these circumstances with little support — and with an incredible amount of judgement about 'their failings.' *Mothering Justice*, in the opening chapter, highlighted how mothers like Fiona Anderson, or in later chapters Jael Mullings and Fiona Pilkington, are often fearful of asking for help, fearful of inviting unwelcome surveillance and ultimately of losing their children (this is revisited and discussed through the voices of the Mothers in forthcoming chapters of this book). As previously highlighted in that book, and sadly here too, the Mothers describe how support was not easy to access in any case, and when support came it was often not in the form women wanted or needed—led instead by what the systems around them felt they needed or had available.

This book hosts the Mothers' voices to describe how hard it was for them to mother through disadvantage, what it felt like to be mothers mothering in a circle of circumstances they felt it impossible to escape from. The Mothers came from a range of backgrounds, crossed multiple ethnicities and ages, but motherhood and maternal emotions were the threads that bound them all together. The Mothers powerfully, and often painfully, described what it felt like to be separated from their children because of imprisonment, or for some to lose their children completely. The Mothers described the 'invisible' mothering that they undertook from behind bars, or the invisibility of being a mother without her children, especially difficult for those Mothers whose children would not be returning to them. The Mothers describe the pain and consequences of the multiple missed and lost opportunities to support them long before they entered the prison space.

CHAPTER 2

Gendered Criminal Justice

'The conduct of the female sex more deeply affects the wellbeing of the community. A bad woman inflicts more moral injury to society than a bad man.' (Hill, 1864: 134, cited in Zedner, 1991)

This chapter concerns the legacy and context of the imprisonment of women (including mothers and grandmothers) and looks at the need for a gendered response. Historically, the treatment of female law breakers in the UK has reflected their position within wider society. This was rooted in beliefs that women were subordinate to, or 'less than' men. Early penal responses to imprisonable women were heavily influenced by reformers such as John Howard, Jeremy Bentham and Elizabeth Fry, and often centred around the 'saving of souls' and a 'return to feminine virtue.' As reformers, they believed in better conditions and responses for *all* criminals, but it was felt that women could be 'saved' or 'corrected,' rather than just punished.

Benevolent ideology informed how women who fell foul of the law were responded to, with many being 'supported' to return, as 'reformed,' to the roles of their gender and the rules of 'civilised' society. If they could not be reformed then there existed a much more 'moral' response to female law breakers: all convicts were perceived as sinners, but women were additionally seen as depraved, deviant, wanton and dangerous.

Thus historically, criminalised women have been defined, evaluated and punished in terms of traditional and cultural attitudes, which became reflected in law. Law, which was written *by* men, essentially *for* men; often designed to protect the traditional family and community, and to 'control women.' It has been suggested that there exists a universal fear of the 'non-conforming woman,' arguing that a criminal woman is the epitome of this.

Notwithstanding criminality, women more broadly were expected to conform and act within their gender role, and within the rules of society, especially motherhood. Whilst feminism does not assume that all men and all women are homogenous or are affected in the same ways by inequality and power differentials, feminism maintains that gender is embedded in all processes of everyday life, in all social interactions and social institutions. In short, the social world is a gendered world.

Pause for Thought

Think about our current criminal justice system and consider the legacy a patriarchal society has had on our laws. See the examples around abortion and prostitution in *Chapter 5* of *Mothering Justice*. Think about the suffragettes — criminalised for advocating and fighting for a right men were able to take for granted, the same for education or divorce or owning property. Additional more recent examples being the anomalous point of law that saw women who were deemed to be exchanging sex for payment (i.e. soliciting) being prosecuted for the offence, but not the men (and it is most often men) involved in the very same exchange. This unequal position was only resolved relatively recently by the Sexual Offences Act of 1985, when persistent kerb crawling became an offence (although it was arguably difficult to enforce until the caveat 'persistent' was removed in 2010). Do you think justice and punishment are equal?

Many feminist scholars purport that gender is essentially socially (as opposed to biologically) created, reproduced and maintained (Renzetti, 2013). It is suggested that the norms of feminine and masculine ideology and associations are generated within a social and structural context in which attitudes, beliefs and behaviours are prescribed. These scripts and prescriptions are then embedded into the 'institutions of society,' such as the family, religion, education, employment, economy and government, thus forming a gendered structure of society (ibid: 8). Feminists suggest that these differentials in a gendered society are not equally valued, neither do men and women have equal access to the rewards or resources of society, defining this differential association as 'sexism.' Sexism thus manifests as discrimination on both interpersonal and institutional/structural levels (micro/macro) and permeates all systems, including the CJS.

Throughout history women have been criminalised and punished, even imprisoned, for things their male counterparts can take for granted even as a right, suffrage being the most obvious. Such traditional and oppressive ideology surrounding women, and especially criminal or 'deviant' women, has had an enduring influence on women's experiences of the CJS. Interestingly, it has resulted in the paradoxical arguments in contemporary criminology that women are treated both more and less harshly than their male counterparts. The 'Chivalry Hypothesis' (i.e. treating women more leniently than men because they are women) suggests that, because women are seen as the weaker sex and as prone to irrational decision-making—often under duress, or under the influence of substances—they are responded to more leniently by law enforcers and the courts (Pollak, 1950). Some studies have offered support for this hypothesis (Daly and Bordt, 1995; Jeffries, 2002), whereas others have challenged this view, arguing that the opposite is true and that women are in fact treated more harshly than men (Edwards, 1984; Eaton, 1986). Evidence has suggested that women who are deemed to be 'less attractive,' from a BAME background, who are violent, or perceived as 'bad' mothers are treated more harshly. Carlen (2002) argued that there is no solid consistent statistical evidence to support either argument, further suggesting that, even if there was, 'such evidence would be difficult to compute because of the difficulties of untangling gender criteria from others, such as those relating to racism and class' (2002: 7).

Contemporary feminist criminologists have asserted that, in either instance, chivalry or harsher responses are not metered out equally or consistently to all female offenders. Motherhood is one variable which affects outcomes for women; the layered identities of women (in terms of race, class, status, motherhood) bear a significant relationship to their experiences within the CJS. Criminal mothers have long been described as 'deviants,' perceived as acting outside of gender norms and their role as mothers. Baldwin (2015) and Clarke and Chadwick (2018) argue that the legacy of such beliefs is still evident, and in attitudes to women who break the law per se, again especially so for those women who are also mothers. Ultimately, not a great deal has changed for women in the CJS: they are still measured against longstanding ideas and ideals of gender norms and femininity, rendering them doubly or even triply deviant.

It is often argued that prison is more damaging to women than it is to men and that the impact on families greater, not least because women are most often the primary carer for their children. Feminist criminologists have argued that women enter prison already damaged and disadvantaged from an unequal position in both wider society and in the CJS itself. Women then become additionally challenged and disadvantaged because they have entered a system that was essentially created by men and designed around the needs of male prisoners (see, e.g. Carlen, 1983; McIvor, 2004).

Moore and Scraton argue that prison simply reinforces the cultural violence and powerlessness, physically and metaphorically, that women are subjected to in society generally. They examine the gendered 'pains of imprisonment' and further suggest that:

> 'In prison, the imposition of discipline and control of women's bodies, their identities and their associations developed a more stark manifestation of the subjugation of women beyond the walls.' (2014: 27)

Contemporary Context and Landscape in the UK

The Corston Report (2007) was widely accepted across the political spectrum and should have been used both as a framework and a platform from which to launch fundamental long-lasting change for criminalised women. Feminist criminologists, and indeed Baroness Corston herself, suggests that the reason the report did not spark the change intended is because women remain a minority in terms of the overall prison population and because the system is male orientated in design and focus. She argued that women often leave prison with additional challenges and in a 'worse position' than before they entered it.

Most feminist prison researchers conclude that prison is not the most effective way to rehabilitate criminalised women. Women commit far fewer crimes than men (PRT, 2020) and, as highlighted in my Introduction, women make up only five per cent of the overall prison population.[1] As it stands the female prison population has more than doubled since 1995, in more recent years it has stubbornly remained around the 4,000 mark (although reduced marginally during the 2020 pandemic). The rise in the female prison population does not appear to relate to a significant rise in crimes by women, but instead to a more punitive neo-liberal socio-political turn which has influenced legislative changes and sentencing patterns.

Short prison sentences disproportionately affect women whose crimes are predominantly low risk and non-violent, and they are oftentimes from an ethnic minority background. The use of short prison sentences for women has attracted widespread criticism, not least because of the significant impact they have on mothers and children. Yet they continue to be used extensively.

Female imprisonment has been the focus of discussion and debate at Government and policy level, informed by multiple reviews and reports which have made recommendations for positive change with regard to the treatment of female offenders. The 2021 announcement that the Ministry of Justice intends to build 500 new prison spaces for women, without a matched closure of unacceptable, inadequate and unnecessary closed prison spaces, has been met with despair and derision by campaigners, academics and criminalised women alike. Furthermore, despite the publication of reports such as The Female Offender Strategy (2018), the female-focussed Farmer Review (2019), and the Joint Human Rights Inquiry Report into Maternal Imprisonment (2019) highlighting the need for community-based responses for criminalised women, there is little indication of forthcoming significant change.

Highlighting missed opportunities for reform, all of the aforementioned, reports stopped short of calling for a radical overhaul of the sentencing framework, instead reiterating the value of an independent

---

1. Bromley Briefings. This fact file collates MOJ information and statistics on the CJS annually on behalf of the Prison Reform Trust;: http://www.prisonreformtrust.org.uk/Publications/Factfile

judiciary; although they did make recommendations for additional guidance regarding the sentencing of women and especially of mothers.

Sentencers are already 'guided' by recommendations from the Human Rights Act 1998 and by Article 8 of the European Convention on Human Rights and United Nations Bangkok Rules,[2] which request that sentencers undertake a 'balancing exercise' to measure the significant harms of prison to women and their children against the necessity of a custodial sentence. Yet, as demonstrated by previous research like that of Epstein (2012) and Minson (2014; 2020), such guidelines are readily and frequently ignored. There remains a real possibility that in the future all of the valuable insights and recommendations I have mentioned here will be hailed as evidence of what *should* happen, but also of what *has not* happened. It is difficult to reach any other conclusions than that the influences of a patriarchally-focussed and structured government and CJS are key reasons why women and their needs remain sidelined.

The disadvantages that all women in the CJS face are compounded for women from ethnic minorities, who make up a disproportionately significant group of the prison population.[3] Motz et al (2020) identified that BAME women were 25 per cent more likely to receive a custodial sentence, meaning that BAME mothers are also disproportionately represented within the prison population. This is especially significant because over half of black families in the UK are headed by single parent mothers (as opposed to less than one quarter of white, and less than one tenth of Asian families). The consequences of this for BAME children is under explored and worthy of urgent attention. As an indicator of scale, former minister-of-state David Lammy found that for every white woman sentenced to prison for a drugs offence, 227 black women were imprisoned for the same offence.[4] Clearly, this requires further investigation and examination.

---

2. The UN Rules for the Treatment of Women Prisoners and Non-custodial Measures for Women Offenders adopted by the UN General Assembly in December 2010 which responded to a long-standing lack of standards re the specific characteristics and needs of women offenders/prisoners.
3. Bromley Briefings.
4. The Lammy Review (2017), David Lammy: https://womeninprison.org.uk/news/double-disdvantage

Currently (2022) 12 women's prisons in England accommodate around 4,000 women at any one time. Six mother and baby units (MBUs) have the capacity to hold 66 babies and 54 mothers.[5] Accounting for five per cent of the overall prison population in the UK, around 9,000 women are received into custody annually (PRT Bromley Briefings, 2019). Research suggests that 66 per cent of those will be mothers of children under 16 years (Caddle and Crisp, 1997; PRT, 2015), meaning that an estimated 17,000 children are separated from their mothers annually, either via remands in custody or sentences of imprisonment (Kincaid et al, 2019). It is important to emphasise that this figure does not include mothers of older children (i.e. over 18 years). Therefore, there is currently no accurate figure representing the *actual* number of mothers held in custody.

Grandmothers and mothers of older children do not feature anywhere in the statistics; if included this 'invisible' population would place the actual number of mothers in custody much higher, nearer to 80 per cent (Minson et al, 2015; Baldwin, 2015). Of the children left behind as a result of maternal imprisonment, only five per cent remain in their own homes; 14 per cent are taken directly into the care of the local authority (LA), and the fate of the remaining 81 per cent is mixed. Some children are cared for by relatives (mainly their grandmothers), others are cared for by their fathers (nine per cent), and the remainder are displaced into the care of other family members and carers (Caddle and Crisp, 1997;[6] Minson et al., 2017; Beresford, 2018). Significantly, these figures originate from the last largescale study undertaken by Caddle and Crisp over 20 years ago.

Currently, there remains no officially recorded data concerning the numbers of children affected by parental/maternal incarceration and the circumstances of their care. However, there are plans for this to change.[7] What *can* be taken from the available statistics is that *most* of the UK

---

5. Including twins, hence the difference in number.
6. Caddle and Crisp's study is over 20 years old, but is the only comprehensive one available in the UK at this time, and is therefore that most often quoted—smaller scale studies, e.g. Baldwin and Epstein (2017) and O'Malley, 2018, present a slightly different picture. In those studies only 25 per cent of the children were cared for by their fathers, therefore we have to accept the possibility that cultural shifts in parent care may have impacted on Caddle and Crisp's 1997 figures.
7. See Joint Human Rights Committee enquiry into maternal imprisonment and the rights of the child (chair Harriet Harmen QC): https://publications.parliament.uk/pa/jt201719/jtselect/jtrights/1610/1610.pdf

female prison population are faced with mothering-related emotions and/or challenges during their imprisonment and following their release.

Women, prison and gendered aspects of incarceration have been extensively researched (see *References and Bibliography*). However, research has tended to focus on gender-based interventions and outcomes in relation to how the CJS and the prison estate responds to male and female law breakers/prisoners. Other research has explored how differently males and females might experience custody. Internationally there is an established body of work regarding mothers and incarceration, particularly in the USA and Canada (see, e.g. Flynn 2014; Enos 2001). However, in the UK, prior to 2015, mothers, and especially grandmothers,[8] had often been 'invisible,' subsumed or missing from research surrounding women and prison. As I have mentioned previously, *Mothering Justice* (Baldwin, 2015) was I believe the UK's first complete book to take *motherhood* rather than just women as a focus in relation to the impact of the CJS.

The academic and policy landscape concerning mothers and prison has changed significantly over the years, especially the last five years, thereby raising the visibility of mothers and grandmothers affected by the criminal and social justice systems by applying a matricentric lens to female criminalisation. The focus on maternal imprisonment has gathered momentum, garnering interest in the UK and Ireland, with studies related to maternal imprisonment, the effects on the children, and alternative means of responding to women/mothers in the CJS, representing a rapidly developing body of work. In addition, maternal imprisonment has been the focus of attention in developments in policy and practice, e.g. the aforementioned Farmer Review,[9] and in sentencing practices following the Joint Human Rights Committee into Maternal Imprisonment and the Impact on the Child (both of which include evidence from my own research). However, despite this increased interest there remains very little research in the UK relating to the *persisting* impact of maternal imprisonment on maternal identity and longer-term

---

8.   Grandmothers under the umbrella term of 'mother' (or Mother) are present in this book as there was no upper or lower age limit placed on the Mothers included in my research.

9.   The importance of strengthening female offenders' family and other relationships to prevent reoffending and reduce intergenerational crime: https://www.gov.uk/government/publications/farmer-review-for-women

mothering, or the relationship with supervision and desistance from offending. Furthermore, maternal imprisonment is often examined in isolation with little reference made to the relationship between maternal criminalisation and broader societal issues. This book seeks to respond specifically to these gaps.

 Pause for Thought

Do you think men and women should be 'treated the same' for the same crime? — Does treating people fairly mean having to treat them the same?

Consider this — In a nursing home all residents are issued with a hair-brush — but a standard hairbrush would be inappropriate and not very useful for African-Caribbean hair — So what is required? — If the African-Caribbean resident is given a specific type of brush that meets her needs, is that fair and appropriate? — Different but equal?

The Need for a Gendered Response

The Corston Report (2007) provided an opportunity to stimulate and provoke the passions of activists and academics working in the field of women's imprisonment. Baroness Corston highlighted the plight of women in prison. Although the report itself did not say anything new, it reiterated what the voices of researchers, feminist researchers and prison sociologists have been saying over the past 30 years: that prison does not work for women. In fact, prison generally further harms women (see also Carlen and Worrall, 2004; Worrall, 1990; Quinlan, 2014; Moore and Scraton, 2014). However, importantly, Corston did specifically high-light the pains of imprisonment concerning motherhood as a distinct area of discussion in its own right, in a way that had previously been less visible in prison research and literature. Corston quoted Baroness Hale in *her report:*

> 'Many women [in prison] still define themselves and are defined by others—by their role in the family. It is an important component in our self-identity and self-esteem. To become a prisoner is almost by definition to become a bad mother.' (Corston, 2007: 2.17: 20)

Corston made a total of 43 recommendations for a 'radical' over-haul of how women in the CJS are responded to. She reiterated the gendered pathways into crime for women, recognising that women are often victims as well as offenders. Because of this, women also need gendered pathways *out* of crime — pathways that ought to include wrap around support and therapeutic interventions which *should,* wherever possible, be community-based and provided by 'one-stop-shop' women-focussed specialist centres. She identified the ways in which the prison estate and its male-orientated design disadvantages women and their need to remain engaged in family life, stating that this can have a nega-tive impact on the health and wellbeing of women. Corston highlighted the fact that women's prisons are geographically dispersed, meaning that many women are between 50 and 150 miles from home, which has an obvious impact on the frequency and possibility of visits from family and friends. She argued vociferously for women to be diverted from custody, indeed from the CJS, wherever possible, advocating instead the development of creative means of providing alternatives to custody and criminalisation.

The Barrow Cadbury Trust, in partnership with Women in Prison[10] undertook research in 2017, 'Corston +10' (see Corston, 2011) with the intention of seeing how far the recommendations of the original report had been implemented. They found that, despite the recommendations being widely accepted and sensible, only two had been fully implemented, and the remainder only partially or not at all (Women in Prison, 2017).

---

10. Women in Prison is a nationwide organization which supports women in the CJS, and also campaigns for positive change for such women: https://www.womeninprison.org.uk/

Since the original report and the follow-on report there have been *some* positive and meaningful changes in the women's prison estate regarding improving physical conditions for women in custody. Such changes have come via the broader ambition for positive change of policy makers, academics and practitioners: to reduce women's imprisonment generally; to increase community pre- and post-prison support; and to maintain family links.

The Female Offender Strategy (2018)[11] launched 'a new programme of work to improve outcomes for female offenders.' The FOS at last included a stated intention to pursue the development of small community-based alternatives to prison, although the details of how this will be achieved in terms of timescale and sources of funding remain unclear some three years later. Although the strategy clearly refers to the importance of family relationships and making positive change, until the female-focussed Farmer Review, there had been significantly less focus or development of policy frameworks specifically related to maternal imprisonment, maternal identity, or mothering during and after prison.

The central role that women often play in the family has led many commentators to present the argument that maternal imprisonment is more disruptive to family life than paternal imprisonment (see also Baldwin, 2015, 2018; Booth, 2017, 2019; Masson, 2019; O'Malley, 2018). As Corston (2007) identified, it is this 'central role' that is often at the root of many of women's anxieties in prison as they continue to attempt to mother and undertake mothering duties whilst incarcerated.

Not all imprisoned mothers will experience prison in the same way or have the same emotional reactions to their experience, nor will all mothers have contact and care arrangements before, during or after prison. Some mothers may see prison as a safe space, or as a positive opportunity to seek support and effect change either for themselves or for themselves and their children (O'Malley, 2018), but research suggests that, for the majority, it may feel more like the end of the world. Individual and emotional circumstances and experiences will have relevance in the lived experiences of mothers in and after prison. However, whether or not

---

11. A programme of work to improve outcomes for female offenders published June 2018, available at https://www.gov.uk/government/publications/female-offender-strategy

mothers had their children in their care prior to custody or when they leave prison, from the limited research examining mothering-related emotions and incarceration it is clear that motherhood and mothering emotions represent an additional layer of complexity, which is of significant relevance to those working with many women in prison.

Certain earlier publications about women serving life or indeterminate sentences have focussed on loss, and how womanhood or gender shapes the prison experience (e.g. Genders and Player, 1990). Crewe et al (2017) and Hairston (1991) argued that mothers experienced profound suffering concerning the loss of their children, their mother status and role. Hairston reported that the mothers found the 'stripping of the mother role' was 'traumatic' (ibid). Walker and Worrall (2000: 28) concluded that female prisoners suffer in distinct and 'special ways,' specifically related to loss of fertility, loss of opportunities to be a mother and loss of children or relationships with children. In this book I have sought to extend the findings of Walker and Worrall (ibid) and Crewe et al (2017) by revealing that it is not only life or indeterminate sentenced female prisoners who experience this difference, but that all mothers in (and after) prison suffer magnified and specific 'pains of maternal imprisonment,' over and above the traditionally accepted understanding of Syke's (1958) work.

In Davies et al (1999), Owen noted that women's physical and mental health needs are often neglected in prison, with many women suffering long-term consequences inadequate care received. Wahidin (2004) found this to be particularly true in her seminal research with older women prisoners. Women described being 'ignored' in terms of their health needs, especially with regard to particular female issues such as post-menopausal care and breast and cervical screening checks. Baldwin and Epstein (2017) found that delays in obtaining medication for anxiety and depression left women vulnerable to self-harm and suicide and, like Wahidin, described menopause related medication being refused. Similarly, women experiencing difficulties in pregnancy also experienced refused or delayed help, resulting in two mothers miscarrying, one alone in her cell and another in handcuffs in the ambulance on the way to hospital (Baldwin and Epstein, 2017).

Abbott (2018) in her important work with pregnant prisoners, found care for pregnant women lacking. She described women neglected in terms of their mental wellbeing and health care needs, even to the point of not having enough food to sustain them through their pregnancy. She describes a mother being forced to give birth alone in her cell because her calls to officers that she was in labour were refuted or ignored. The baby was born breech, a particularly dangerous situation for both mother and child. Her research was published in the context of four separate instances occurring where women had laboured alone in their cells, resulting tragically in the deaths of three babies — two died during the cell delivery,[12] one in an undisclosed location within the prison, and the other en route to hospital.[13]

Confirming that prison is a gendered experience, women are more likely than men to be sent to custody for short periods (Baldwin and Epstein, 2017; Minson, 2018), and as such they are often unable to access any of the therapeutic or rehabilitative interventions offered to those on longer sentences. As Corston described, the short sentences may not be long, but they are long enough to cause women significant harm — long enough for women to lose homes, children and jobs, often compounding their already challenging circumstances. Thereby creating a situation where women are at an increased likelihood of reoffending. Particularly in the aftermath of the Transforming Rehabilitation (TR)[14] agenda, when more women became subject to post-release licence supervision. Something criminologists and sociologists have described as setting women up to fail (Gomm, 2016).

---

12. Russell Webster Criminal Justice Blog 'Why has another baby died in prison?' — and 'Why do we still imprison pregnant women?' Both discuss the babies' deaths.
13. Bronzefield incidents: https://www.theguardian.com/society/2019/oct/04/baby-dies-in-uk-prison-after-inmate-gives-birth-alone-in-cell and https://www.theguardian.com/society/2019/nov/22/hmp-bronzefield-baby-death-prison-births
14. Transforming Rehabilitation (TR) was the name given to a White Paper issued by the MOJ in 2013, and to a programme of work from 2013 to 2016 to enact the strategy outlined in that document. It was concerned with the supervision and rehabilitation of offenders in England and Wales and was initiated by Chris Grayling, then Secretary of State. It involved the splitting and partial privatisation of probation services. New provisions meant that all prisoners serving a sentence of 'more than one day' would be subject to post-prison licence — whereas previously only those serving 12 months or more were.

Mothers and Prison — What Did We Already Know?

Motherhood and motherhood ideology is more extensively explored in the next chapter and so I will focus here specifically on the 'criminal mother.' As alluded to earlier, mid-to-late-nineteenth century perceptions of women and mothers were rooted in patriarchal ideology and ideas of femininity. Shame and judgement directed at all women who fell afoul of the law (and social norms) were magnified for those women who were mothers, 'because in their role as mothers, they were identified as the biological source of crime and degeneracy' (Zedner, 1991: 14.308). The lasting influence of such beliefs has resulted in a pervading sense that mothers who break the law are classed as doubly and triply deviant.

The types of crime a mother commits can also influence perception and reactions to her both formally and informally. Roberts (1993) argued that the law punishes women according to the extent to which their acts deviate from 'appropriate' female behaviour, resulting in mothers being punished (and judged) more harshly, especially mothers who commit offences against children, more so if the children are their own. Lockwood (2018: 157) suggests that imprisoned mothers are afforded less sympathy than other prisoners, or than mothers who are separated from their children by orthodox means (even by state removal to the care of an LA). This despite that maternal imprisonment can 'severely alter, disrupt, or even terminate' mothering (ibid). Minson (2020) also posits that mothers are afforded less compassion in the criminal courts and are judged more harshly. Furthermore, criminal mothers' separation from their children is treated more casually than in the family courts. At least in part because the assumption is that a criminal mother is, by definition, a bad mother. Prevalent gendered ideologies surrounding the 'institution of motherhood' mean that most, if not all, mothers enter prison from a society that perpetuates these views.

Mothering from prison — Maternal identity and role

Previous research suggests that separation from their children is thought to be a challenging and damaging aspect of women's imprisonment, not least because of the disruption caused to the mother role and because motherhood and mothering is firmly embedded into the female identity. Lockwood (2018) suggests that mothers separated from their children by imprisonment are often seen as abandoning them through 'choice'; informing her claim that imprisoned mothers are afforded less sympathy than is shown to mothers separated by 'involuntary' means (ibid: 157).

Notwithstanding this, despite facing multiple disadvantages, many—if not most—imprisoned mothers will regard their children as their primary concern throughout their incarceration. Particularly those who had the care of their children pre-prison. The more involved mothers were able to be during their imprisonment, then the more likely they were to continue to 'feel like a mother.' My earlier work identifies the significance of maternal emotions in prison and how they are inextricably linked to disruption of maternal identity and role (Baldwin, 2015). Enos (2001), argued that maternal identity for mothers in prison is closely linked to the mothering role, i.e. *doing* mothering was key to *being* and *feeling* like a mother and this is resonant with my findings in *Part II*.

Most research around maternal imprisonment has demonstrated that women who are mothers find prison much more demanding than prisoners who are not mothers, and that such prisoners struggle more to adjust and cope (see Carlen, 1983; Enos, 2001; Loper and Turk, 2006; Rowe, 2011; and Lockwood, 2014). Motz et al (2020) and Walker and Towl (2016) have all identified a link between mothers' separation from their children and mental health issues and self-harm. Mother and child separation through prison has been described as a 'profound hurt' which involves constant renegotiation of maternal relationships and the challenge of striving to maintain an active mothering role (Datesman and Cales, 1983: 142).

Most studies on maternal imprisonment speak about 'mother guilt' and the shame felt by mothers as a result of their incarceration and suggests that mothers in custody adopt a range of mechanisms to help them to cope with the emotional fallout of being a mother in prison. Again my earlier work (Baldwin, 2015), echoes previous findings concerning the emotional challenges for imprisoned mothers, highlighting the need for maternal emotions to be factored into responses to mothers in criminal and social justice settings. The findings set out in *Part II* of this book extend that work and provide evidence for the absolute *necessity* of working positively, compassionately and supportively with mothers in prison regarding their maternal emotions, maternal identity and maternal-role. This is important whether or not mothers currently have the care of their children or may be likely to care for them in the future.

Custody provides some mothers with opportunities for reflection and motivation relating to motherhood, rehabilitation and recovery (O'Malley, 2018). In such circumstances, they might, sometimes for the first time, take advantage of the substance misuse support services available in prison. Something that maybe they were not ready to engage with before prison or that may not have been available to them in the community (often due to systemic failures and cuts to funding for services).

There is little doubt that the conditions in which a mother is imprisoned have a significant relationship with how she adjusts to and copes with prison, and they also impact on her ability to maintain a maternal-role and her relationships with her children and wider family (Booth, 2020; Masson, 2019).

Challenges concerning maternal contact

There are far fewer women's prison than men's in England and Wales (12 as opposed to 105),[15] meaning that many women are imprisoned far from home. Consequently, many receive fewer or no visits from friends and family. Financial costs, unsatisfactory visiting conditions, and strained relationships with carers are additional barriers to positive experiences of visitation.

Costly and time-consuming visits with children (in terms of travel time for families), harsh rules of the institution, e.g. no touching, hugging, not allowing the prisoner out of their seat or children on their mother's knees, mean that some mothers, particularly those who are on shorter sentences make the difficult decision not to have visits at all (see also Baldwin and Epstein, 2017; O'Malley, 2018). Meaning telephone contact becomes vital in the pursuit of an ongoing maternal role (Booth, 2018). However, not all prisons in England and Wales have in-cell telephones

---

15. Prison Statistics 2018/19: https://www.instituteforgovernment.org.uk/our-work/performance-tracker/prisons

and calls from wing phones are expensive, restrictive, lacking in privacy and completely subject to the prison regime (Booth, 2018).

Each prisoner is given a 'status' within the nationwide prison-based Incentive and Earned Privileges Scheme (IEPS). This allow access to or denial of, e.g. visits, phone calls, in-cell TV, or other rights, entitlements or restrictions. IEPS has three levels: basic, standard and enhanced. Each comes with lesser, added or denied privileges the more favourable of which are 'earned,' i.e. conferred or taken away based on good or poor conduct, compliance with Prison Rules and so on. Such privileges are also dependent on the prison regime itself being able to properly function.[16]

Mothers in Irish prisons have pre-paid access to daily phone calls home to their children (O'Malley, 2015). Booth's (2018) research highlighted the significance and importance of telephone contact with children, revealing how mothers' efforts to retain contact were often frustrated through no fault of their own. Mothers have recounted feeling especially challenged by frustrated contact during the early days of custody. It is not well understood or sufficiently explored how these interruptions to mothering and maternal relationships recover (or not) and how this then impacts on the mothers' long-term mental wellbeing in and after prison, however this book offers some understanding of the long-term impact of maternal imprisonment.

Booth's research (2017; 2020) focussed on the impact of maternal imprisonment from the perspective of the family, though she makes important contributions to our understanding of the specific impact on mothers themselves. She highlights the systemic and institutional failures that contribute to the specific pains of imprisonment for mothers, under-lining how the structure and regimes of prison can impact on mothers and their children. As with the Mothers in this book, most of the mothers in that research were involved in the care of their children prior to custody and therefore felt the wrench of separation. However, Booth found that, regardless of whether mothers had had care of their children or not, they were deeply affected by the stigma of being a prison-experienced mother

---

16. For further information and the merits or otherwise of IEPS, see, e.g. https://www.doingtime. co.uk/how-prisons-work/how-do-prisons-actually-work/incentive-and-earned-privileges-ieps/; http://prisonreformtrust.org.uk/wp-content/themes/chd/old_files/Documents/IEP%20 Briefing%20Prison%20Reform%20Trust.pdf

and their attempts to continue to play a mothering role with their children was repeatedly frustrated by 'the system.' She concluded that when a mother is imprisoned it becomes a 'family sentence' (2020: 16) and as such requires a family focussed response, calling for additional research around the deconstruction of maternal identity and the long-term implications for successful reunification and reintegration — to which this book seeks to provide a response.

Most studies on maternal imprisonment have highlighted the significant role of caregivers, i.e. those caring for the imprisoned mother's children during her incarceration. In the UK, around 18,000 children are separated from their mothers annually because of imprisonment (Kincaid et al, 2019). However, neither these figures nor the care needs of the children affected are represented in official inquiry. The Joint Human Rights Inquiry into Maternal Imprisonment (2019), and the female-focussed Farmer Review (2019) both made recommendations for this to change and explored how this could best be achieved. It is hoped that if all the recommendations are actioned, this will alleviate some of the current stresses and strains impacting on mothers in custody and their families outside. Not least, issues around overcrowding in blended homes, financial support, shared care, contact and disrupted education of children (see Pitman and Hull, 2021; Kincaid et al, 2019; Baldwin and Epstein, 2017; Masson, 2019; Booth, 2020). However, based on the failure to implement similar recommendations from numerous previous reports, it is difficult not to be pessimistic and suspicious that the promises made will not come to fruition.

Imprisoned mothers have described strained relationships with their wider families, and particularly with those family members who are their children's caregivers. Becoming what Booth describes as 'gatekeepers' concerning access to their children. Research suggests that caregivers are most often the maternal grandmother, although more recent studies have indicated that fathers are playing a more significant role (Baldwin and Epstein, 2017; O'Malley, 2018), perhaps due to a slight shift in societal expectations around fathers and childcare.

O'Malley found in her study that biological fathers constituted her largest group of carers for children of imprisoned mothers. This echoes

Baldwin and Epstein's (2017) study which also found a significant number of father caregivers (again as is evident in this book), indicating the need for an updated study regarding caregiver circumstances of children on imprisoned mothers. However, O'Malley's (2018) findings in her Irish-based study need to be understood in a context where Catholicism is still the dominant religion and therefore where marriage is more common. Indeed, in O'Malley's study most of her mothers were in long-term marriages or partnerships, which is not necessarily typical of women in prison elsewhere.

Research suggests (disregarding demographic factors) that close mother-caregiver relationships, contact with their family during imprisonment and the expectation of regaining custody of their children upon release all impact positively upon imprisoned women's mothering identities (Barnes and Cunningham-Stringer, 2014: 3). However, almost completely lacking in the literature are reference to the experiences of older mothers and grandmothers and their experiences of contact with their adult children and grandchildren (with the exception to an extent of Wahidin (2004) and Baldwin (2021)). There is much to be learned about how this generation of mothers fare in prison. As I have already indicated this book responds to that gap, extending knowledge and understanding of criminalised mothers *and* grandmothers through prison and long after release.

Post-release motherhood and maternal supervision

Although several international studies exploring the experiences of post-release women and mothers exist (see, e.g. Eaton, 1993; Arditti and Few, 2006; Huebner et al, 2009; Sheehan, 2014; Bachman et al, 2016), there remains little published in the UK about women leaving prison, and even fewer focussed specifically on mothers (with a few exceptions: see Sharpe, 2015; Baldwin and Epstein, 2017; Masson, 2020).

Research suggests that mothers in prison are often naïve about the issues they will face on release. Previous research has found that mothers often expect things to 'return to normal' in home and family life. Baldwin and Epstein (2017) and Masson (2019) found that mothers imprisoned, even for short periods, were deeply affected by imprisonment and that the impact of prison lingers. Despite the challenges they face while incarcerated, many women continue to regard themselves as mothers and believe they will be reunited with their children post-release. However, Eaton suggests that most women exiting prison will feel 'disorientated,' 'excluded' and degraded' (1993: 56). She argues that women feel subject to gaze and judgement and have a feeling of being under 'constant surveillance.' Opsal (2009) identified that the supervision of post-release women centred on 'surveillance' rather than the 'tenets of rehabilitation and reintegration' originally intended as a focus for supervisors (ibid: 308).

Historically, many women had previously escaped post-release supervision due to the brevity of their sentences; however, post the TR agenda revisions, all prisoners who have served more than one day in prison are now subject to post-release supervision of at least 12 months. Thus, not only must post-release women worry about meeting their basic needs, as previously described, but they must also be compliant with supervision and reporting requirements. Non-compliance may result in a breach of licence and recall to prison and further separation from children, so the stakes are high. In the UK, since the implementation of TR, breach and recall for women has dramatically increased (WiP, 2017). The increased punitiveness of supervision has impacted negatively on the 'one-to-one' relationship between the supervisor and supervisees in relation to women (Annison et al, 2015), although the impact specifically regarding mothers under supervision is unknown.

McIvor et al (2009), in their Australian-based study, found that women (60 per cent of participants were mothers) exiting prison particularly benefitted from supervision when they engaged with practitioners whom they felt exhibited 'genuine concern' (ibid: 347). Like Masson (2019) and O'Malley (2018), their research also highlighted issues related to lack of compatible housing (see also McMahon, 2019) and revealed mothers were troubled by many issues related to their children and their reunification or persisting separation. They noted many missed opportunities to prepare mothers for release more effectively.

Unsurprisingly, McIvor et al's (2009) findings concluded that women who enjoyed the benefit of multi-agency support, and those who had a positive supervisory relationship, were most likely to continue to desist from crime. However, what McIvor et al did not do was to explore ways in which mothers could be more effectively supported and how the statutory services could, and arguably should, adapt their service to better meet the needs of mothers under supervision. O'Malley (2018) also found that these failures to respond to the needs of mothers during and after custody bore some relationship to whether the mothers reoffended and returned to custody, i.e. due to their desistance or otherwise, especially regarding mothers with addiction issues. Similarly, Sheehan (2014) argues that a multi-agency support approach is fundamental to family reintegration following maternal imprisonment, highlighting that mentoring and peer support can play a key role in successful reintegration.

Opsal's (2009) study of women's experiences of parole investigated how women manage surveillance and how they 'made sense of living under a system framed largely by monitoring their actions rather than meeting their needs' (ibid: 313). Many of Opsal's participants were mothers; the women described feeling like they were 'on a leash' and 'waiting to be caught out' (ibid: 318), generating fear and anxiety about recall. Opsal argued that the women's relationship needs, i.e. particularly those as mothers, were neglected or ignored altogether — findings echoed in this work which extends Opsal's work by exploring how the additional layer of motherhood interacts with the already heavy weight of surveillance felt by the women under supervision. In addition, the informal surveillance of family friends and agencies concerned about mothers' maternal capabilities adds to the burden; again, this is further explored later.

Re-entry, renegotiation and repair
It is accepted wisdom that prisoners post-release will experience challenges, not least stigma, disorientation and shame, as they re-enter society post-prison. However, it is argued that the post-release experience is a gendered one. Leverentz (2013) acknowledges that both men and women are very likely to experience challenges related to housing, employment, reconnecting with family and financial support, but that women are additionally likely to face challenges related to past trauma and substance misuse, mental health issues, together with reconnecting/reuniting with/fighting for their children (see also Wright, 2017). Richie

(2001) and Buncy and Ahmed (2019) also emphasise the fact that imprisoned mothers are often already struggling with their multiple identities generally, relating to gender, ethnicity, culture and economic status. Thus, their ex-prisoner status increases their marginalisation within already marginalised communities.

Masson (2019) identified many practical obstacles faced by mothers in their return to normality, however the majority of Masson's participants were fewer than three years post-release, and none were more than five years post-release. (In this book 61 per cent of the participating Mothers were more than five years post-release, and 47 per cent more than seven years post-release, the longest being 46 years post-release). Nonetheless, Masson's study makes an important contribution to the understanding of the immediate and medium-term post-release impact of maternal imprisonment, particularly concerning the 'collateral harms' caused by a first short period in custody. Mothers in Masson's study described the loss of their homes, jobs and financial security, all of which impacted heavily on their children, losses experienced by many, if not most, ex-prisoners, both male and female. Masson concluded that the 'morally significant' harms (ibid 228) caused to mothers and their children by short periods of maternal imprisonment were disproportionate and unwarranted.

The literature suggests that the central concern for many mothers leaving prison is reunification with their children (O'Malley, 2018). There are multiple variables which bear some relevance to how successful reunification may be. For example, length of sentence, ages of children and housing situation. Mothers have described a long-lasting impact on their relationships with their children (Baldwin and Epstein, 2017). Research has shown that there is often a honeymoon period, or a 'euphoria of freedom' (Bernstein cited in Hayes, 2009) but beyond this, mothers face numerous challenges that they may not have anticipated.

Booth (2020) did not interview her participants post-release, but mothers in her study spoke about their fears and anxieties surrounding re-entry into family life. Like O'Malley (2018), she found that mothers who had a history of substance abuse and had secured therapeutic support in prison, were motivated and reflective concerning their relationships with their children. As such, they were keen to re-engage with their maternal identity and role. Baldwin and Epstein (2017) described how post-release mothers felt their relationships with children had 'forever changed,' especially those with older teenage children. Like Masson (2019), Sheehan (2014) argued that short custodial sentences are especially harmful to women because of their impact on employment and housing, with little return by way of rehabilitation, pre-empting Masson's findings that early support would be a more appropriate and effective approach to avoiding criminalisation.

'Reunion narratives' of post-release mothers were characterised by difficulties (Bachman et al, 2016: 223). Chiming with Eaton (1993), who found mothers struggled to regain status and authority. Mothers who have misused substances may face specific challenges related to motherhood that non-substance misusing mothers do not face, or perhaps face in different ways (O'Malley 2018). Additional factors such as race, culture and community acceptance of ex-prisoners mean that many BAME mothers, experience an intersectionality of inequalities and varied experiences, especially around faith and culture (Bachman et al, 2016; Buncy and Ahmed, 2019). For example, Buncy and Ahmed (ibid) found that when a Muslim mother had been imprisoned, very often her children were simply told that mum had 'gone away,' and so visits would not have occurred at all whilst mum was in prison. Moreover, they also stated it was not unusual for communities to completely reject Muslim mothers who had been to prison and to keep children from their care, serving only to add to a mother's trauma.

An emerging area of research is the trauma prisoners leave prison with, triggered by or originating from the prison experience (Piper and Berle, 2019). Research investigating the relationship between trauma and prison itself tends to focus on potentially traumatic events (PTEs) that might occur in prison such as prison rape, witnessing violence or witnessing suicide rather than the trauma of separation or the prison experience itself. Due to the lack of published research in the area Piper and Berle (ibid) undertook a systematic review exploring the relationship between prison experienced trauma, PTEs and PTSD outcomes.

Moore and Scraton (2014) specifically recognise incarceration as a traumatising experience for women, one that is often experienced as 'destructive and debilitating,' however how that translates post-release is not explicitly examined. The level of trauma women generally, but specifically mothers, feel after prison as a direct result of their incarceration remains underexplored, though this book aims to begin this conversation and provides evidence of PTSD in mothers *directly* related to imprisonment and separation from their children.

What is apparent from the Mothers' accounts, even where not explicitly mentioned, is the relationship between successful re-entry, support, positive reunification and desistance. Wright's study (2017: 29) (where some participants were mothers) observed a relationship between motherhood and desistance, or at least 'the pathway towards desistance.' Wright found that the hopes, ambitions and dreams of mothers were repeatedly frustrated and undermined by the very interventions and punishments that were 'designed' to support them on their path to desistance. As a feminist researcher she powerfully concluded that this 'frustrated desistance,' rather than 'persistent offending,' is where we need to cast our activist gaze. When we focus on the women who 'persistently offend,' we focus on 'the offender' rather than the wider structural inequalities and penal responses which have presented individual challenges to women in the first instance and impacted on their offending behaviour.

The failure of multiple services to have a 'joined-up approach' in understanding the needs of post-release women impacted on their desistance journeys (Sheehan, 2014). Mothers who are supported in their release, and whose reunification with their children goes well are less likely to reoffend. This book provides new evidence to support this claim, echoing and extending existing research.

Summary of *Chapter 2*

As highlighted, research has evidenced the 'profound hurt' of maternal imprisonment, revealing challenges for imprisoned mothers concerning separation from their children and their ability to maintain positive relationships with children and caregivers. Less is known about the post-release experiences of criminalised mothers, especially beyond five years. Understanding of mothers' and grandmothers' own perceptions of post-prison motherhood in the UK is limited. Mothers of older children, and grandmothers, have attracted very little attention and there is little understanding about the layered or intergenerational impact of maternal imprisonment.

Research surrounding the post-release period has focussed on material loss (home, employment) which, although devastating and impactful are also dynamic situations which apply more generally to all ex-prisoners. Less visible is an understanding of the long-term impact of imprisonment on mothering, maternal emotion, and maternal identity.

Knowledge concerning the relationship between criminalised mothers' experiences and desistance is limited and understanding sparse, resulting in missed opportunities to fully understand and/or support the custodial and supervisory experiences and desistance journeys of mothers. I believe that what follows in *Part II* of this book contributes to knowledge and understanding about this discussion.

CHAPTER 3

The Making of Motherhood

'[The] all importance of mother love has been fuelled by a giant
collective wish for perfect mothering.' (Thurer, 1994: xvi)

This chapter focuses on the context in which criminalised mothers live. It
highlights their standards, beliefs and ideals, or as I call it, the 'Mothers'
Code of Conduct' against which criminalised mothers are judged. It is
important to understand our criminal justice structures and responses
to women to understand the impact of these on mothers themselves.

Motherhood has been described as the 'unfinished business of feminism' (O'Reilly, 2016: 2). The chapter examines the contributions of
decades of motherhood scholarship and investigates the notion of the
'good mother.' Rich (1976) suggests that 'motherhood' is a term universally recognised as the 'institution' surrounding mothering. Social
constructionists and feminist thinkers like Parsons (1937) and Kelly (1955)
suggest that the 'good mother identity' is shaped as a result of socially
constructed ideals relative to dominant cultural norms, values and expectations. These ideals inform the norms associated with motherhood which
are influenced by patriarchy, religion, biology and dominant ideologies.

So I will explore the early foundations of maternal thinking, revealing
the often complex relationship between motherhood and feminism,
together with recent (i.e. post-war) perspectives on mothering ideology,
concluding with a discussion of O'Reilly's (2016) 'matricentric feminism.' Moreover, I will also examine perspectives on maternal identity
and associated maternal emotions.

Motherhood studies and research have tended to concentrate on non-
criminalised mothers, however criminalised mothers and mothers who go
to prison are no less exposed to the rules and expectations surrounding
motherhood, operating within the confines of a patriarchally influenced society. Therefore, I will lay down the matricentric foundation

for understanding the experiences, assessment and treatment of criminalised mothers, from internal and external perspectives.

Foundations of Motherhood Ideology

As motherhood scholarship has observed, since time immemorial the world has been bombarded with images of mother and child, deemed 'purest' love. Philosophy, mythology and theology have all laid a foundation for the mother-child relationship to be regarded as the most important human relationship, long before psychology and psychoanalysis began to explain and discuss the significance of motherhood. The mother-child relationship has been presented as the basis of the subsequent healthy development, both physically and mentally, of children and the adults they become.

Early representations of mothers were revered and the burden and responsibility for society's children and their future lay firmly at the feet of mothers (Thurer, 1994). Freud (1941) suggested that the mother-child relationship was 'unique' in that it set down a lifetime pattern for all love relations to follow. Weitzman et al (1985) suggest this simple premise was the foundation of future psychological development theory, including Bowlby's (1958, 1969) attachment theory, which remains influential today.

Bowlby's (1951) theory of attachment is based on his assertion that the mother-child relationship is uniquely important and biologically driven. Although he accepted that other figures *could* have significance and form a 'primary bond' with a child, it was *always* preferable that the child's primary caregiver should be their mother. He defined this vital and close bond with one figure as *monotropy*. He believed that failure to initiate, prolonged interruption, or a severing of this bond could have serious and lifelong consequences, particularly if they occurred within the first two years of a child's life. Bowlby's theory of monotropy led to the development of his arguments surrounding maternal deprivation (1953). He believed that a person's experience of being mothered contributes to their understanding of the world, their self, and others, and that it informs a person's developing expectations, responses and evaluations of contact with others, i.e. it shapes an individual's internal working models.

Along with other developmental theorists this position set in motion a dominant ideology about the importance of positive mothering, especially in the early months and years of a child's life. Weitzman et al (1985: 3) suggests that this led to maternal behaviour and mothering practices being 'scrutinised, analysed and measured' like never before. Mothers, as the 'primary source of emotional sustenance' (ibid), were viewed as the foundation of a well-adjusted or maladjusted adult. Weitzman et al emphasise the responsibility placed on mothers, who 'were told they held not only the fate of their own children in their hands, but also the fate of the world' (ibid: 30).

I quote Thurer at the start of this chapter concerning the all importance of mother love and the collective wish for 'perfect mothering.' Although undoubtedly influenced by her psychoanalytical background, she recognised that mothers are not the omnipresent influence that exclusively determines their children's future, instead 'poverty, sexism, racism or war can undo any mother's best efforts' (ibid). Thurer states that she published *The Myths of Motherhood: How Culture Reinvents the Good Mother* to free mothers 'from an uncritical dependency on an ideology of good mothering that is ephemeral, of doubtful value, unsympathetic to caretakers, arbitrary, and literally man-made' (1994: xxv). It was this notion that motherhood was socially created and perpetuated by a patriarchal society which further demonstrates how motherhood has become a 'feminist issue' (Rich, 1976).

Motherhood and Feminism[1]

Early feminism (or first wave feminism) was concerned with emancipating women from men and challenging inequality between the sexes, which had manifested in the denial of women's basic rights, such as rights to education, to suffrage, to own property and to be able to divorce, and even rights over their own bodies. Feminism was not at this time so explicitly focussed on motherhood (Friedan, 1963). However, Reid (1983) suggests that it is difficult, if not impossible, to completely separate

---

1. For a fuller discussion of feminism and motherhood, see Baldwin L. (2021).

discussions about motherhood from feminine and feminist ideology, i.e. how women should and should not behave or are expected to behave. This in turn is impossible to separate from patriarchal ideology and structures that have long defined and confined women.

Weitzman et al (1985) argued that the 1940s and 1950s were dominated by a 'maternal ideal' that trapped women in the pursuit of perfect motherhood. However, during the 1960s and 1970s second wave feminism broadened its reach, retaining its early commitment to equality of women's rights, but also now becoming more concerned with addressing issues that still affected women, but that were controlled and influenced by patriarchy. This included domestic violence, responses to rape, marital rape, reproduction, and motherhood, which all now became the focus of feminist activists. Women began to demand control and rights over their own bodies, which inevitably led to the spotlight beginning to shine on motherhood.

However, motherhood has not always enjoyed an easy relationship with feminism, particularly when intersected with race and class (Collins, 2005). Motherhood is a contentious issue that has split feminist movements and caused tension between women otherwise united in the pursuit of equality (Neyer and Bernadi, 2011). On the one hand, it has been regarded by women as a source of agency and power; a reason to celebrate the uniqueness of womanhood, the wonder of biology, and a means of uniting women through age, culture and race.

Paradoxically, motherhood has also undoubtedly been a means of excluding women and reducing their status. Furthermore, it has provided anchor points for discrimination, inequality and disadvantage (Smart, 1996), which were problematic to feminist thinking. It is from this latter vantage point that mainstream feminism, particularly from the end of WWII until the 1970s, took a critical stance concerning motherhood, arguing that for the subjugation of women to be overturned, motherhood should be rejected (De Beauvoir, 1949).

In 1976, Adrienne Rich published *Of Woman Born: Motherhood as an Experience and an Institution*, widely regarded as the first book on feminist motherhood and mothering. Rich's book influenced a whole generation of scholarly work on motherhood in an area of womanhood she felt had been neglected. She wrote, '[W]e know more about the air we breathe, the seas we travel, than about the nature and meaning of motherhood' (ibid: 11). Rich maintained that motherhood through the ages has been culturally and continuously 'redesigned' in response to economic and societal factors, arguing that modern dominant mother-hood practices were rooted in industrialisation and the need to support the male breadwinner and therefore women were imprisoned by soci-ety's need to protect the patriarchal status quo. She suggested that people found it difficult to see motherhood as the 'prison of patriarchy' because, she argued, neither men nor women wanted to view the mothering of society's children through this lens. She believed that women perpetu-ated the patriarchal status quo by allowing themselves to be conditioned into accepting that they *should* have children, and for believing that they were somehow going against the feminine grain if they did not.

O' Reilly (2004: 2) states that Rich provided, for the first time, the 'analytical tools to fully study and report upon the meaning and experi-ence of motherhood.' Rich (1976: 13) made the distinction between the 'two meanings of motherhood, one superimposed on the other,' i.e. the institution of motherhood, and 'mothering' which refers to women's own experiences of being mothers. She argued that motherhood *as an institu-tion* is male defined and controlled much like all other institutions which, she suggests, is how power is 'maintained' and 'transferred' (or not), and which 'guarantees that it [power] shall reside in certain hands but not in others' (ibid: 279–280). Echoing De Beauvoir (1949), Rich believed that *motherhood* is sustained by patriarchy, and also by women becoming mothers, thus securing their place as secondary citizens. Whereas the act of *mothering* refers to women's experiences of 'doing' mothering, which if women-centred and defined could be potentially empowering to women/mothers — albeit within the oppressive confines of the socially constructed patriarchal institution of motherhood.

Rich's (1976) distinction between the *institution* of motherhood under patriarchy, with all that that entailed, and the *experience* of moth-ering, which was more amenable to being shaped by feminist mothers themselves, left an important imprint and legacy in terms of the recog-nition of maternal power. The coexisting oppressive and empowering dimensions of mothering have been a challenge and focus in feminist motherhood scholarship ever since. O'Reilly (2004: 2) citing Umansky, presents the 'two competing views of feminist motherhood' as the 'negative discourse, which focuses on motherhood as a social mandate, an oppressive institution, a compromise to women's independence,' and the positive discourse, which offers the view that motherhood can be a unifying, empowering site of liberation, nurture, creativity and agency, if released from patriarchy. However, even with this distinct split being recognised, it is difficult to disentangle one view completely from the other, as inevitably both 'camps' have areas of shared opinion. The challenge to presenting discrete arguments may explain why feminism has a 'complicated' relationship with motherhood (O'Reilly 2016: 2).

'Intensive Mothering' and Beyond

The 1980s and 1990s continued to be represented by conflicting perspectives of feminism and mothering. Feminism had begun to accept that 'liberated' women could also be mothers but continued to be clear that this would only be possible if mothers denounced patriarchy and 'fought back.' As such, more women than ever appeared to 'reject' full-time motherhood and entered the workplace, although many actually did so because of economic need, especially BAME women (Bailey, 1995; Collins, 1994). Nonetheless, some women did so because now came the message 'we can have it all,' i.e. be a mother and have a career. Slaughter (2015) highlighted how this created a divide between mothers: there was judgement from mothers who were employed outside of the home, towards women who were 'only' full-time mothers and who chose not to work, and judgement from stay-at-home mothers, who perceived working mothers as 'selfish' and as placing their own needs above their children's.

Hays (1996) highlights the emotiveness of discussions around motherhood, recognising that it has a polarising effect even amongst women—something she calls the 'Mommy Wars' (1996: 131). Arguably, this represents a significantly challenging period in history for mothers, who were damned if they did (work) and damned if they did not.

In the 1980s and 1990s, dominant motherhood ideology continued to demand that mothers adopt a selfless devotion to their children, meeting their every need through the absolute devotion of time, money, effort and emotion. Persistent idealised notions of motherhood made it challenging for mothers who were struggling with multiple identities or multiple realities (such as mental illness, addiction, or domestic abuse), to seek help and support, not least because they feared the judgement of professionals that they were bad mothers; ultimately mothers feared the risk of losing their children if they were seen not to be coping (Baldwin, 2015). Mothers simply 'got on with it.'

Hays (1996) analysed socially developed ideas of motherhood which she, too, believed is a constructed ideology, serving not only men but also capitalism, at least for the white middle-classes. She observed (ibid: 6) that more women than ever were entering the workplace but doing so whilst remaining influenced by and beholden to the dominant ideology of 'intensive mothering,' which she argued is rooted in an ideology which suggests that children need their mothers more than anyone else (see earlier discussion), and that mothers must remain selfless, i.e. by putting their needs behind those of their children. She argued that, in a society where 'the logic of self-generated gain seems to rule behaviour,' it is a 'cultural contradiction' that women and mothers were also now expected to succeed in the workplace without being freed from the constraints and expectations of motherhood. Mothers were now, argued Hays, expected to work a 'double shift,' one as a mother, one as an employee. She has, however, been criticised, perhaps obviously, by developmental psychologists, but also for not listening to the voices of mothers—mothers who feel they have agency and power in motherhood and who do not want to lose the 'ideals' of motherhood, but instead want to gain support to mother well and to work outside of the home, if they choose, yet equally to be valued and supported in a choice not to (see, e.g. O'Reilly, 2006). However not all women are faced with equal 'choices' or share the same beliefs about mothering practices.

Crenshaw (2017) coined the term 'intersectionality' in 1989, initially to explore the oppression of women of colour but later expanded it to include race, gender, sex, sexuality, class, ability, nationality, citizenship and body type. Although not fully utilised by feminists until the 2000s, intersectionality became a key feature of third wave feminism. For the first time, the multiple realities and experiences of women and mothers were explored and gained entry into feminist discussions of motherhood. Collins (2005, 2007) believes that the 'anti-motherhood' bias in mainstream feminism alienated black mothers and was a serious impediment in the development and theorising of a black motherhood scholarship. She highlights that in black mothering (particularly African-American/ African-Anglo mothers) there are often 'other mothers' raising children, and mothering is not solely the responsibility of the birth mother; furthermore, that black motherhood is often 'both dynamic and dialectical' (Collins cited in Takševa, 2018: 184). This is further evidence to support O'Reilly's assertion that a universal approach to understanding motherhood is inadequate (as discussed below).

In this millennium, motherhood arguably remains as influenced by dominant motherhood ideology as it ever was, but with additional pressure on mothers to be 'perfect.' Social media has added a whole new area of judgement for mothers, and the 'celebrity' and 'influencer' culture has arguably placed even more pressure on mothers to not only 'love and adore their child' but also, to provide the best pram, designer clothes and toys, to 'snap back' into their pre-pregnant body shape (obviously thin!), and to transition into motherhood in a bubble of maternal contentment (Chae, 2015).

Nevertheless, the multiple realities of mothers and motherhood have gained ground, and scholarly motherhood literature has been bolstered by semi-scholarly literature written by non-academics who are nonetheless influential. Publications on a theme have regularly appeared on best seller lists: books such as *The Good Mother Myth: Redefining Motherhood to Fit Reality* (Norman-Natham, 2014); *Misconceptions: Truth, Lies and the Unexpected Journey into Motherhood* (Wolf, 2003); *'Shattered: Modern Motherhood and the Illusion of Reality'* (Asher, 2012); and *Making Babies: Stumbling into Motherhood* (Enright, 2005). Such publications share several themes, that true equality between the genders does not exist and potentially never will because women give birth. In addition, they offer rousing admiration for mothers who are doing a fantastic job (although, arguably, the focus remains on middle-class, white mothers), and, finally, an acceptance that there is no such thing as the 'perfect' mother. However, women continue to aim for the ideal of the perfect mother, engaging in negative self-evaluations as they inevitably 'fail' to live up to perfection.

The continuing complicated relationship between motherhood and feminism persists. Purely scholarly writing in the twenty-first century on motherhood was quiet, and in fact, O'Reilly (2016) has documented the 'vanishing' percentage of maternal scholarship publications. O'Reilly herself is a prolific writer on motherhood and founded the Association for Research on Mothering in Canada in 1998, which later became the Motherhood Initiative for Research and Community Involvement (MIRCI). It was through her progressing scholarly activity in motherhood studies and listening to mothers that O'Reilly (2004) developed her concept of 'empowered mothering' and 'matricentric feminism,' both of which concepts are central to this book.

Matricentric feminism

O'Reilly (2016: 1) argued that matricentric feminism (MF) was born from an acceptance of the position that 'mothering matters.' She stated that she was not saying that mothering 'is all that matters or matters most,' but that any true *understanding of women's lives is incomplete without a consideration of how becoming a mother shapes a woman's sense of self and how she sees the world*. She continued:

> 'I can say with confidence that for women who are mothers, mothering is a significant, if not a defining dimension of their lives, and that arguably, maternity matters more than gender…Mothers need a feminism that puts motherhood at its centre.' (O'Reilly, 2016)

Illustrating her comparison with gender, O'Reilly highlights that, although there has been significant progress in terms of equality and reduced discrimination between the sexes, discrimination for mothers has remained consistent. She argues that, although not completely eradicated, the 'sticky floor' and 'glass ceiling' that impede women in the workplace have been, to a degree, successfully challenged, but that the 'maternal wall' remains to limit and challenge women in the workplace (O'Reilly, 2016: 2). She cites Crittenden (1998) who stated, 'once a woman has a baby the egalitarian office party is over.' O'Reilly asserts that, despite over 40 years of feminism, mothers remain marginalised and disempowered. She suggests (2004: 10) a 'counternarrative' of motherhood would involve reimagining and implementing a motherhood that is 'empowering to women as opposed to oppressive.'

Within empowered mothering, the emphasis is on the mother's own experiences and meanings; importantly that the mother, and her culture ascribe to so that motherhood becomes a site of power, a site through which the mother and the mother role can influence future generations from the home 'through new feminist modes of socialisation and interactions with daughters and sons' (O'Reilly, 2004: 10).

O'Reilly (2016: 2) argues that MF ought not to replace traditional feminist thought, rather that its role is to recognise that the role and category of 'mother' is distinct from 'woman.' She maintains that maternal issues relating to economic, political, social, psychological, cultural and emotional spheres are 'specific to women's role and identity as mothers.'

Di Quinzio (1999) argued that mainstream feminism and motherhood have a complicated relationship, primarily because of the need and want to challenge the oppression of patriarchy and patriarchally favoured structures, balanced against the want and need of individualist but still feminist mothers who want to celebrate the experience of mothering and the power and agency of motherhood. This is in part why O'Reilly (2016) argued, that motherhood should have a feminism of its own.

O'Reilly (2016: 6) states that, as a relatively new, emergent and collegiate feminism, MF is 'difficult to define,' and instead she offers 'central and governing' principles and aims. These are:

> '...that motherhood, mothers and mothering as a topic is deserving of sustained scholarly activity and inquiry that will establish itself as a legitimate and independent and productive discipline; that it identifies mothering as 'work' which is important but not the sole responsibility of mothers; that it challenges patriarchal oppression of motherhood, thus seeking

maternal identity and practices that are empowering to mothers; that it seeks to contest the child-centredness defining much of the scholarship and activism on motherhood; that it develops a research activism centring the voices and experiences of mothers; that it recognises mothering experiences to be diverse and in the context of race, class, culture, ethnicity, sexuality, ability, age and geographical location; that it will actively pursue and seek social change and social justice concerning mothering—whilst regarding motherhood as a site of power wherein mothers can and do create social change through feminist childrearing and activism.'

Matricentric feminism recognises that 'motherhood matters,' and that it is an individual as well as a collective experience that occurs in a cultural context within mothers' multiple realities, creating a space in feminism where motherhood is better understood and valued. It also centres motherhood in a broader societal context and demands a political, social and structural response.

Like Kitzinger (1994) before her, O'Reilly argued that mothers must be supported to have the 'freedom' to choose whether to have a career or not—and not to be judged as a better or worse mother for either choice, and in the context of this book—that whether a woman is a mother or not should have no bearing on how she is judged within the CJS (yet motherhood is nonetheless relevant to how she will experience the CJS). Key to understanding MF is the acceptance of the notion that to women—whilst subject to aspects of gender roles that are to some extent socially constructed—their motherhood matters and 'maternity is integral to a mother's sense of self and her experience of the world' (O'Reilly, 2016: 204).

Important messages from within MF (as also evidenced in my findings in *Part II* of this book) are that motherhood needs to be supported, politically and socially, by society's structures, policies and practice; that mothers, and motherhood, should be supported and that women who choose not to mother, or who cannot have children, are not made to feel inferior. Women need to know that whatever contributions they may wish to make to the children of the future, whether as aunties, godmothers, mothers, grandmothers or friends, their input is valuable and appreciated. O'Reilly (2016) argues that gender difference has been the 'elephant in the room' which has 'shut down' much needed conversations between feminism and motherhood. To redress the balance and give motherhood its rightful place in feminism, O'Reilly (2019: 60) argues, matricentric-feminists must be recognised as scholars and activists, that they and MF should have 'a room of its own in the larger home of academic feminism.' In summary, O'Reilly (2016: 20) is not suggesting that only motherhood matters, or that it is motherhood that defines the self or makes a woman a 'real' woman, or even that as a variable of 'self' it is the most important: but is saying that 'motherhood matters' and is integral and central to 'understanding the lives of women as mothers and their maternal identities' (2016: 204).

Thus, she concludes, mothers need a feminism of their own, both in theory and practice, for and about their identities and experiences as mothers. I argue that the same is true of criminology, i.e. that there is a place in academic study for a 'matricentric-feminist criminology.' Accordingly, in relation to this book, I maintain that criminalised mothers need to be recognised *as mothers*. As O'Reilly argues, 'motherhood matters' and motherhood and maternal identity needs to be understood in the context of criminalised mothers' pathways into crime, their criminalisation itself, their imprisonment, and their pathways out of crime. Under the following sub-headings I identify how motherhood scholarship, and the sociology of motherhood has contributed to our understanding of how a maternal identity is developed and shaped, thus providing a backdrop and theoretical lens through which the experiences of the criminalised Mothers in this book can be examined and understood.

Maternal identity

Arendell (2000: 1192) argues that definitions of mothering share common ground, i.e. nurturing and caring for dependent children; 'mothering' is also an adjective defined as 'actions related to being a mother, especially in being protective, caring and kind' (*Oxford English Dictionary*, 1989). Thus, mothering is focussed on *doing* mothering, but also can involve the experience of *being* a mother. A transition into maternal identity can be influenced by experiences during pregnancy, and of pregnancy itself, and these bear some relationship to the development of a healthy and affirming maternal identity. Spending time with other pregnant friends and other mothers, and attending antenatal appointments, bonds mothers to other mothers — all of which assists in the development of a maternal identity.

Many criminalised women, especially from ethnic and/or working-class backgrounds, are living in challenging circumstances (including criminalised women), where the maternal experiences described may not be possible. Many women do not have the luxury of a safe, planned, uneventful pregnancy with regular antenatal appointments/classes because their reality might be trying to survive through domestic abuse, or as a migrant seeking asylum, or simply working every day making regular antenatal appointments impossible. These diverse experiences of pregnancy are bound to impact maternal identity and provide a context in which to understand the challenges of an incarcerated pregnancy.

Stryker and Burke (2000) suggest that identity theorists from anthropology, sociology and psychology have offered various explanations through the decades about what contributes to the formulation of identity or identities, many of which are rooted in Mead's social interactionism (1935). Although competing theoretical perspectives remain in terms of specifics, Mead's premise of 'society shapes self, shapes social behaviour' (cited in Stryker and Burke 2000: 285) is largely accepted although 'highly simplified.' It suggests that for a mother, her maternal identity is made up from and affected by both internal and external forces, which are in turn influenced by a multitude of variables, to include her upbringing and personal circumstances, class, ethnicity, culture, relationships with others, perceptions of motherhood, the responses of others to her (as a mother and as a woman), and her own assessment of herself as a mother.

Hughes (1945), an American sociologist, was the first to speak about 'master status' in terms of identity. He was referring to aspects such as gender, race, and occupation, which he argues could all co-exist as master statuses. Master statuses can be ascribed or achieved; an example of an achieved status is that of mother. It is suggested that when one aspect of identity influences all others or 'overpowers' the others, it is determined

71

as a 'master status.' For many women 'mother' becomes their 'master' (ironically) status. Equally, for a BAME mothers, 'black mother' can become her master status (as has been demonstrated, this can be influenced both internally, i.e. by the mother herself, or externally, i.e. by wider society). More recently this has been referred to as 'identity salience.' Lockwood (2020) identified that mother status remains the most important aspect of identity to criminalised and imprisoned mothers.

'Maternal identity,' although difficult to define exactly, involves the assimilation of the maternal role into a women's self-concept, to include how she would evaluate and describe herself in the mother role (Mireault et al, 2002). A mother's own self-evaluation of her maternal identity, and her 'internal working model of caregiving,' is related to her own assessment of her 'performance' as a mother, which is related to a number of other variables, to include uncertainty, lack of confidence, experiences of being mothered, and external factors such as poverty, class, and the ability to engage in mothering activities (George and Solomon, 1996).

Becoming a mother for the first time involves learning new skills, accepting bodily changes and constructing or negotiating a new, special and permanent self-concept, confirmed through normal pregnancy tasks and rituals. Many of which would be unavailable to pregnant mothers in prison or mothers living in the challenging circumstances with limited agency as previously described. McMahon (1995, cited in Abrams and Curran, 2010: 2), conceptualised motherhood as a 'rite of passage' through which women generate and attain an identity associated with a 'maternal or loving character.' Abrams and Curran (2010) highlight that 'successful' motherhood is often wrongly measured against supposedly 'universal' maternal standards and the 'production' of a healthy well-adjusted successful child, which is only able to be assessed fully when the 'child' becomes a successful adult.

Unsurprisingly, a number of factors have been shown to impact on the development and sustaining of a positive maternal identity, to include a history of trauma, early parental loss, substance misuse, domestic abuse, mental illness, poverty, teenage mothering, and finally, active mothering or doing. Rittenour and Colaner suggest that, although motherhood is often cited as a source of joy and fulfilment for women, it is not without sacrifice. They suggest that motherhood is often accompanied by financial burden, emotional and physical costs in terms of health and wellbeing, work and family conflict and considerable self-sacrifice, and yet many women choose to be mothers and 'experience great satisfaction' at being a parent (Rittenour and Colaner, 2012: 352). They go on to suggest that mothers' satisfaction in their role is influenced by the aforementioned factors, but also by mothers' commitment to the role of mothering and their 'maternal identity,' and fundamentally their love for their child. Thus, mothering even in challenging conditions and circumstances (like criminalisation and imprisonment), can still bring joy and agency to mothers if they are supported to do so.

Takševa (2018) questioned decades of dominant theorising of motherhood and the relationship to maternal identity, arguing it is fundamentally flawed because of its failure to incorporate diverse voices and experiences (e.g. black mothers, imprisoned mothers), and suggested these omissions 'have serious intellectual and institutional implications.'

Takševa suggests that to assume that the 'knowledge' we have thus far of feminism and maternal identity is true is essentialist and reductionist in that motherhood is seen though a heteronormative, white, middle-class lens (ibid: 179). This in effect denies and renders invisible the experiences of lesbian mothers, single mothers, working-class mothers, surrogate mothers and mothers from diverse backgrounds and cultures. It imposes or risks a negative maternal identity on/for women who may not actually share that experience or perception of themselves.

For many women, just *being* a mother and doing her best in that role in the set of circumstances in which she lives is enough to have a positive sense of themselves and a positive maternal identity as a good (or good enough) mother. Many of the problems and challenges for mothers in terms of their 'good mother' identity come from external judgement, fundamentally because their maternal identity is often 'under attack and vulnerable to the 'external gaze' (Ruddick, 1983) of other mothers and wider society. Universal standards and ideals of motherhood, (e.g. 'quality time') are not so simple for mothers who might be working multiple jobs simply to provide the basics for their children. Key to note is that experiences of 'becoming and being mothers are inextricably linked to 'race,' social class, and socio-cultural location and lived experiences — and as a result are diverse and fragmented' (Miller, 2008: 46, cited in Odum, 2017).

Rose (1989: 123), argues that childhood is 'intensively governed,' and mothers are closely scrutinised at different times throughout the journey of childhood/motherhood, by a range of professionals concerned with the health and wellbeing of children. She suggests, and as feminism has also highlighted, this is because mothers hold the 'destiny' of the nation in their hands. Rose (ibid: 131) argues that from the turn of the twentieth-century, 'legal powers and practices of judgement' began to identify and judge some families and family structures as 'troublesome.' Often this would be single parent families and families existing in challenging circumstances. Thus, through normalisation and surveillance emanating from external agencies and institutions, the family, especially mothers and maternal identity, continues to be directed, controlled and judged.

In addition, Rose argues that through the increasing influence of the state, via normalisation through institutions and state agents such as education, Social Services, psychology services and governmental bodies, childhood — and ergo the mother — this has 'been opened up for regulation in new ways' (ibid: 134). The mother must mother according to society's will and fashion. Such high levels of surveillance (Foucault, 1979; Rose, 1989) denotes that, despite the 'gains' of feminism, despite the liberation of women and the increasing recognition of the importance and value of motherwork and mothering, to a greater or lesser extent, mothers remain at best influenced, at worst controlled, by the state. Furthermore, if they do not 'perform' well, there are likely to be consequences that are internally felt and experienced, (i.e. feeling like failed mothers, or inferior), or externally felt and experienced (i.e. externally judged with potential sanction — e.g., the prosecution and imprisonment of mothers who 'fail' to send their children to school). Or as Thurer puts it:

'In a time where society [finally] values the fulfilment of women persons, we have an ethos of maternity that denies them that very thing, or at least judges them harshly if they are not perceived to be meeting the needs of their children first and foremost.' (Thurer, 1994: xxvii)

When the stakes are this high, the consequences and losses are potentially great. This is especially so for mothers mothering children in adverse circumstances, but also for those who are not, so it is not surprising that motherhood is an emotionally challenging experience. The plethora of emotions associated with mothering can feel all-consuming especially, but not exclusively, to new mothers, and only to be repeated when grandmothering occurs. The relationship between mothering and emotion is an enduring one.

Maternal emotion

The relationship between motherhood and emotion has stimulated research and discussion, particularly in relation to 'good' mother, 'bad' mother labels, and emotions such as guilt (Sutherland, 2010; Rotkirch, 2009). Maternal identity is rarely, if ever, separated from emotion/emotions. Mothers are by definition—or at least are expected to be—selfless, compassionate, giving, tireless, nurturing and, perhaps above all else, 'good.' In addition, the association between motherhood and powerful emotions is commonplace. It is often said that there is no love, greater than, more nurturing, enduring or forgiving than a mother's love. Of course, such beliefs are generated from the aforementioned ideas, ideals and expectations of motherhood, patriarchally shaped and influenced, but also from mothers themselves, as mother love and motherhood can be a source of agency and power.

In the context of this book, maternal emotions (emotions the Mothers interviewed associated as being related to their motherhood and mothering), are compounded by the location, i.e. prison and prison space (Baldwin, 2018; Jewkes and Laws, 2020). For example, should a child win a school prize then a free mother might feel (and be *expected* to feel) pride and love; a mother in prison might well feel the same pride and love, but might also feel guilt, shame and sadness at not being present to share the experiences and the emotions of the occasion—*as she is supposed to* or as is *expected* of her.

Similarly, a mother in prison might be feeling love and loss in terms of missing her child, but she also might feel relief at being imprisoned and thus be able to access support and to focus on her own needs whilst she recovers, without the pressures of motherhood (O'Malley, 2018). Yet, she may feel reluctant to disclose that 'relief' because she is beholden to the ideal that children and *their* needs are *supposed* to come first, thus triggering guilt.

The expectations of motherhood are such that a mother's ambivalence, contradictions, and inconsistency towards her children are deemed anomalous, which develops into a theoretical strand of maternal theory in its own right, i.e. 'maternal ambivalence.' Widespread acceptance of the 'maternal ideal' makes it challenging for women who do not live up the ideal (or want to) to admit to. Meaning mothers who feel that they do not do so either in thought or action find it difficult to discuss or reveal and they can become trapped in a cycle of guilt and shame (ibid). For some mothers (including criminalised mothers) this can trigger addiction or damaging mental health issues, and/or an unnecessarily harsh self-critical evaluation of their own mothering and maternal identity (Baldwin et al, 2015).

Parker (1995) argues that although mothers are encouraged into silence or minimisation by expectations of motherhood, all women experience some degree of maternal ambivalence. Almond (2010) cited in O'Reilly (2016: 63), suggests that 'too many women suffer in their attempt to be perfect... or maternally correct.' Mothers are literally driving themselves crazy in their quest for maternal perfection which can only be proven by the perfection of their 'offspring' when they become successful adults. This presents particular challenges to mothers mothering through challenges and adverse conditions (like prison). Parker (1995) and Thurer (1994) both highlight the harm of 'maternal shame,' which they argue comes from the prevalence of 'mother blaming' which appears to be inherent in society and which they claim is rooted in patriarchal motherhood ideology. This fear of external judgement and negative intervention can also mean struggling mothers do not ask for help. This is especially true for mothers who are trapped in a cycle of trauma, addiction, offending, child removal, guilt and additional trauma- and so the cycle can perpetuate.

In her ground-breaking book on motherhood, Rich (1975: 217) summarised motherhood as an experience that elicited terrific guilt: 'the guilt, the guilt, the guilt,' something most mothers, even 45 years later, would still identify with. Indeed, Sutherland (2010: 310), also believes that motherhood is synonymous with guilt, arguing that maternal guilt is 'so pervasive' in contemporary culture that it has become considered 'natural.'

Motherhood literature suggests that expectations of mothers, together with the assumption that motherhood is absolutely fulfilling, is universal across class, cultures and ethnicity (O'Reilly, 2016). However, most mothers will describe a vast range of emotions felt during their experiences of mothering and grandmothering their children. Mothers, whether they mother well according to their own internal or society's external standards, will be aware of the emotions expected of them. Ergo, feelings of failure as a result of not living up to these standards can hit mothers hard (Sutherland, 2010). The 'mandates of motherhood' serves to 'inform women of the right way to mother' (ibid: 212). The intensive mothering, according to Hays' (1996) dominant ideology, as previously described, inevitably leads to negative emotional states because of the 'unreasonableness' of its demands.

Sutherland argues that however 'natural' or inevitable maternal guilt might be, pervasive guilt impacts on the physical and mental wellbeing of mothers and can be counterproductive. In her observations, maternal guilt was often connected to social disapproval and judgement and to the 'myths of motherhood' or dominant motherhood ideology.' She highlighted the difference between maternal guilt and maternal shame (ibid: 311), arguing that guilt often refers to a 'specific act or behaviour,' whereas shame often relates to 'a negative evaluation of self, a more core reaction to public disapproval, with a focus on the entirety of the self.' Sutherland also argues that while for some mothers the terms guilt and shame are interchangeable, they can also be distinctly different, albeit related and coexisting. Shame, she suggests is felt in relation to others, or to external values, ideas, ideologies, and standards, and guilt is often an internalisation of that shame.

Sutherland also argued that mothers 'exist under the gaze of society,' which she believed renders women (as demonstrated in this chapter) subject to definitions of what constitutes a 'good mother.' She goes on to say that being a good mother is directly related to 'the representation of a moral self.' She found that 'doing motherhood' as society told mothers it *should* be done was nigh on impossible, which women 'knew'; and yet, paradoxically, mothers continued to strive for the impossible, and thus also accepted guilt and shame at not meeting those impossible ideals, an 'inevitable' aspect of mothering:

> '...the guilt that many mothers feel is endless and tyrannical. Guilt for providing too much attention or not enough, for giving the child too much freedom, or not enough, for spanking, or not—these feelings are common yet often hidden. The guilt of the working mother, the guilt of the mother who does not have to work, the guilt of the mother who tried to do both—work part-time and mother part-time—and feels both jobs suffer because of it...the guilt of the mother whose child is showing signs of disturbance, unhappiness, physical illness; the certainty you've somehow damaged your child permanently, no matter what you've done or fail to do' (Sutherland, as cited in Swigart, 1991: 66)

Garey (1995) found that some mothers 'buffer' guilt differently by interpreting cultural norms, allowing themselves to justify or reshape their guilt. For example, women who work might work only on a night shift or when children are at school—thereby not technically leaving their children and minimising any opportunities to be accused of maternal neglect.

For mothers for whom working is a necessity, they are 'providing' for their children, a basic requirement of motherhood. Sutherland (2010) similarly found that mothers would attempt to manage their maternal emotions of guilt and shame by focusing instead on their positive maternal emotions (love, pride, joy) and the needs of their children they were meeting. Her findings were extended by Liss et al (2013) who explored the relationship of maternal guilt and shame explicitly to a fear of negative evaluation. They believe that the distinction between whether mothers are feeling guilt or shame is important, 'because shame has more serious repercussions' and suggest that (ibid: 1113).

'…one explanation for maternal guilt and shame is that women experience a discrepancy between their actual sense of self and their ideal sense of who they think they should be as a mother.'

They go on to argue that, as mothers, women are open to public and private scrutiny — that they feel guilt and shame as a result of a failure to live up to their internalised standards. They, like Sutherland (2010) argue that guilt and shame are challenging to disentangle, citing Gilbert (2000) who argued that fear of public exposure (and judgement) and a sense of inferiority are specifically related to shame. This led Liss et al (2013) to conclude that fear of negative evaluation is related to shame explicitly, which Higgins (1987) had noted can lead to 'self-punishment.' Liss et al also highlight the significance of the 'fear' of negative self-evaluation which then enhances and magnifies the sense of failure and a negative focusing on potential or impending judgement and evaluation (which can be worse for mothers who are either already lacking in self-esteem or who are very socially self-conscious). Put simply:

'[F]eelings of guilt and, especially, shame that may result from discrepancies between actual and ideal maternal sense of self may be exacerbated if women fear negative evaluations from others.' (Liss et al, 2013: 1114)

They suggest that this is important because the experience of guilt and shame have negative consequences for mothers, particularly in terms of depression and broader mental health issues (see also Motz et al, 2020; Walker and Towl, 2016; Covington, 2007). In the context of this book, this is significant because such issues, entwined with other criminogenic factors, can have a relevance to women's pathways into and out of offending (see *Chapter 6*).

Liss et al (2013) conclude their study by stating that maternal emotions, especially negative ones, can be moderated if mothers are supported to have more realistic expectations of what it means to be a 'good' mother, which would in turn act as a protective factor against guilt and shame. Adjustment in individual and societal maternal expectations and ideology would be beneficial.

From the limited literature available pertaining to maternal emotions, there is a distinct ethnocentric focus, which Collins (2005) argues leaves BAME mothers under-represented and misunderstood. Collins argues that there are cultural differences in terms of choice and necessity which impact maternal practice and maternal emotion in such women. For example, in families additionally challenged by poverty, it might be culturally usual, and also necessary, for childcare to be shared amongst family members, where individual 'quality time' between mother and child is deemed a luxury. Many mothers in challenging situations can ill afford such time, often being between working multiple jobs, and doing so as a single mother. Although there might be an assumption in terms of white middle-class values and dominant mothering ideology that such a mother would (and should) feel guilt, she is perhaps more likely to simply feel exhausted by trying to do the best for her child, and grateful to her wider family and community for supporting her, if indeed they have.

Maternal guilt is not the monopoly of the white middle-classes, but it is often only ever examined there. There is a dearth of literature concerning the mothers' own views of what it is like to mother in poverty, with/ through mental health issues, in domestic abuse situations, through homelessness, or as a criminalised mother. This occurs even less if multiple categories apply, and the mother is also from a BAME group. This book at least responds to the knowledge gap in the literature concerning the emotions and experiences of imprisoned and post-release mothers; those mothers whose own view of themselves as mothers, and others' views of them as mothers, altered or affected by their 'criminality.'

I acknowledge that a great deal more research is required concerning motherhood and multiple realties. As Odum (2017) reiterates, the traditional Eurocentric model of motherhood, as previously discussed, is not fully representative of African/Afro-Caribbean (BAME generally) families, and she emphasises that class, race, age and gender greatly influence understandings of the maternal experience, particularly of maternal identity and maternal emotion. BAME, and other marginalised, mothers are often left out of motherhood discussions (McDonald-Harker, 2016), but mothering occurs within interlocking structures and contexts, and must be analysed as such (Sutherland, 2010).

Although her research specifically related to guilt felt by working mothers, Collins (2020) found that public policy has a role to play in reducing maternal guilt, and there is no reason to assume that the knowledge and conclusions resulting from her study are not more widely transferable. Thus, like O'Reilly (2016) and matricentric feminism, Collins argues that increasing the societal value of motherhood, politicising motherhood and supporting motherhood at policy and individual levels, would contribute to the reduction in negative maternal emotions and experiences, thereby maximising the chances of positive outcomes for mothers, children, and wider society generally.

Summary of *Chapter 3*

This chapter has highlighted the complicated relationship motherhood has had with feminism and presented the argument for why a 'matricentric feminism,' is necessary and reveals why I felt it useful and important as a framework for this book. The chapter underlines that the stakes are high, not least because it remains a desire of most women to have children: whether that is born from a biologically driven desire, socially expected desire, or personal choice. It highlights that motherhood, (and non-motherhood) attracts gaze and judgement arguably like no other status. This watchfulness over motherhood is deeply informed by patriarchally influenced, 'traditional' norms, values and motherhood ideology.

The chapter reveals how absorbed motherhood ideology and maternal expectations have far reaching implications for mothers concerning the formation and maintenance of a healthy maternal identity and mothers' internal and external experiences. When viewed in the shared context of *Chapter 2* ('Gendered Criminal Justice') this provides a foundation on which to build an understanding of the experiences of criminalised mothers and mothers who mother from and after prison.

Investment in *all* mothers is important, including, and perhaps particularly, criminalised mothers. In recognising that feminist motherhood is consistent with 'broad feminist ideals of female empowerment and social justice' (Takševa 2018: 180), motherhood should also be considered not only in further research, but more visibly and centrally in wider policy and practice, and specifically in relation to criminal justice.

In line with a feminist stance it was important to me that the Mothers were not left 'invisible.' I did not want them to be 'reduced' to a series of disembodied quotes, or worse simply and only a table in an *Appendix*. I wanted to present a sense of the women as mothers, as individuals, and I hope the pen portraits of them of them in *Chapter 4* begin to do just that. This book is for them.

 Pause for Thought

Think about the messages you have absorbed over time about motherhood — What do you think a 'good' mother looks like? — Do you judge mothers more harshly?

Think about how the media reports the crimes of women — Consider that an article about a woman's crime will most often lead with 'Mother of two, etc' ... 'Grandmother of ...' But when men commit crime we rarely see the headline begin 'Father of ...'

Why do you think this is? — What does all this tell us? — What should we do as a consequence?

CHAPTER 4

The Mothers

'Being in prison made me feel like I was just a rubbish mum ... I
know [my daughter] felt abandoned, she missed me, that's all
she kept saying, I need you she'd say ...' (Annie, *Chapter 6*)

As I describe in my *Preface*, a total of 43 Mothers contributed to the
investigations underlying for this book: 15 who were still imprisoned, by
letter (the 'letter writing Mothers'), and 28 post-release, who took part
in one-to-one interviews (the 'interviewed Mothers'). Just over a quarter
(eight) of the interviewed Mothers were grandmothers. I had no way of
knowing how many of the letter writing Mothers were grandmothers,
but three of them revealed that they were.

The Mothers' individual circumstances are contained in the snap-
shots below. I did not specifically ask any of them about their offences,
although most chose to disclose something. Reflecting the typical, all bar
two of the Mothers disclosed offences that were non-violent in nature.
From what was known (i.e. disclosed), they crudely fell into one of three
main categories, i.e. those:

- who had issues with addiction and had offended to fund their habit;
- in poverty who stated they had offended to provide/survive; and
- who had made a 'one-off mistake' (of varying gravity).

Most of the Mothers disclosed traumatic histories, again typical of
women who experience prison.[1] Importantly, however, most also demonstrated strength and resilience and were emphatic that they had 'survived'
prison. Most were involved in or had access to their children prior to
custody, either via shared care, visitation or as a primary carer. This aspect

---

1. See the Corston Report (2007) for a general description of women who find themselves in the
   CJS/prison.

was however not so typical and often many women in prison have previously lost children to the care system or are no longer their main carer. This is often linked to substance misuse or as a result of concerns about children being in homes where domestic abuse occurs.

During their Mothers' imprisonment most of their children were cared for by grandmothers. Six of them lost the care of their children either permanently or temporarily to their local authority (LA), as a direct result of their sentence (three were eventually returned to at least partial maternal care).

The Mothers' accounts, memories and assimilated experiences, recent or past are respected, trusted, represented and authentically reproduced in the book. This chapter now introduces the interviewed Mothers via pen portraits to avoid them being 'reduced' to a series of disembodied quotes in text without any sense of them as women or individuals. Whilst being equally as important and contributing significantly to the findings in *Part II*, less is known about the details of the letter writing Mothers' broader circumstances and experiences and so actual pen portraits were not possible for them and their backgrounds are instead summarised.

Pen Portraits of the Mothers

Annie, 33, mother-of-one (aged 12), four years post-release. Annie was sentenced to 12 months in custody for fraud for her first offence and first ever time 'in trouble.' An ex-professional with mental health issues (bipolar disorder), she had experienced domestic abuse and her ex-partner remained controlling. Annie was experiencing a severe depressive episode at the time of her offence. She had not expected a custodial sentence, it was a complete shock to her. She went to prison not knowing who would pick her child up from school that day. Her ex-partner prevented any contact with her daughter for the first five weeks of her sentence and would not allow the child's immediate return to Annie on her release.

Beth, 19, the youngest Mother I interviewed, 12 months post-release. Beth was sentenced to four months in prison for shoplifting when her child was three months old. Beth was not in contact with her family as there was a history of domestic and sexual abuse which was unresolved. She had left home at 15 and had a history of substance misuse. Social Services were involved prior to her sentence. When Beth was imprisoned her child was taken into LA care and fostered. Beth had been determined to get her back. However, on release her child did not know her (there had been no contact during her sentence as Social Services refused to bring her daughter to the prison). She was now allowed only supervised access in a contact centre. Tragically, I later found out that Beth, aged only 20, had taken her own life. Her daughter is in the process of being permanently adopted.

Kady, 28, a mother of two girls, eight years post-release. A student she was 17 at the time of her offence (theft). Kady gave birth to her first daughter as a prisoner. She was sentenced to immediate custody for her offence (30 months). Kady had one previous-offence, committed when she was a juvenile. For which she had been given a community sentence, when she was fully compliant. She applied for an MBU space when she entered prison but did not discover the outcome until several-hours after her baby girl was born. Kady and her baby spent five months in the MBU. She now studies law and hopes to work with women affected by the CJS. She recently gave birth to her second daughter. Her eldest daughter is unaware that she spent her first half-year in a prison MBU, or that her mother has been to prison.

Dee, 29, mother of four, five years post-release. Dee has experienced ten periods in custody and previously had a history of drug and alcohol misuse, which she described as being like her own mother before her. Her children ranged from two to 15 years of age at her last custodial sentence. They had various caregivers during her sentences; on one sentence her sister initially had care of Dee's children but latterly gave them over to LA care. Dee is still trying to get one of her children back from care. Her offences were drug/alcohol and breach related. She once absconded from court after being told she would be remanded, in order to secure care for her children whom she had dropped at school, again not expecting a custodial sentence. Dee now works in a women's centre as a women's support worker and plans to attend university.

Queenie, 64, mother of three, grandmother of three, ten years post-release. Queenie was given her first custodial sentence (for fraud), only one day after telling her children she had been on police bail for over 12 months. Her family are very religious, and she was nervous of their reaction. Her relationship with her children is now strained because of her ex-prisoner status and she is no longer permitted to care for her grandchildren in the same way she had. Her grandchildren do not know their granny has been to prison. Queenie is trying to establish a business venture which will support ex-prisoner women into paid work on release.

Tarian, 29, mother of five (one child deceased), five years post-release. Tarian on reception into prison (for drug-related offences) found out she was pregnant (women are routinely tested). This was her first prison sentence but not her first offence. She was successful in gaining a place on the prison MBU where she resided for most of her sentence. Her children outside were informally cared for by their fathers and maternal and paternal grandmothers. Tarian's partner and father of her youngest child committed suicide not long after her release. Her children still spend time living with various relatives informally and with Tarian. Her oldest daughter died of leukaemia some time before her sentence.

Sophie, 21, sent to prison for arson, six years post-release, for her first and only offence (she maintains her innocence). She was in a domestically abusive relationship and she alleges it was in fact her partner who had set the fire. Her infant daughter was taken into care because she was in the house when the fire was set. Post-release, Sophie fought hard to regain custody of her daughter after a difficult period of gradually increasing contact. With the support of an advocate, she was successful, and mother and daughter are happily reunited. She feels that, had she not fought hard for her daughter, challenged social workers and had the support of an independent housing provider, she would have lost her daughter permanently. Sophie now wishes to work with women adjusting to life after prison.

Ursula, 48, mother of five, grandmother of four, all under 18 when she was sentenced to eight years (for drug-related offences), approximately ten years post-release. This was not her first offence, but her first custodial sentence. Her offences were committed with her husband, who did not receive a custodial sentence. Her first grandchild was born whilst she was in prison. Ursula served four years in custody and four years on licence. She states that when on licence, despite being a mother of five, no-one ever asked her on how her re-entry and reunification was progressing. Ursula now works for an organization campaigning for reforms in criminal justice.

Rita, 36, mother of-four, four years post-release. Rita is diagnosed as living with bipolar disorder. Her youngest child was 18 months old when she was sentenced to custody for fraud. Rita became pregnant whilst on bail and waiting for her case to come to court. She had not expected a custodial sentence for a first offence. She was not immediately informed of her right to apply to bring her youngest child into prison with her to reside on an MBU. When informed, Rita made the decision not to apply for a space, because he was 'settling.' This would have meant separation from siblings and a further distance for them all to travel — potentially reducing the number of visits. Rita has started her own business and community initiative which employs women after prison.

Maggie, 61, mother of-four, grandmother of two, sentenced for a first offence (theft), nine years post-release. When her offence was committed her family were experiencing financial difficulties, including the potential repossession of their home following her husband's retirement on health grounds. She was his full-time caregiver and childcarer for her grandchildren when sentenced. Maggie was diagnosed with depression in custody. Her grandchild was hospitalised with cancer whilst she was inside and she was refused ROTL to visit him. Maggie now volunteers with women in the CJS.

Nicola, 41, mother of three, eleven years post-release, has two children who were taken into care several years prior to her sentence and one taken into care during her most recent sentence. Nicola had a long history of substance misuse and mental health issues. Her two older children had previously been removed from her care. She had been sober and well for several years, relapsing prior to her sentence following the death of her mother. Her offence was related to funding her alcohol abuse. Nicola had previously experienced custody but was not expecting a custodial sentence this time as it was over ten years since she had been before the courts. She challenged but lost the application for her son to be placed for adoption.

Mary, 65, mother-of two, 38 years since the sentence from which, she lost her children, and 26 years post-release from her last sentence. Mary served several short custodial sentences and remand periods, mainly for alcohol and public order-related offences. She was sentenced to 18 months in prison when her sons were aged seven and nine. They were taken into care and in a series of foster homes over many years, they themselves later serving time in prison. Mary decided her children were *better off* without her. She gave up both seeing them and her parental rights. She did not see her sons for over 30 years. In their 40s, they eventually found her and were reunited. They now have a tense, fragile, but improving relationship.

Carla, 45, mother of two, six years post-release. Carla had a long history of domestic abuse, substance misuse and MH issues. She had served three previous short sentences. She shared care of her children with her mother prior to custody and this arrangement had continued after previous sentences; on her last release, her mother would not agree to shared care and the children now reside permanently with their grandmother and Carla visits them. Her home was repossessed during her last sentence, she lost everything and lived a transient life for 14 months. She was eventually housed in a one bedroom flat, where she still lives; she attends a women's centre for support and hopes to volunteer there in the future.

Margot, 32, mother of one, two years post-release. Margot had previously served a short period on remand. Her 14-year-old daughter was severely bullied about having a mother in prison. Margot struggled to deal with this inside and states that she self-harmed as a means of coping. She served 18 months at what she felt was the most important stage of a teenager's life and feels their relationship has suffered enormously. She struggles to accept her daughter's maturity and independence and describes their relationship now as strained.

Lauren, 26, single mother of a two-year-old, four years post-release her first custodial sentence (not her first offence). Lauren disclosed mental health issues stating she had begun self-harming in prison. Her son was taken into LA care at the point of her sentence as she was estranged from her family at the time. Post-release, Lauren's son was eventually returned to her (after 12 months). They now live together with Lauren's mother. During her sentence Lauren accessed support not available to her in the community and found it a positive experience—this also resulted in her securing support on her release which helped her to reunite with her mother and child. Lauren is employed and engaging with mental health support.

Mavis, 60, mother of two adult children, grandmother of two, six years post-release. Mavis, a retired teacher, had been the full-time childcare provider for her grandchildren before going to prison. Her son is a legal professional, his wife works for the government. Mavis is no longer permitted to care for her grandchildren. Despite previously being close, her son and his family have little to do with her. Mavis believes this is because they are ashamed and embarrassed. She has a better relationship with her daughter, although it is 'still not as it was.' Mavis has been prescribed anti-depressants since her release.

Karen, 44, mother of three children aged eleven and 17, ten years post-release. Sentenced for a serious driving offence. Karen was a professional with a good support network. Her husband cared for her children in their family home during her sentence and they were reunited post-release.

Karen stated she struggled with her experience of the CJS and with the stigma of being a middle-class mum who had been to prison. She could no longer work in her previous profession and is hoping to re-train in an alternative profession where her prison experience can be turned into a positive.

Sandra, 46, mother of four, grandmother of two, 12 months post-release, Sandra had a long history of alcohol and substance misuse, she stated she used to block out childhood trauma. Sandra's teenage-daughters became pregnant during her first sentence, something she blames herself for. Her family cared for her children during her sentences. One child 'refuses' to return home and now lives with his grandma permanently. Sandra states that she is now clean 'for her grandchildren' and wants to work with women exiting prison.

Shanice, 30, mother of two aged two and eleven, five years post-release. Shanice has served three custodial sentences with large gaps between them. One was only a few weeks; the others were around six months. Her eldest child has behavioural difficulties and is on the autistic spectrum. Shanice believes this is partly attributed to her substance misuse and prison sentences. She is now clean and sober but struggling to stay this way. She states she feels 'under surveillance' from Social Services. She and her mother no longer speak due to tensions concerning the children arising whilst she was in prison. Shanice is a graduate and wants 'eventually' to work with women in the CJS.

Tanisha, 31, mother of three aged four, six and 12, seven years post-release. Tanisha served her first custodial sentence at the age of 17 (she was 'looking after' drugs for her much older and violent boyfriend), her first son was born during a custodial sentence. She served one further sentence when she was pregnant with her second. Tanisha stated that at points in her life the LA have taken her children into care through concerns about domestic abuse in the home (by Tanisha's partner). She also had a period of shared care of her children with family members. She now has the full care of all her children and is with a non-violent partner.

Tanya, 27, mother of two aged six and seven, two years post-release. Tanya had two periods in-custody, eight-weeks on remand and 14 months as a sentenced prisoner following an assault. Before prison, she informally shared care of her children with her mother, their caregiver during her sentence. Post-prison, Tanya stated the children 'chose' to stay with their grandmother most of the time with Tanya having them usually only for overnight stays once or twice a fortnight. She and her mother remain in conflict about the children.

Cynthia, 50, mother of one, four years post-release, has a long history of alcohol abuse, and mental health issues. She experienced extreme trauma as a child and young adult describing being 'forced' into prostitution to fund her addictions. Cynthia now has a 'close' relationship with her adult son, who is 'very protective and nurturing' towards her. He himself suffers from MH issues and lives with anorexia, which his mother believes was caused by their repeated separations because of her multiple short custodial sentences.

Tamika, 26, mother of three, aged 12, two and four, five years post-release. Tamika was pregnant during her last sentence (her second). Her baby was born post-release. Tamika stated she had 'a problem with anger.' She put this down to unresolved emotional issues following her abuse. Tamika had spent time in care (where the abuse occurred), resulting in anger issues with her mother whom she blamed for *putting her into care.'* Her children had been cared for by grandmother (GM), during her sentence. Tamika has now resumed care of her children but with 'strained' support from GM.

Tia, 26, mother of two aged 12 and four, five years post-release. Tia, a graduate, had been addicted to heroin prior to her traumatic arrest at her daughter's school gates. She had been what she described as a 'functioning addict' but was 'dealing' to fund her own addiction. Her mother and ex-partner cared for her children, so were separated for her sentence duration. As a result they are not now close, a constant source of guilt for Tia. Her daughter feels Tia 'lost the right' to be a mother. They now have a fragile, strained but developing relationship. Tia feels she has a 'second chance' with her son, who was very young when she was jailed. Tia went on to secure voluntary work, leading to paid work with prisoners and ex-prisoners struggling with addiction.

Margaret, 66, mother of two and GM carer of her grandchildren, whilst their mother was in prison. Margaret was 46 years post-release at interview (the longest post-release period of all of the mothers). Her now adult children were not born when she served her sentence; she had been pregnant when sentenced but her baby was adopted shortly following her release. Margaret's sentence and her first baby are a 'secret' from her grandchildren, and she feels 'deeply ashamed and guilty' about this. Margaret feels responsible that her own daughter went to prison, too. She feels she was not a positive role model.

Jaspreet, 36, mother of 18-month-old twins with special needs, one-year post-release. Jaspreet, a professional prior to her first and only offence, maintains her innocence but was found guilty at trial. She served five months. Prior to her sentence, she stated she had not expected to be able to survive the separation from her children. Jaspreet bears what she describes as additional cultural shame at losing both her profession and her respectability in such a publicly 'shameful' way. Her mother-in-law and husband cared for her sons during her sentence, and she described relations as strained — slowly improving.

Rayna, 36, mother of two aged six and eight, two years post-release. Rayna served three-and-a-half years for her first offence. Rayna is a foreign national. The Home Office were seeking a deportation order on her release. She appealed this decision, won her case and now has indefinite leave to remain in the UK. Her husband cared for her children during her sentence; however, they have since separated. Rayna's mother, to whom she was very close, died during her sentence after a short battle with cancer. She is struggling to integrate and readjust and feels traumatised by the separation from her children.

Marjorie, 61, mother of one, grandmother of one, eleven years post-release. Marjorie served 12 months of a two-year sentence for fraud. Her son was 18 when she was sentenced and still lived at home. Her first grandchild was born whilst she was in prison, something Marjorie states she cannot get over or forgive herself for. Her son subsequently offended and served a short prison sentence during which she shared the care of her grandchild (as per her son's pre-prison arrangement).

Tahira asked to withdraw from the project, and asked for none of the content of her interview to appear in print. My transcript was destroyed. However, she asked that her chosen pseudonym and presence/withdrawal be documented. She specifically asked that her withdrawal be reported as follows:

> 'Although I enjoyed participating … and think and feel it will be of importance, my husband has asked that I, and all my given interview details be withdrawn from the investigation. My offence and imprisonment caused me and my family great shame, to that end we would, on reflection prefer to leave the past in the past. We seek peace and solace in this rebuilding period and therefore wish to keep our experience a very private one. We wish you every success … With very kind and respectful regards.'

Backgrounds of the *Letter Writing* Mothers

I received a total of 25 letters from 15 different Mothers who were writing from prison; they each had at least one child, most more than one. It was difficult to confirm the actual number of children for this group, as not all Mothers fully disclosed this in their letters (nor were they asked to). However, this group had between them at least 27 confirmed children. The Mothers were: Taranpreet, Emma, Alexandra, Rosie, Natacha, Danielle, Diane, Erin, Sandy, Helen, Jennifer, Adel, Sam, Pham and Melanie.

Not all of the letter writing Mothers disclosed details about their offences or sentence length (and were not asked). Information collated from those who did offer the information was as follows: six were serving sentences of less than six months, two disclosed sentences of less than three months. Two disclosed that their sentences were over four years but did not specify length. One was a life sentenced prisoner who was several years into her sentence. Several mentioned they were within weeks of release. The disclosed offences ranged from murder, fraud, assault, theft, recall and 'debt' in the shape of non-payment of fines. Most of the disclosed offences were minor and non-violent, as is typical of women in prison.

Three Mothers were foreign nationals.[2] I do not have accurate information about the ages of the letter writing group, but the ages of their disclosed children ranged from a few months to 45 years old. Obviously, these Mothers were writing about separation from their children in 'real time' and contributing their experiences as they were occurring, along with their hopes and fears for release and reunification.

One of the Mothers, Emma, imprisoned for shoplifting and breach of a previous order, wrote several times. She had wanted to also give an interview. We had planned to do this following her release. We did meet several times but were waiting until she was more 'settled' to record her interview. However, before we could do so, tragically Emma died aged 36 from pneumonia just five weeks after her release from prison. I had supported Emma into new permanent accommodation via my contacts. She had found voluntary work, was drug free, and had been hoping to reunite with one of her children, a teenage daughter she had not seen for some years (her youngest child had been permanently adopted). Her older daughter attended her funeral, as did I.

More About the *Interviewed* Mothers

The 28 interviewed Mothers were geographically widely spread across the UK, ethnically diverse and representative of the wider prison population. Most Mothers were interviewed in their own homes (at their request), all had been out of prison for at least 12 months. The longest

---

2. Rosie, Natacha and Adel.

period post prison was 46 years; the remainder of the post-release periods varied, with 61 per cent being five years or more post-release, and the women were aged between 19 and 66. Periods in custody ranged from two to four years. Fifty-six per cent of Mothers were either serving their first custodial sentence for their first offence or were serving their first custodial sentence but had previous offences; the remaining 38 per cent had multiple offences/sentences.

Pause for Thought

What are your observations/thoughts when reading the Mothers' short biographies — Does anything surprise you? Why? Why not?

Prior to beginning this book, in the UK there was a distinct lack of scholarly representation concerning mothers' internal experience of mothering per se. Mothers' own voices are often silenced, muted, unheard or invisible in research and policy. Bassin et al (1994: 2) again highlight the importance of mothers' own voices, stating that it is 'critical to fighting against the dread and devaluation of women,' and, further, that 'listening to the maternal voice disrupts deeply held views of women and motherhood' (1994: 10). This book, at least in terms of post-prison and criminalised Mothers, seeks to respond to this omission and quite deliberately and heavily features the voices of Mothers, grandmothers and their experiences.

Using a matricentric-feminist lens, I explored the experiences the 43 Mothers affected by imprisonment. I examined maternal identity and role through their concepts of motherhood; specifically, 'good' motherhood, within the context of prison and post-release, and whilst retaining a critical matricentric-feminist position. The Mothers accounts were examined in the context of feminist criminological thinking and with reference to longstanding feminist ideology and maternal theory, thus creating a bridge across two currently distinct and separate disciplines to generate and develop a matricentric-feminist criminology.

The research underpinning the book was approved by De Montfort University Faculty Research Ethics Committee (FREC) and was additionally supported by two national organizations that work with women in and after prison.[3] Those organizations agreed to host information and invited potential participants to contribute to the research, thus leading to my first line of Mothers, many of whom contacted friends on my behalf to encourage them to participate also. Other Mothers responded to calls for involvement made via relevant press or posters in women's centres and probation offices.

Having introduced the Mothers and provided a whistle stop tour of women and criminal justice, I now turn to my 'findings' which reveal the profound impact of maternal imprisonment. They are presented via themes emerging from the knowledge and understanding gained and the chapters are organized accordingly.

---

3. Women in Prison; and Women's Breakout (an umbrella organization supporting 53 women's centres nationwide—now merged with Clinks; https://www.clinks.org/community/blog-posts/womens-breakout-new-chapter).

PART II

FINDINGS

The chapters in this part contain direct, first-hand evidence by the Mothers gathered in interviews or letters. Although it is not always easy to compartmentalise what the women told me, I have tried to marshal the chapters to allow common themes to emerge chronologically as follows:

- Before prison: *Chapter 5.*

- In prison; *Chapters 6 to 8.*

- After release: *Chapters 9 to 11.*

Where the Mothers' comments coincide with (or deviate from) the writings and research of others, I have pointed the reader to the *References and Bibliography* section at the end of the book. I hope the overall effect is to combine and validate new discoveries and insights by comparing what is already known about women (and sometimes mothers) in prison.

I believe that by allowing readers to listen to the Mothers' stories this book provides new knowledge and more nuanced understanding regarding mothers' and grandmothers' pathways to prison and how incarceration intersects with their maternal identity and role in and long after prison.

CHAPTER 5

Pre-Prison Experiences

'Before prison my life was shit. I never had a life like normal people
have, it was drama, chaos, abuse and more drama. It was really shit
you know; prison just made my already shit life more shitty.' (Sam)

The Mothers felt that their in-prison and post-prison experiences were
only part of their 'story' and that these were informed and shaped by their
lives and experiences *before* prison. So, to accurately represent their voices,
these pre-prison circumstances must be always be kept in mind and
acknowledged as well as the broader structural inequalities and discrimi-
nations which provide the backdrop and context to those experiences.
The layered nature of grandmothers' and older Mothers' experiences, as
detailed here, are an important contribution to an overall understanding
of the experiences of *all* criminalised mothers. Therefore, grandmothers'
experiences are interwoven.

Mothers' experiences and descriptions of being mothered before
custody are previously underexplored but are presented here via the
Mothers' described experiences. As previously discussed, women who
enter prison usually do so from 'challenging circumstances.' They have
frequently experienced abuse and violence; they may have mental health
issues, and/or problems with addiction; they often have experienced
poverty and neglect. Many such circumstances were described by the
Mothers. They tend to bear some relationship to each other so are often
impossible to disentangle and discuss as discreet topics. However, I have
organized them under the headings that follow.

Poverty and Mental Health

Several Mothers were living in severely disadvantaged circumstances in
areas of high unemployment and few opportunities. Many were struggling with mental health issues, often compounded by their financial

circumstances. They described how they felt they were '*failing*' (Tia) by not being able to provide their children with not only the basics of living but also the latest TV, trainers, and video games, seemingly increasingly important to a consumerist society and which present added pressures on mothers to provide.

Contemporary motherhood is bombarded with media-driven images and messages of 'must have' toys, gadgets, even certain baby bottles, dummies and, especially, 'the pram.' The pram is often seen as a status symbol and perhaps one that sometimes belies the true financial position of the mother (Thomsen and Sorenson, 2006). Tarian:

> 'My pram was the best you can get, it was over a £1,000, my little Quenisha, she was my show pony. I wanted her to have the best of everything.'

Mothers have always been under pressure to provide and provide well for their children, but in single parent families, which 26 of the Mothers were, mothers bear that pressure alone. Thomsen and Sorenson (2006) argue that providing the 'desired' trappings of motherhood contribute to an image of an elevated financial position, assisting in the construction of a positive maternal identity—or a negative one if mothers are unable to provide the basics in terms of food and clothing, but also those commercially suggested 'essentials':

> 'It's ironic really, you fall into bad ways partly because you want to provide things for your kids, and you end up in prison and it all goes to shit anyway…I feel like a worse mum for being in prison than I did for being skint, but I just wanted them to have nice things you know, not even flash things…just nice things.' (Tanya)

Some of the Mothers, particularly those who lived a 'good lifestyle' (Tarian), had originally begun offending to 'earn more money than I ever could have legit' (ibid). Tarian, Kady, Maggie and Tia all explicitly stated that their original motivation to offend was to mitigate their poor financial position, provide 'nice things' (Tia) for their children, or to try to reduce a level of debt that was having an impact on their lives.

Kady described offending to 'save the family home.' She felt she had had 'no choice' but to offend as the family were facing eviction:

> 'What was I meant to do? My mother hadn't told me about the debt, so I found out with two weeks' notice, where was I going to get £1,000 in two weeks, bank loans aren't options for people like us man…I know I did wrong…but how else man? How else could I have got £1,000 pounds in two weeks? It was wrong though, I know. But well…we kept the house.'

Living in poverty was not (many of the) the Mothers' only challenge but it was significant. They described the hopelessness and powerlessness of living on benefits. Facing benefit sanctions, unstable employment[1] or unemployment compounded their often already difficult circumstances:

> '…it was no one thing really, it was all of it. It was all shit, but it all looks worse with no money, don't it.' (Beth)

Parenting through poverty takes a great deal of coping energy (Ghate and Hazel, 2002). Parents, and especially single mothers, face multiple disadvantages and often are parenting with already depleted personal resources in a society not structured to support them. It is not surprising that mothers in such circumstances, sometimes, in the midst of the 'desperation' described by Ghate and Hazel, fall foul of the law. What is more worthy of note is how many women actually *do* manage to parent their children alone, and parent them well, despite the multiple challenges they face in our structurally unequal society.

It is not uncommon for poverty to be a factor in relation to mothers' imprisonment. In Baldwin and Epstein's (2017) study, several mothers were imprisoned as a result of offences associated with debt, or poverty-related issues, including stealing nappies. Experiencing poverty or addiction issues was relevant to the Mothers imprisonment impacting on their view of themselves as mothers:

---

1. The number of people on zero hours contracts has drastically increased in recent years—with significantly more women than men being on them: https://www.statista.com/statistics/398576/number-of-employees-zero-hour-contracts-gender/#statisticContainer

'How could I call myself a good mother when I couldn't give them what they needed, let alone what they wanted.' (Nicola)

The multiple challenges they faced contributed to poor mental health, exacerbating existing mental health conditions. Triggering feelings of 'depression,' 'emotional fatigue,' 'stress,' and 'desperation.' The discrepancy between their 'ideal' mother self and the mother they were able to be in their circumstances was a contributing factor to their mental wellbeing. The relationship between poverty, mental health and maternal identity was clear:

'When they cut my benefits because I missed an appointment, I just felt like giving-up, you know not being here, I just felt what's the point. I felt useless as a mother...useless.' (Nicola)

Many Mothers struggled to secure support for their mental health issues, adding to the complexity of their situations. This is typical and symptomatic of structural failures to support services disproportionately affecting women (Hackett, 2015). For several Mothers, their mental health issues interacted with their limited financial resources, trauma-filled histories and controlling or abusive relationships, creating a 'perfect storm.' Rita, Annie, Nicola, Emma, Sam and Cynthia all disclosed that they had been diagnosed with bipolar disorder or severe depression. Annie and Rita both offended whilst in a 'full-blown bipolar episode':

'I had this fine to pay and I was just obsessed with it...really paranoid. I was facing eviction because I hadn't paid my bedroom tax, I couldn't cope — my brother would just tell me to pull myself together 'cos he couldn't see I was ill, I'd tried suicide and failed, everything, everything was just too much.' (Annie)

Cynthia disclosed that she had felt suicidal on at least two occasions, she had at various points been received into secure psychiatric care as opposed to prison. She openly stated that some of her offending was in fact 'cries for help,' including setting fire to herself, for which she was imprisoned (because she had been in a public place):

> 'I've done [prison] nine or ten times, twice in a [psychiatric] hospital instead of prison, sometimes came out homeless so then it would never be long before I was back, but mostly I did deliberate acts to get help, self-harm and public disorder to get help, arson to get help, shoplifting to get help. The last time, the judge didn't want to sentence me, he said I needed help, but probation couldn't find a place for me because it was arson … serious isn't it, see? … so I had to go to prison. There was nowhere else, see.'

A further six Mothers disclosed mental health issues. Most were not in receipt of adequate support prior to their prison sentences. All bar one had requested support: some had received intermittent support and three were prescribed anti-psychotic medication (Sam, Annie, Cynthia). Seventeen volunteered information (they were not asked about medication) that they were prescribed anti-depressants or had been in the past. For most Mothers their mental health issues were deeply rooted in trauma and abuse, which for some had resulted in 'self-medicating' (e.g. Dee), which often in turn led to addiction.

Abuse, Trauma and Addiction

Couvrette et al (2016) highlighted the complex and interwoven relationship between trauma, addiction and motherhood, suggesting that addiction/substance misuse provides an additional 'layer' of judgement over mothers. Most addicted mothers are 'deeply traumatised,' not only by whatever prompted their substance misuse in the first instance, but also by the additional guilt they feel as 'failed' mothers. Of the 16 Mothers who had issues with addiction, all disclosed abuse or trauma histories, which they linked to their substance misuse. This is not untypical. Over half of all women who enter prison have experienced abuse in some form.

For many women, the only way they can cope with the traumatic legacy of abuse is to obscure their memories and associated feelings with substances like alcohol and drugs; for many it is the only alternative to suicide (Walker and Towl, 2016; Motz et al, 2020). Beth, the youngest Mother illustrated this as follows:

> 'Sometimes just being alive was hard. I was so wrapped up in trying to cope with my past it was hard to live in the present you know … hard to be the mum I should be.'

Similarly, Lauren and Nicola traced their substance misuse back to their traumatic experiences:

> 'Nothing went right in my life from the minute it [childhood rape] happened you know, I was a good kid you know, I had plans, I was going places … but after that I just couldn't cope, I was on a slippery slope to nowhere.' (Lauren)

As a direct consequence of her addictions, Nicola's three children were taken into care, aged two, several years prior to her most recent offence and one at her most recent sentence. Nicola had a long history of substance misuse and addiction which had begun in her teenage years. She had been a victim of sexual exploitation as a teenager and struggled to cope with her experiences and emotions. She was bullied at school due to local publicity surrounding her case. In her words, she felt everyone 'knew' she was 'dirty.' Her childhood was troubled. Nicolas' mother had also experienced child sexual abuse and Nicola described her parenting as 'shit.' Many Mothers described circumstances which warranted help and support, which for most was not forthcoming.

Nicola, like Beth, Shanice, Dee, Cynthia, Mary, and Carla, explicitly attributed her addictions and mental health issues to past experiences of abuse and/or to her childhood trauma, a common phenomenon:

> 'The only time I could cope was when I was off my head … the rest of the time it was just too painful … it's a lot to come to terms with you know … all that stuff … it tortures you.' (Beth)

'I hated the fact I'd become my mother, I needed alcohol to cope with everything…everything from my past and actually everything I was living in…it blocked it out, dulled the pain…I tried counselling but that literally did my head in…pardon the pun…so I just went back to drinking.' (Mary)

Cynthia had a long history of drug and alcohol abuse and had also used substances as a means of 'coping.' Others described 'dealing with' (Ursula) or 'blocking out' (Lauren) their emotions and trauma as a result of abuse of one description or another:

'I was dealing with so many issues, so many issues, it was all brushed under the carpet…the abuse I mean…no-one listened to me, so I drank, and I took drugs, I know drinking and drugs are self-harm really but I didn't know how else to deal with it.' (Cynthia)

Despite their substance misuse being described as a coping-mechanism, some of the Mothers struggled with the consequences of engaging in an activity they saw as incompatible with motherhood. Mothers repeatedly described how being a mother who misused substances was 'at odds' with how a mother 'should behave' (Shanice). Challenging their maternal self-esteem. Mothers who misuse substances and break the law are often perceived as 'triply deviant,' because they are deviating from societal, feminine and motherhood norms. Zedner (2010: 332) suggests this is not something that male addicts, even those who are fathers, experience in the same way, arguing 'lack of sympathy' for women who 'escape misery' in addiction is commonplace.

The Mothers were very aware of the contempt and derision they received as mothers using substances. They felt that as addicted mothers they were perceived as 'selfish,' not 'putting the needs of the kids first' (Sandra), and therefore as undeserving of support. They negatively evaluated themselves as mothers, internalising shame and guilt concluding they were 'bad mothers,' leading to further substance misuse in order to block out their feelings. This triggered a perpetual cycle of substance misuse, maternal-guilt and shame, further substance misuse to bloc-out maternal guilt and shame—and so on, creating a 'cycle that I just couldn't escape' (Beth).

Alongside their own internal performance assessments, Mothers were subject to widespread formal and informal scrutiny. This impacted on their willingness to seek help and support. For some, the stakes were high, and they attempted to secure support for their complex needs whilst trying to navigate their way through systems that at every turn had the potential to remove their children. Mothers described being wary of asking for help, fearing formal negative evaluation or state assessment or surveillance that might result in their being deemed a 'mother not coping,' 'not able to protect her children,' or simply just not 'good enough':

> 'I really wanted help but knew if I asked then the spotlight would really be on me, and I just didn't want to risk losing my kids.' (Shanice)

Not all Mothers who misused substances necessarily viewed themselves as bad mothers despite widespread disapprobation. Particularly if their drug-related offending brought financial benefits or if they were still able to meet their children's basic needs. This was true for some Mothers, for others there was a process of realisation that addiction was not compatible with motherhood and that it had impacted on their ability to mother, and mother well:

> 'You don't see it when you are living in it…you know what I mean…in it, living it you don't think about the times you are not there for them…but I do now.' (Ursula)

Similarly, Dee and Tia talked about a developing awareness that they had not been 'emotionally there' (Dee) or 'emotionally available' (Tia), when they were in the midst of their addiction. Being 'available' and present as mothers was something discussed by several Mothers, and some struggled with the fact that their addiction or their imprisonment had impacted on their availability. Which in turn impacted on their perceived self-esteem and worth *as mothers*.

Some mothers reshaped their guilt or provided justification and 'evidence' of positive aspects of their mothering whilst minimising their substance misuse and its impact on their children, 'They never saw me use, ever; I was careful' (Tanya);

'I don't feel guilty because I know I was providing for them through my dealing. They went without nothing.'

Motherhood can be a valuable source of moral worth and self-esteem (Aiello and McQueeny, 2016: 34), and some Mothers were steadfast in their determination to retain a positive maternal identity. They defended their 'good mother' status by offering 'proof' of how much they loved their children, and their maternal achievements (vicariously through their children).

'They [Social Services] called me a functioning addict, that was the term, and I did function, I fed them, I clothed them, I took them to school, I didn't use in front of them...well they were upstairs, but they only saw me do it once. I always thought the kids were alright, they've got family providing stuff for them too, providing love and affection for them that I wasn't providing for them.' (Dee)

'My social worker said they are very "resilient" children, and that's down to me...I mean they went through 12 raids and were okay, they can take certain situations... when I knew I was going away [to prison], I gave them a good Christmas, they got everything they wanted...but then they have always had the best trainers, best everything. I've done this [sold drugs] so we can all be a bit more comfortable. Like our Mario, he would have a sleep over and there's not many mams would say oh well order anything from the pizza place you want...most would get a Tesco pizza if they were lucky.' (Tarian)

Echoing earlier studies (Baldwin and Epstein, 2017; Masson, 2019), there were many missed opportunities to help and support the Mothers. Several described explicitly asking for help:

'I needed help, but I didn't need to go prison, if the help had been there I wouldn't have, and I wouldn't have been separated from her [my daughter].' (Annie)

Dee described once asking for help 'before things got really bad.' She described being so 'off her head on crack,' she had 'passed out' on the sofa and the social worker had climbed in through the window to see her. Dee disclosed to him she was smoking crack, that her partner had died and that she 'needed help.' She described how he looked in her cupboards, and over the next couple of days phoned the school to check on the children's welfare:

'He came back—climbed in the window again and said, "Dee your house is clean, there is food in the cupboards, everything seems to be fine with the kids and school. I really don't know how I am supposed to support you." My life fell apart after that.'

Dee provided yet another example of where severe cuts to public sector funding has resulted in a reduced service of both staffing and resources (Barnes, 2015). Thus resulting in implications (especially for women), regarding the point at which a service can intervene or provide support. In effect, much of social service provision has become firefighting or crisis management as opposed to primary or preventative work that would provide better outcomes for mothers and their children (Morriss, 2018).

Several Mothers felt their imprisonment was a result of being inadequately supported in the community. They articulated clearly that it was in the community where their issues began and where their maternal identity had already begun to spoil. Schram (1999), and Gunn and Canada (2015), suggest that for addicted mothers there are multiple traversing stigmas that go beyond social, gendered and motherhood norms, which then taint the ideals of both 'good woman' and 'good mother.' This occurs on multiple levels, contributing to the 'spoiling,' of the maternal identity. Interestingly, despite acknowledging the failure of the 'systems' to intervene and support them, the Mothers internalised their 'failure' as mothers rather than contextualising the broader structural failures to support mothers (and women) per se. Despite motherhood arguably being the single most important safeguard for society's future generations, and the most governed (Rose, 1999), there remains a failure to adequately resource, fund and maintain the services that support women, especially woman with children.

Mothers Not Mothered

Although commonly noted as a relevant criminogenic factor in the backgrounds of women in prison (Carlen, 1983), women's experiences of being mothered has not yet been well investigated or evidenced in the literature. The Mothers' assessments of their own mothers, and their own experiences of being mothered were clearly based on the widely accepted ideas and ideologies of traditional motherhood. Providing the Mothers with a double-edged sword, i.e., they measured their own mothers against these established criteria, yet they were the same criteria with which they assessed themselves; and a fact of which the Mothers were all too aware; the same criteria that others used to judge *them*.

Nicola, like 14 other mothers, reflected on her experience of being poorly mothered. Concluding this had an impact on her own ability to mother. Importantly, also, on how she had coped (or not) with her past trauma:

> 'My mother was shit really; I know that sounds bad, but she was. She wasn't like other mothers … she just seemed blank most of the time. When what happened to me happened … she wasn't really there for me you know, I think the social thought about putting me in care 'cos they could see it … that she struggled with it and didn't help me, but I dunno I think they just forgot about me in the end. Anyway, so yeah … I didn't learn how to be a mum from her.'

Mothers who spoke of being poorly, negatively or inadequately mothered and the impact this had had on them often described being 'determined' (Sam) not to repeat the 'mistakes' their mothers had made. Several Mothers became reflective during the interviews. Making connections, sometimes for the first time, about their past experiences of being mothered and their own experiences of mothering. Stewart (2015) argues this is very important in terms of 'breaking cycles,' being a key feature of her work as a forensic-psychotherapist with mothers in prison.

> 'My mother was crap. Crap childhood, crap mum, crap life, what do my girls have?…crap mum, I really wanted to do it better.' (Emma)

Mothers who had experienced poor mothering were angry with themselves that they had not 'done better' (Sam), but equally seemed to accept or believe that there was an inevitability about their own 'failure' (Nicola) as mothers:

> 'My mother wasn't there for me, I lost her to addiction, she died to addiction and we went into foster care, I learned through counselling that my addiction…all that happened to me…it wasn't all my fault, I've made bad choices yeah…but it wasn't my fault…not with my life, with my childhood, you know what I mean?…with my mum…two dead addict parents, addiction it's genetic innit?…what chance did I have really, your childhood traumas, they come back…they get you…they gave me addiction, addiction made me a criminal, being a criminal gave me prison…all traceable back innit?' (Dee)

Similarly, Sam, whose emotionally abusive mother would regularly leave the family home for months on end without them, telling them it was their fault she was leaving, reflected:

> 'I didn't want to be like her, she was a cow really, pure and simple, what kind of mother behaves like that? I was determined to be better than her, I hated her because she left me, but then when I think about it what did I go and do? I left my daughter too, I went to prison, I suppose my daughter must have felt the same way I did really. Just not important enough.'

Stewart (2015) reiterates the importance of recognising the significance of mothers' own experiences of being mothered. She argues that for many criminalised mothers this bears some relationship to their life chances and choices and their own ability to mother. Particularly to widely accepted, expected, exacting external standards. She observed in criminalised mothers with whom she worked the frequency with which they had not experienced 'good enough' mothering (Winnicott's term), or had a 'deficient' maternal relationship. Stewart argues that when early years are marred by neglect and chaos the child does not develop well 'physically, emotionally, or cognitively.' Making them more likely to act emotionally and on impulse. Diane, who was serving a life sentence for killing her abusive husband, was very angry with her own mother, directly attributing her adult experiences and her offence to her childhood.

'I had the most horrendous upbringing from age four, beaten starved, abused by my mother and stepfather and all of her boyfriends in between. Witnessing all her sour relationships. I stepped out into the world and into violent relationships of my own. I had no chance.'

Hackett (2015: 45) suggests that mothers experiencing mental distress to an extent that it limits their own mothering abilities, are 'othered.' In agreement with Stewart, Hackett suggests that women often find themselves in these multiply disadvantaged and challenging positions, not always because of personal or individual failure, but because 'they are often disadvantaged as a result of discrimination, inequality, weakened socio-economic positions and victimisation' (ibid: 46). There is little doubt that many Mothers experienced a lack of 'good enough' mothering by mothers impoverished by their own circumstances, or that this had an effect on their mental wellbeing. Mary, who had struggled with mental health issues from an early age, left home at 14 in an attempt to 'escape' her addicted and abusive mother:

'I only really remember my mother as just being "there", not absent, but not present either. Drunk more often than not and she was obsessed with her pills [...] They definitely meant more to her than I did, I can't imagine her getting that stressed if she couldn't find me. I always felt like I was a burden, in the way, an irritation. So as soon as I was able to, I left. I left home just before I was 15.'

Mary's subsequent transient lifestyle left her vulnerable to abuse, and without the resilience and wisdom that Stewart suggests comes from a stable mother (or mother substitute), Mary found herself in a series of relationships with abusive men (i.e. replicating the cycle). Mary goes on to say how she got pregnant very quickly but was pleased because she felt that having a child 'to love' and for it to love her 'right back' gave her, her 'own family.' Nonetheless, Mary describes how her life swiftly spiralled out of control. Through a period of deteriorating and painful circumstances, Mary became addicted to alcohol. She experienced multiple violent and controlling relationships, lost the care of her sons to the LA, and found herself in prison. All of this Mary felt was traceable back to her childhood and her relationship with her mother. She felt she 'didn't have any self-worth to fight with' because she had never 'felt loved':

'It's probably not surprising that I entered the world I did. I never sold myself for sex, […] but the drink got me too. In some ways I understand her a bit better now, maybe she used the drink to block it all out too—I get that. I would end up trusting men who would hurt me, ply me with drugs, try to get me on the game, knock me about. It was like I had a sign on my head saying, "Do this, treat me like a cunt, I'm used to it."

Similarly, Cynthia, whose childhood was also marred by her expressed experiences of maternal neglect, reflected on her pathway into an offending and substance-reliant lifestyle:

'I'm not saying it was her fault…but we never got no affection from our mam, not even when we were babies, she was a drinker, see. If my mam had said that [I love you] to us when were young, us girls and a boy, well maybe we would have turned out different…who knows…but I think we would have.'

Early experiences of mothers who are distracted, addicted or abusive can have a devastating and lifelong impact on a child; but as also argued by Stewart, it is important not to solely lay the blame for such experiences in the laps of the mothers, but rather on 'a society that fails to support them' (ibid). Earlier discussion demonstrated how additional circumstantial factors mean that many mothers—even those entering prison for a first offence—do so 'already feeling they have failed as mothers because of their life chances and life choices' (Baldwin, 2017: 233). Their maternal identity is already spoiling (Goffman, 1963). Criminalised and imprisoned mothers are often struggling to hold on to a positive sense of self as a mother in a world seemingly trying to undermine that view.

Summary of *Chapter 5*

The Mothers came from quite diverse backgrounds and ranged widely in age, sentence length and time out of prison. Many of them entered prison with an already spoiling maternal identity. Most from disadvantaged backgrounds where they had faced multiple challenges which impacted on their maternal identity and maternal self-esteem. Their narratives revealed the many missed opportunities to support them, either as children or as adults. The Mothers were reluctant to seek support *as mothers* for fear of being negatively assessed and they feared losing their children. Earlier support might have prevented them being criminalised at all. Yet as individuals they were the ones paying the price for the failure in society and society's structures and systems to support them—either now as adults in need or when they were children.

In *Chapters 6* to *8* I look at the Mothers time in prison and reveal how the prison space and the dynamics within it can contribute to a highly stressful, frustrated and painful experience of incarcerated motherhood. The chapters in that section show the ways the Mothers sought to use the 'skills of motherhood' (Kitzinger, 1994: 242) to navigate through the prison system via relationships with each other, with prison staff, and through their children and outside contacts.

Pause for Thought

Are you able to recognise the points in the Mothers' stories where a practitioner might have been able to intervene? — What are the barriers to them supporting mothers more fully? — What would you have done personally within the boundaries and resources available?

What would be the value of earlier intervention? — How can services promote an atmosphere of safety and trust to encourage mothers to seek support? — What would/should that support look like?

CHAPTER 6

Entering the Prison Space and Early Days

'It wasn't the smell that hit me, or the fear or even the humiliation of being searched. It was the realisation I was separated from my children. Physically unable to reach them. Separated by walls and bars and distance.' (Karen)

Demonstrating O'Reilly's fundamental matricentric principle that 'motherhood matters,' this chapter explores the Mothers' described experiences of prison. The previous chapter revealed how they would have entered prison with an already spoiling and negative maternal identity, this chapter takes up that narrative from within the prison space. It centres the Mothers' voices on how the maternal experience is assembled and challenged in and through the carceral space thus germinating an 'enduring spoiled maternal identity.'

Conflicting opinions exist about whether the maternal in-prison experience can be an opportunity for positive and focussed reflection, a reprieve from external and oppressive pressures, a cruel, disproportionate, and largely unnecessary punishment and separation from children. Or perhaps most controversially, that it is no different from the experience of prison for non-mothers (Loper, 2006). Loper suggests it is 'no more difficult to be a mother in prison than it is to be a non-mother' (ibid: 93). This book provides evidence to dispute this stance, emphatically. The Mothers described how they struggled specifically as mothers to adjust to prison life, and how they felt that prison for a mother is 'a million times harder than if you're not a mother' (Jaspreet).

The chapter demonstrates how imprisoned mothers become *more* 'spoiled' in their maternal-self through the 'abasements, degradations, humiliations' and deprivations of prison. Which interacted with their motherhood and imported beliefs about 'good' motherhood. Through this and the following two chapters ('Mothering and Grandmothering from a Distance' and 'Regimes, Rules and Relationships') the women's reactions to entering prison *as mothers* and the impact on their maternal identity are explored.

The prison environment brought specific challenges, opportunities and experiences discrete from the separation from the Mothers' children. This included the actual prison space itself, whether the prison was open or closed,[1] how it was organized, the regime, and Mothers' relationships with prison staff and each other. These factors either mitigated or aggravated the pains associated with their maternal experience. The maternal experience was disrupted, altered, or destroyed by prison. For many Mothers, their mothering activities and consequently, their mothering role was significantly reduced or stripped away by the prison, rendering the mortification of motherhood complete.

Reception and early days — 'it just hit me'

The Mothers spoke of the shock, horror, fear and shame they felt on entering the 'total institution' of the prison space. Most of them found this and the early days and weeks of their sentences profoundly painful and harmful. As mothers, the punitiveness and harm of the experience was exacerbated and magnified. Like many prisoners, Maggie described how she entered reception and immediately felt a sense of bewilderment and shock at being there at all. She contextualised this by stating her bewilderment was immediately coupled with a feeling of shame that related to her children '… that's it … I've let them [her children] all down.'

Other Mothers described similar feelings: for some this started in the court or in the 'van,' the prison transport that conveyed them from court to prison, and was confirmed on arrival at the prison. Kady described how she was completely disorientated having been abused by fellow

---

1. In the female estate, prisons are defined only as 'open' or 'closed' as women are not categorised in the same way as male prisoners. Ten of the 12 women's prisons in the UK are closed-prisons, despite more than 80 per cent of the women being in prison for non-violent offences. See also: https://commonslibrary.parliament.uk/research-briefings/sn05646/

male prisoners in the van for 'hours,'[2] and after being 'shamed' in court, but said that was 'nothing' compared to how she felt when she arrived:

'I was exhausted after that awful journey, I cried for most of it. The things they said were vile…I didn't think I could feel any worse…but man was I wrong…nothing can prepare you for it [entering the prison] nothing.'

The Mothers' feelings of powerlessness, shame and disorientation during their early days in custody were compounded by and interrelated to their mother status:

'Going to prison as a mother is I think the worst thing…I genuinely can't think of anything worse as a mother to do to your children…I felt like I was watching it as if it was someone else. I was numb with shock but at the same time all I could think about was my children.' (Jaspreet)

Diane stated that entering prison made her feel like 'the worst mother in the world.' Annie, like many mothers, had not expected a custodial sentence and was sent to prison in shock after taking her daughter to school that morning. She expected to be able to make calls to her family to find out where her daughter was, who had picked her up from school. She was not given her reception phone call.[3] This caused her untold stress:

'I was supposed to get a reception phone call but I didn't get it because there was so many of us on the prison transport that day. I was literally going crazy crazy, crazy. It was driving me mad not even knowing she was safe. It was hours and hours before I finally got an officer to check for me that she was safe. I genuinely thought I would have a heart attack from the stress.'

---

2. Although guidelines seek to guard against mixed prison transports, it is not uncommon for female prisoners and male prisoners to travel in the same vehicle — verbal abuse/threats between prisoners, especially male to female, is also not uncommon. Women are usually the 'last drop off' as they will often be travelling to prisons furthest away for longer periods of time.
3. See guidance regarding reception phone calls: https://www.gov.uk/government/publications/early-days-in-custody-psi-072015-pi-062015 see also http://www.prisonreformtrust.org.uk/Portals/0/Documents/Prisoner%20Information%20Pages/04%20Keeping%20in%20contact%20with%20family%20and%20friends.pdf

Annie's experience was not unusual, echoing various findings by Her Majesty's Inspectorate of Prisons (HMIP). Fourteen of the mothers stated they had experienced delays in accessing their reception phone call. Mothers described how the delayed contact, especially with their children, impacted negatively on them. Making their first days in custody, when the Mothers were at their most vulnerable, even more challenging. Tia, who experienced a traumatic arrest at her daughter's school and in front of her children (discussed later), was remanded immediately. She spoke of her desperation to speak to her daughter, saying, 'I just wanted to know she was safe, to apologise to her, to ask her to forgive me … It was all I could think about.' Rita did have her reception call, but all of her children were out 'trick or treating.' Revealing the complex emotions mothers in prison often struggle with, she spoke of feeling 'relieved' that 'life just carried on for them,' but 'torn' because she wanted them to miss her, and then also 'guilty' for thinking that.

Mothers spoke of not being able to 'settle' (Sophie), 'think straight' (Cynthia), 'concentrate on anything' (Karen), 'sleep' (Annie), or 'eat' (Sophie), until they had seen or at least been in contact with their children. Missing their children permeated every aspect of their prison life and to many it was all-consuming, especially in the early days and weeks. Taranpreet, who had convinced herself that her toddler children had not recognised her on their first visit, wrote 'I'm totally broken […] I'm literally dead inside […] the mere fact my own children don't recognise me has torn me apart […] I've lost everything.' Like several Mothers, she struggled to get through her first days and weeks in custody.

Six Mothers spoke of feeling suicidal during that period, sadly not unusual for mothers in prison (see Baldwin and Epstein, 2017). It was the most emotionally intense period for most of them. Beth stated, 'I just didn't want to be here anymore, I felt like I'd lost her [her baby] forever, if I wasn't a mother anymore what was the point of me?' Some Mothers made explicit reference to suicide:

> 'I must admit I did have very negative thoughts, I'm ashamed to admit it crossed my mind to take my life … obviously I didn't!' (Mavis)

Kady felt that it was 'only' the fact than an officer 'was kind' to her and 'made time' to support her as a newly pregnant mum that she 'got through that first week.' She felt that, but for that officer, she might have taken her own life.

Visits as well as phone calls were often delayed. This had a huge impact on the Mothers' wellbeing (and likely their children's wellbeing). Tia was sentenced just before Christmas and had not yet seen her children after three weeks in custody. She was told she was being moved to another prison the day before her children were due to visit. She was already more than two hours away from home; the prison she moved to was a further 150 miles away (almost three hours) from her home:

> 'They shipped me out to [........ Prison the day before the visit] Just because the prison was full they said — simple as that ... I said "I can't go, I can't go on the ship out I haven't seen my kids yet ... they are coming tomorrow," and they just said "The visit will be cancelled." There is no emotion, no sorry ... the answer was just "Tough you are going, you are booked on the van". I was devastated, I couldn't believe it.'

Tia goes on to say that staff forgot to cancel the visit and her children (aged four and 12) arrived at the prison expecting to see their mother, whom they had last seen when she was arrested at the school gates three weeks before. Tia stated '... to say they were devastated is an understatement, apparently Theo [the four-year-old] could be heard crying right through the hall, I was told.' Tia's move meant that the children and their caregiver would have to stay overnight in a nearby hotel to facilitate a visit, adding further financial burden to a family already struggling. Nonetheless, the visit was booked, the accommodation was booked with the cheapest 'no refund' option. Three days before this visit Tia was told she had a further court appearance in a court near her previous prison. However, when she arrived, she was told her presence was not required. As she had been travelling for a total of five hours by this time she was asked if she needed a 'toilet break.' Yes she did. The transport from that particular court only served her previous prison. So that was where she was taken and readmitted, despite her children's replacement visit being booked at her new prison and where all her belongings were. By the time new visiting arrangements were made, six weeks and Christmas had passed without Tia's children seeing their mother.

Tia's experience was not unusual. Several Mothers identified that being separated from their family was generally 'hard,' but that prolonged periods of separation from their children was worse. Rita, who also had to wait weeks for a visit, summed-up how many of the women felt by stating:

> '...at that point, I would have given up all access to all the rest of my family, even my own mum, for that one visit from my children...I didn't feel I could function without seeing them, for the first time in my life I considered self-harm for no other reason than I had no idea how to handle the pain.'

About a third (13) of the Mothers disclosed they had self-harmed at some point in their lives. Four Mothers spoke of self-harming *directly* related to their mothering pain, especially during the early days and weeks, often the most vulnerable period for mothers. Sam described self-harm 'as a way of coping [with missing her son] ... letting out the pain.' Mothers who self-harmed, as most other prisoners, had additional factors contributing to their self-harming behaviour, such as pre-existing mental health issues and trauma histories (and see Walker and Towl, 2016). Nonetheless, maternal emotions were a factor. Nicola had previously lost two children to the care system and her third child was taken on her reception into custody, '[Y]eah I thought about ending it, the pain was too much, another child, gone...I felt dead.'

Clearly, Mothers who self-harmed, missed their children and the associated guilt and shame of being a mother in prison was a trigger for both suicidal ideas and self-harming actions. Rita spoke of being in the cell next to a 'girl' who attempted (unsuccessfully) to take her life after being informed that her child would be adopted. Rita spent the 'next few days trying to talk her out of killing herself.'

Mothers are supposed to be asked about and tested for pregnancy on reception (MOJ, 2020). As noted in earlier chapters, pregnancy is an important aspect in relation to developing a healthy maternal identity (and obviously a healthy child). Being in prison frustrated Mothers' efforts to view themselves in a positive light as mothers. Kady, who found out she was pregnant on reception into prison, struggled to articulate her feelings at first but her meaning was clear:

'I dunno…it was like…aww man…like pregnancy is a pure time innit…becoming a mum. Its special…and to be in prison for it…I can't describe it. It just felt wrong…more wrong than if I weren't [pregnant].'

Eight Mothers were pregnant for some part or the whole of their incarceration. Not only did this provide yet another opportunity for additional surveillance by the authorities, but also for additional, internal and external judgement and shaming. This was heavily influenced by traditional motherhood ideology, with the additional layer of imported values and beliefs about pregnancy.

Importation of 'Traditional Motherhood' Values and Beliefs

The Mothers' worries about their families and especially their children 'outside' was the biggest adjustment for them in prison. Some women, and especially mothers, never do fully make that adjustment. Inextricably bound to challenges in adjustment for mothers were imported beliefs about motherhood and a conscious or unconscious acceptance of traditional motherhood ideology:

'Almost as soon as I went into the prison I knew I would forever be looked at as a bad mother…and I felt like one too to be fair…there can't be much worse than a mother who goes to prison can there?' (Rita)

Throughout history, mothers, including imprisoned mothers, have internalised attributes and circumstances important and acceptable to mothering. More explicitly to *good* mothering. Arguably the most fundamental of these widely held beliefs is that mothers 'are, or rather should be, just good' (Baldwin, 2017: 233). How well prisoners adapt to prison life is influenced by the deprivations of prison life, and pre-prison characteristics which are imported into the prison (Dhami et al, 2007).

The Mothers felt the deprivation of their maternal role keenly but were also greatly affected by the traditional motherhood values and beliefs they imported into the prison space. The traditional motherhood ideological framework which underpinned all of the Mothers' experiences was at the root of a great deal of guilt and shame. Primarily because the Mothers were measuring themselves against the aforementioned exacting and almost universal standards of motherhood or mothers' 'Code of Conduct.' The Mothers' perceived failure to 'measure up' triggered guilt and shame which permeated their narratives.

Many of the Mothers spoke about the 'expectations' and 'normals' (Maggie) of motherhood and how accepted ideology of motherhood is fundamentally at odds with going to prison. The Corston Report (2007) famously stated that many mothers who go to prison automatically feel like and are deemed to be 'bad mothers,' and Lockwood (2018: 157) identifies that imprisoned mothers are afforded less 'sympathy' than mothers separated by 'other' means. Embodying Sykes' (1958: 79) concept of a 'morally acceptable identity,' many of the Mothers struggled to retain a healthy and affirming maternal identity because of the self-imposed principle that you cannot be a 'good' mother *and* go to prison.

Queenie spoke about how her daughter 'shamed' her as a mother and questioned how she could 'as a mother' allow herself to be in a position where prison was 'even a possibility.' Queenie went on to say that as a grandmother, this was 'layered,' and that her motherhood *and* grandmotherhood were measured against her daughter's friends' mothers and mother-in-law. Who were — by definition due to the fact that they had not been to prison — 'better' than her:

'I'm compared to the other nanny all the time — the granny who hasn't been to prison — I can never be as good as her — because she hasn't been to prison … I'm the runt in the mother department now.'

Similarly, Maggie, also a grandmother and feeling the burden of expectations of motherhood, grandmotherhood, and age, stated:

'I was a good Mam, well I did my best…when I went to prison I felt like that was all wiped out, I'd failed…even worse because I'm a Nanna and a Mam, I'm meant to be respectable at my age…'

As previously in this book, it is argued that 'guilt' is synonymous with motherhood. Internally, most mothers feel guilty about their 'failings' because they are set-up to fail due to impossibly high societal standards. Further, and importantly, 'maternal guilt' is often compounded by society's failure to deliver structures and policies that actively support motherhood (Rich 1977), and prison is by and large no different.

For the Mothers, guilt as 'prison mothers' (Danielle) went above and beyond the guilt familiar to most mothers. Prison provided the hook on which to hang a sense of guilt, shame and perceived failure. Liss et al (2012: 1113–4) suggest that although shame and guilt are often used synonymously, they are distinct emotions. Arguing that guilt 'involves a negative evaluation of a specific behaviour,' whereas shame 'represents a more global negative self-evaluation' and social evaluation (ibid). The Mothers used the terms interchangeably but referred to guilt more often in the 'in'-prison context, in relation to their physical absence in their children's lives, and also regarding their children's own expressed pain at missing their mothers.

Ursula described her deeply felt guilt, which pervaded her whole narrative, particularly triggered by one specific painful conversation with one of her daughters:

'And then I remember Irie coming, so she's my middle daughter,…the one that's the gymnast, coming on a visit, I went to hug her at the end of the visit and said oh I love you Irie. And she goes "Mum don't do that again." And I said what do you mean…what do you mean? She goes, "Don't say you love me". And I said oh, what do you mean? She goes, "Mum, I'm going to tell you this, I'm going to tell you this once only…if you ever knew what love is you as my mother would have never put yourself in a position where you could have been taken away from me. So don't ever say you love me again". And I think it was like a dagger in my heart that day. It felt like a dagger. The guilt man, the guilt…It felt like the worse pain ever and…I suppose it brought me to life in a way, you know, maybe … I'm one of these people that probably needs painful experiences to learn. I went back to the cell and I really thought about it and I thought she's right, you know, here's the reality, I'm a shit mum because I'm in prison. At the end of the day how can you be a good mum, how can you even pretend to yourself you're a good mother, because you're actually separated from your children. You are not there for them and your children are in intense pain and you are not there, you are not available to them to ease their pain. So there isn't really anything that I can respond to that other than sit here and hold that. I suppose the only thing to be done is to make sure that I'm never in that position again and just hope that they'll forgive me at some point.'

Similarly, Rosie described her guilt and its relationship to her spoiled maternal identity:

'I've missed so much, the guilt eats away at me knowing I wasn't there for her first period, her first boyfriend, her first day at big school. She will always remember I wasn't there. I feel guilty every single day. I feel like the worst mother in the world.'

Rayna was explicit in rooting her 'biggest guilt' in the separation from her children, despite the fact that her mother was ill and subsequently died during her sentence:

'Yes I felt guilty about my mother and not being there for her, for the family, of course I did, I don't even know how to process that … but my biggest guilt was about not being there for my children. When they needed me most, I wasn't there.'

Tamika and Tanisha both mentioned the 'additional' (Tanisha) guilt and shame they felt as pregnant mothers in prison, especially on occasions such as attending 'outside' hospitals for maternity appointments in handcuffs. However, their 'shame' was not confined to outside appointments:

'Being pregnant in prison is awful, you can feel people eyes on you judging you, I tried so hard to hide my bump all the time — I was scared for my baby, but I was mostly just ashamed.' (Tamika)

Most pregnant women in prison spend their pregnancy feeling powerless and fearful of miscarrying or giving birth in prison, or alone in their cells, fears echoed by the pregnant Mothers. These complex concerns add to the guilt and shame by 'reminding' mothers that they are pregnant in abnormal circumstances. Arendell (2000) suggests that the 'tasks of pregnancy' and preparing for the birth are important aspects for a mother in developing a maternal identity. Mothers in prison are essentially denied this experience, at least until (and if) they secure a place on the prison MBU. Places are often not secured until very late in pregnancy, or even after the birth[4] (Sikand, 2017). Thus, pregnant women in prison do not always go through the process of 'becoming a mother' in the way that free mothers do, via attending antenatal classes or buying baby clothes or preparing a nursery. This can have a profound effect not only on a mother's maternal emotions and maternal identity, but also on the mother-child bond. Which can have lifelong implications.

'I was so concerned with keeping my belly safe in there I didn't really think about it as a baby or even me as a mam … so when the baby was born I felt quite disconnected. I didn't feel like he was even mine.' (Tanisha)

As demonstrated above, many of the Mothers had felt their maternal identity was already spoiling prior to them coming to prison. Some Mothers described a further spoiling having occurred in the courtroom and via judges' comments related to their motherhood, illustrating Collins' (2020) points about shame and social evaluation, and Liss et al's (2012) about fear of negative evaluation:

---

4. From July 2020 following a review of pregnancy and new mother provisions in custody, measures and recommendations were implemented seeking to improve outcomes and process MBU applications earlier and easier. Staff received training and guidance for working with pregnant and new mothers in custody, as directed by the MOJ: the author has been involved in their development and implementation. See https://assets.publishing.service.gov.uk/government/uploads/system/uploads/attachment_data/file/905559/summary-report-of-review-of-policy-on-mbu.pdf

'I would play over and over in my head what the judge said in court, he basically said I was not fit to be a mother, after he said that I didn't really hear anything else. My head was swimming.' (Carla)

Nicola's lawyer had informed the judge that her son would in all likelihood be adopted if she was given a custodial sentence, hoping that would be a mitigating factor. However, Nicola felt it served to 'seal her fate':

'The judge knew my other two were taken off me and so I think assumed that that would be best for my son, he took no notice of the fact that I'd been clean for years, that all had happened ... my relapse was because of my mum [who had died], but he just said that social services had decided I wasn't a good enough mum to keep my other kids so why would I be good enough now ... he actually said my son would be better off without me ... words to that effect. It broke me. Everyone in that court looked at me like I was scum, a shit mother ... scum.'

Maggie had offended as a way of trying to alleviate debt and had paid back most of what she had stolen. She was hoping for a non-custodial sentence, especially as she was a primary carer for her terminally-ill husband and one of her grandchildren. Nonetheless, the judge had said to her, in words that Maggie stated she would never forget, that she could not 'hide behind her husband's illness, or her grandchild.' Shockingly, the judge went further, stating:

'You didn't think of these things when you stole, as a mother and a wife you should have been thinking of your family's needs. You were not. You took those risks knowing the potential consequences, and now Mrs Brown, those consequences have found you out.'

For most of the Mothers their identity as mothers was truly spoiled, and their motherhood was mortified, once they were imprisoned. Several Mothers used the phrase 'the worst mother in the world,' revealing not only the strength with which they felt their failure, but also the significance of their comparison to other mothers and wider mothering 'standards.' Several Mothers felt their maternal identity was fully spoiled as they entered custody. For others it was gradual. Maggie described how, from the moment she entered prison, she knew that as a mother she had let her family down and that for her and her children she 'knew it would never be quite the same again.' Similarly, Annie described how for her, being in prison was incompatible with 'good' motherhood:

'Being in prison made me feel like I was just a rubbish mum…I know she felt abandoned, she missed me, that's all she kept saying, I need you she'd say…that was the one, I need to smell you, I don't know what you smell like anymore…what kind of mother can put her child through that and still think they are a good mum[?]'

Ursula described a gradual 'dawning,' she had felt, as did Tarian and Dee, that when she first went to prison, she 'did not want to examine [her]self as a mother.' Like Dee, Tia and Tarian, Ursula stated that, despite her lifestyle and conviction, she had held on to a positive maternal identity and continued to describe herself as a 'good mum.' However, once in prison they all struggled to retain the same view: 'that became impossible' (Tia). Ursula, when speaking about the aforementioned visit from her daughter Irie, had previously 'held' on to her belief for some time, but for her it disappeared in a 'moment':

'In terms of how I felt about myself as a mother, I would say that when I first went to prison I was still of the mindset that I was a good mother […] I don't think I really wanted to really look at my mothering and so I just thought this is an occupational hazard, selling drugs…the kids are fine and they're not in care, they're with their dad, everything's fine…But then, because in that moment of understanding that I wasn't a good mother, nothing else about me made sense, did it. It's like my whole life fell away in that moment in the prison.'

Many of the Mothers expressed very clearly that they felt that prison life was 'different for mothers' (Mavis), that prison would have been 'piss easy if I weren't a mother' (Shanice). Even those who had current partners who were 'good' fathers to their children felt that their role as mothers was more significant to their children, and to society, than that of the fathers. They were not all saying this explicitly (although some did) but that the 'traditional' expectations and roles of motherhood meant they would be 'missed more' (Karen) by their children than if it were their fathers who were incarcerated:

> 'It's not him they go to when they are ill, or when they have forgotten their homework, or when they have an issue with friends, it's me, it's not him who takes time off work when they are poorly, it's not him who knows their favourite colour, or their best friends' names...it's me...They go to him for money and lifts...don't get me wrong they love him just the same I think...but it's me they rely on; me they depend on to always just be there.'

Annie put it simply, 'mums make it better.' 'Being there,' or availability, was something raised by most of the Mothers. Simply because of their absence and unavailability they felt they were failing their children. This challenged their maternal identity. Most of the Mothers felt their children and grandchildren were in good hands and that their alternative caregivers would be 'doing a good job' (Rita). Nevertheless, they worried about how their children would cope with their absence, and also spoke of how this served to reduce their own sense of self as mothers. As Ursula stated, 'I just wasn't there... that was the problem, I just wasn't there.'

Being physically separated from their children was traumatic for the Mothers. Both the source of their pain and 'confirmation' that they were *bad* or *failed* mothers. Not all described feeling a sense of guilt or failure: Tarian and (to a lesser extent) Dee both felt that their actions and offending helped them to be better mothers and refused to 'wear' the judgement of others that they were by definition of their substance misuse and imprisonment necessarily and automatically 'bad mothers.' Tarian stated:

> 'I've never been a mamsie mam, I'd cook and clean and obviously I was a provider, but never been one to get on the floor and do puzzles with them and stuff...but we don't all have to be the same do we? Doesn't mean I love

my kids less…do I feel guilty about my life no…they were always okay I made sure of it.'

Similarly, although Dee did talk about her own feelings of guilt, she also spoke about how she felt the responsibility for her situation was not solely hers:

'I'm not going feel guilty about it all…it is what it is, life happened to me you know…I didn't choose all that…and it all had consequences so why should I feel guilty about it all…I did my best with the shit hand I was dealt.'

Powerfully evident was the Mothers' resilience and hope. Many of them had continued to mother well through complex and challenging circumstances. They had great hope of continuing. Despite facing a possibly uncertain future, imagining and planning for their maternal future was an important part of the Mothers' hopes. As their narratives will further illustrate, hope was the antidote to guilt for many and provided the bridge between their past and present experiences and their anticipated 'better' futures.

A significant observation in the Mothers' absorption of traditional motherhood ideology was a collective sense that motherhood gave the women a feeling of agency and power. The Mothers might have felt powerless in being unable to undertake as much active mothering as they would have liked (being subject to the power of the prison). Yet they found strength in just *being* mothers. Mothers felt that *as mothers and grandmothers* they had achieved something that 'men can't do' (Annie), something that could not be easily replicated, something 'special' (Mavis). They were separated from their children or may even have had children removed from their care, but they were still mothers; they had borne children — and it mattered:

'I might never see them again, but I have sons, I am a mother, and I will always be a mother, no-one can take that from me.' (Nicola)

The Mothers took comfort and had a sense of marvel and achievement because as mothers they felt they were 'better than dads' (Taranpreet).

Where a Mother had been able to retain a sense of a positive maternal identity, she felt a sense of pride and would get angry and frustrated at attempts to minimise or reduce her mothering role. Beth, like others, felt, 'It's the only thing I'm good at.' As O'Reilly (2016) succinctly states, 'motherhood matters,' and it most certainly did to the Mothers.

A significant factor of the everyday lived prison experiences of mothers in prison is the support they receive from 'outside' (Dye and Aday, 2019). Demonstrating traditional models of motherhood and family, the most common source of support the Mothers referred to came from their own mothers—who were often their children's caregivers and despite sometimes having troubled relationships with them. Traditional models of family and mothering evoke 'natural order' and a series of expectations. Expectations like—in times of need, mothers 'should' and will provide support, encouragement, guidance, motivation and hope throughout their children's lives. For some of the older Mothers and grandmothers, this significant source of support was not always available: four of the grandmothers' parents were already deceased, others had quite elderly parents and two had very sick parents. The expectation was that they as daughters would and 'should' take on the caring role—'return the favour' (Margaret), by looking after their own parents in their advancing years.

This was yet another source and layer of guilt for the mothers who were grandmothers, and a source of worry for the older Mothers. They worried about their parents' health and their own absence and subsequent inability to provide care and support for them; and within that, should their parents become ill, then who would look after their own children? Maggie's elderly father died whilst she was in custody, and she felt that her mother blamed her for 'causing the stress' that 'killed' him. She was angry with Maggie for not being there 'like a daughter should be.' They rarely spoke after Maggie was released. Such thoughts and emotions occupied the minds of the grandmothers, together with the parallel worries and feelings that they (as per the expectations of motherhood) were failing their own adult children, *and* their grandchildren, *and* their own elderly parents.

Being physically apart from their children and grandchildren was a source of universal pain, as was not actually being able to 'do' the tasks associated with mothering (and daughtering). This also had a significant impact on the mothers' maternal identities and maternal self-esteem.

 Pause for Thought

How would you feel if your children were being bullied because you were a 'prison mother'? — What would it make you feel like if in court the judge said, 'What kind of mother are you?' or that you should have thought of your children? — If your children had no food and no warm clothes what support networks could you call on? — What if you had none, what would you do?

What was your reaction to the mothers who are 'repeating' patterns from their own upbringing? — What might have helped them to have a different outcome?

Do you judge a criminal mother differently to other criminals?

Summary of *Chapter 6*

For the mothers, their already spoiling maternal identity was confirmed as soon as they entered the prison space, and further compounded by the reduction or removal of their maternal role. The Mothers struggled to adapt to being away from their children, describing how the structural barriers to contact impacted them negatively. At times risking their mental health and wellbeing. Most of the Mothers, regardless of the circumstances concerning the care of their children, remained preoccupied with all matters maternal. Whether that be the loss of their maternal role or the actual loss of their children. The Mothers and grandmothers measured their 'performance' as mothers against traditional models of motherhood, grandmotherhood and mothers-to-be that were imported into the prison with them — and importantly that were shared by others. The next chapter continues to explore how the Mothers own assessments of their mothering intertwined with the perceptions and reaction of others to their incarcerated motherhood, and how this served to frustrate or support the Mothers' in prison experiences.

CHAPTER 7

Distant Mothering and Grandmothering

'Going home is all I think about, the joy and love, to be able to
cook his tea, hold him, to know what his day has been like, to dress
him, to choose his clothes, to know what time he goes to sleep,
to hold him, to smell him. Just be a mother really.' (Lauren)

As already described the Mothers felt their maternal identity was fully
spoiled once they were imprisoned. Contributing to that perception was
the fact that they no longer 'felt' like mothers, and the reason they gave
for this was the lack of ability to perform their mothering role.

All of the Mothers articulated that there was a distinction between
'being' a mother and actually 'doing the job' (Beth) of mothering. The
actions of mothering or, as O'Reilly (2006) calls it 'motherwork,' was
hugely important to the Mothers and grandmothers. The 'stripping away'
of their maternal role and identity was incredibly painful:

'There's a massive difference in actually being a mother and actually doing
it, anyone can get pregnant, anyone can have a kid, but that's not the doing
bit is it? Being there for them, being reliable, being on their side and putting
them first, loving them more than anything or anyone, that's being a mother
and doing the job.' (Beth)

This chapter explores the challenges the Mothers faced concerning
their maternal role and examines how their contact with children and
relationships with caregivers could magnify or mitigate those challenges,
thus facilitating active mothering or rendering the Mothers and their
mothering 'invisible.'

Reflective, Active and Invisible Mothering

Enos (2001) suggests that 'roles' in life re-affirm who we are by what we do; thus as a fire fighter fights fires, and a nurse nurses, she argues that mothers need to mother in order to 'feel like' mothers. It is clear from previous research, and echoed in this book, that the disruption to their mothering role was hard for the Mothers *and* grandmothers to bear. Losing their mother role illustrates what Goffman (1961: 11) called 'role dispossession,' which he suggested is a by-product of 'total institutions' like prison.

For the Mothers, the actions associated with mothering, i.e. 'doing' mothering, were important. Not being able to do mothering made them feel like failed mothers. For those mothers who had already lost care of their children or for whom the return to them of their children was in question, the challenge to retain a positive maternal identity was even greater. Danielle spoke of 'missing' all of the 'jobs' of motherhood, saying that it drove her 'demented and tortured' not knowing where her son was or how his days were being filled. Even though she had a good relationship with her own mother, who was his caregiver and with whom she was in contact every day, she said:

'…it's not the same as doing, or knowing, I don't feel like a mam anymore, how can I be when I'm not there?'

The Mothers' anxieties and guilt were at their height when they felt their children 'needed them most'; often, but not always, this would be on special occasions or for specific life events. Shanice spoke a lot about missing the 'little things' she associated with motherhood and described how she felt her role as a mother was 'diluted' by not doing them. She felt replaced and displaced as a mother, jealous that her own mother had taken on her mothering role. Although Shanice phoned home daily, she described those calls as difficult. Stating that, afterwards, she would reflect and feel like she was an outsider looking through a window at 'what used to be my life.' She described how she would try to do some small 'jobs' of motherhood during contact, such as her daughter's hair, or to assist with her homework during phone calls; but her daughter would always tell her it was 'okay' and that her 'nanny had done it.' Shanice said this made her feel 'pointless.' These frustrations and deprivations (Sykes, 1958) were similarly described by several of the mothers:

> 'It was hard man, you miss so much of their lives, things you don't even think of on a day to day basis, but they are the things that make you a mam. Things like walking to nursery with him, picking my daughter up from school, those journeys in the car where we did most of our talking really. I missed that...watching cartoons with them. Just hearing about their days, even watching them fight and bicker, I never thought I'd say it, but I even missed that!'

Ursula described a phone call in which her daughter was very distressed because she had a gymnastics competition, and her leotard was not washed, and they had run out of soap-powder. Ursula knew that if she'd been at home she simply would have 'washed it with shampoo or soap, or actually not run out of soap powder at all!' She found this particular phone call distressing because she could not 'mother,' she could not solve the problem. This made her feel 'powerless, hopeless' and 'disconnected.' Ursula hung-up the phone in 'utter despair.' Annie and Shanice described how not being 'actively' involved in their 'motherly duties' (Annie) made them feel like 'less of a mother' (Shanice). Annie described how she didn't recognise herself, 'when that gets taken away from you, you don't know who you are. You have lost who you are because that is me, I am a mum.' Similarly, Shanice stated:

> 'It's the little things that get you, not taking them to school, not knowing how their day has gone, not being able to see what they are wearing that day, not making their packed lunches. You expect to be upset at birthdays and Christmas, not going to parents' evening, that kind of stuff, you expect to miss that and it's not a shock, but honestly the worst pain is in the little things.'

Echoing previous research on mothers in prison over an extended period of time all of the Mothers were preoccupied with thoughts of their children. Whether those thoughts related to missing them, hoping to reunite with them, worrying about them, anxieties about resuming their mothering role, or even coming to terms with the loss of their children to LA care, motherhood related issues were of primary concern. Reflecting on their mothering and 'thinking about' their children was something the mothers engaged in 'all the time' (Jaspreet). Tia described this as 'invisible mothering.' Tia felt that it was an important part of her prison experience and was possible only because she was clean and away from the pressures of her substance-misusing peers and her old lifestyle. She also felt that the reflection she undertook in prison was an important part of preparing for release and 'doing better' in the future: Emma also spoke about how reflecting on her motherhood helped to motivate her:

> 'I've been thinking a lot about it lately, I want to be a better mum I want to see my daughter. If I go back to my old lifestyle before I came to prison…well it's just drugs, drugs, drugs, heroin…I don't want that. I'm getting too old for that game and I just want to see my girl…but I wouldn't let her see me on the gear.'

The Mothers spoke of how they mothered 'in the background' (Sandra) of their children's lives, physically invisible or out of reach but still trying to organize and manage caregivers and how they 'brought up [their] kids' (Jaspreet). This sometimes caused friction with caregivers and the Mothers stress and worry. Karen spoke of how she was determined to ring her daughter's school when her daughter was being bullied, stating, 'I was still her mum.' It was important to Karen, that, even if she could not directly mother her children in the same way as she had prior to coming to prison, she would still be able to maintain some of the tasks she felt were her responsibility.

Echoing Lockwood's (2018) research, the Mothers felt that the more involvement they lost in their children's lives, the more their positive maternal identity reduced. To counter this, they would 'micromanage' (Rita) from prison, trying to 'foresee' all of the potentials.

Several Mothers who had known in advance that they were going to prison and who therefore had a period at home before sentencing, had tried to prepare—or mother—in advance. For example, Rita 'cooked loads and filled up the freezers,' even buying sanitary products for her pre-teen daughters 'just in case they started while I was away.' Others had bought birthday and Christmas presents, or they had 'sorted out the bills and left loads of notes' (Maggie). Most had worried about how 'they would manage without me' (Maggie) and had assumed or worried that their families would 'fall apart,' 'descend into chaos' (Rita) or 'break down completely' (Jaspreet). This brought up mixed emotions for the mothers: they wanted their families—and especially their children—to be cared for but, as Rita put it, 'I also wanted them to miss me.' When most of the families survived their absence, to a greater or lesser extent, the mothers worried about how it would be when they returned to them, and what their role would then be (the focus of the next chapter).

Tarian, who spent time on a prison MBU with her son, reflected on her desire to be a 'different kind of mam' when she was released. She said that her life outside as a 'drug dealer' and mother-of four other children had been frenetic and focussed on drugs. She stated that had she not found out she was pregnant when she came to prison, she would have been a 'very different kind of prisoner,' admitting she would have kept 'ducking and diving' and being 'a player.' As she wanted to keep her new baby with her, and knew she was being 'watched and assessed' informally even before she put in her application for the MBU, she 'played the game.' Actively preparing for the impending birth like a 'perfect mother.' She was successful in her application and found herself really enjoying the intensive active mothering of her baby in a non-chaotic space in a way she had never experienced with any of her other four children. Ironically, the prison space provided Tarian with a sanctuary from her home chaos and created a space where she could 'just be a mother.' Sadly, her MBU experience was not universal amongst other Mothers who had spent time on a prison MBU although they were grateful that their children were not removed into care, they had found the 'constant threat' of their babies being removed, and the additional surveillance, stressful (Kady).

Six of the Mothers had experienced one or all of their children going into either temporary or permanent care of the LA, and all of them described this background/invisible mothering, even though they may not — or were not expecting to — regain custody of their children. The Mothers all described their mother identity as significant to them.

> 'I thought about my kids every day, in that sense I was no different to the other mothers.' (Nicola)

Beth, who was still breastfeeding her three-month-old baby when she was sentenced, described the 'agony' of having full and leaking breasts 'but no baby.' She stated that she:

> '…thought of my daughter every single minute of every single day, it was awful. I didn't want to be here most of the time, I felt like nothing…I missed her so much.'

One of Dee's children was living with Dee's sister but her sister 'couldn't cope' and so handed Dee's daughter to the LA. Dee stated she was 'beside herself' and 'worried all the time' that she would not get her daughter back. The loss of a child to the care of the LA has far reaching psychological effects (Morriss, 2018) and the Mothers in this situation struggled to deal with their emotions, which were compounded by them being in prison. Morris describes mothers who have lost a child to care as 'haunted' and highlights the lack of compassion and empathy afforded to mothers who lose their children in this way in contrast to a child dying. Nicola described herself as 'an invisible mother now.'

Even when a mother does not lose her children to the care system on imprisonment, the impact of maternal imprisonment on their children and the wider family is huge. Not least because she is most often the primary caregiver of her children. Maintaining contact and navigating caregiver relationships is challenging. Contact with children and caregivers was sometimes supportive and assisted the Mothers in maintaining an active and involved maternal-role. At other times it was fraught with difficulties and served to remind the Mothers of their separation and undermined them in terms of their maternal-role and identity.

Contact

Contact with children was often bittersweet. Mothering from the confines of prison generated a number of challenging issues for the Mothers and their families regarding contact. Her Majesty's Inspectorate of Prisons (HMIP) directs that all prisons must promote and facilitate easy and regular access to visits and phone calls. Furthermore, the Farmer Reviews (2017; 2019) reiterated the importance of 'family ties,' arguing that families have a significant role in the rehabilitation and desistance of prisoners. Despite now having devolved budgets and some freedom to develop family-friendly initiatives, prisons do not always reflect this significance in their policies and practices regarding families or contact (Booth, 2020).

Experiences of contact between the Mothers and their children was varied and challenging, influenced somewhat by institutional challenges, also by their own emotions and relationships with their children and caregivers. For parents, especially mothers, contact with children is particularly important. In fact, more than one Mother felt it was a matter of life or death:

'…if I hadn't been able to see them, I just wouldn't have survived, it's that simple.' (Rita)

Most of the Mothers had the care of their children pre-prison and most, though not all, were expecting to resume care on release. Communication with children and grandchildren provided the most important and concrete strategy for maintaining relationships and an affirming maternal identity:

'…just hearing her say mummy was the best, I missed being called that so much.' (Sophie)

Visits and phone calls were an opportunity for the mothers to engage in 'active mothering,' which was important not only to meet the needs of the children, but also to affirm the Mothers' maternal identities and assist their coping. However, contact was often fraught with difficulties. Echoing previous studies (e.g. Booth, 2020; Masson, 2019), regular contact for the Mothers was often compounded by circumstances beyond their control, reinforcing their sense of powerlessness concerning their children:

'...you knew a visit could be taken away or ended at any point, it was like a knot in your stomach all the time.' (Tanya)

The Mothers described contact with their children as 'complicated' (Mavis). Not unusually, some, especially those on shorter sentences or in closed-prisons (see later discussion), chose not to receive visits from their children (Baldwin and Epstein, 2017). This was for a myriad of reasons, some related to practicality (i.e. cost of travel, time, distance from prison), or the non-child friendliness of the visiting experience, sometimes because it was 'too much' (Shanice) either for themselves or for their children. Mothers made what they saw as a 'protective' decision not to allow their children to visit (Baldwin, 2015; O'Malley, 2018):

'I didn't want him to visit because I thought...I didn't want to upset him because I know he wouldn't understand what was going on. I would be the one breaking down when he had to go, and I didn't want him to see that and be upset. Because he wouldn't understand why mummy couldn't come out. I didn't want him to. I didn't want that for me or for him. It would be just too painful.' (Shanice)

Or because the children did not know their mother was in prison. Mignon and Ransford (2012) suggest that this reluctance to disclose is sometimes related to embarrassment and the avoidance of stigma and/ or judgement:

'I don't let my children come to visit; they think I am away at work, a few of us have done this…I wouldn't cope if I saw them. How could I stay here and let them go at the end…how? But anyway I just don't want them to know I did bad things.' (Alexandra)

Similarly, Danielle told her son she was working away, although now she regretted that decision because of the impact it had had on her son:

'But now he thinks I've chosen work over them and he hates me, so I probably should have just been honest.'

Shanice described how she witnessed mothers coming back from visits and self-harming, or just breaking down and not coping at all. Like Rita, Taranpreet spoke of a mother in the next cell to her who had tried to take her own life after a visit with her six-month-old baby. Visits were a source of both joy and pain for the Mothers and described as a 'mixed blessing' (Rita), and 'bittersweet' because of the complex emotions they triggered in both themselves and their children. The Mothers described complex and competing emotions before a visit, such as anxiety, foreboding, worry, excitement, guilt, shame, sadness and happiness—with a similar range of emotions occupying their thoughts post-visit.

On the one-hand, the Mothers were desperate to see their children. Wanting to simply 'hug them and tell them I love them' (Tanisha), but on the other hand Mothers wanted to 'protect them from the shame of a prison' (Mavis), or to protect and control their and their children's feelings and emotions:

'I was scared of the emotional fall out of visits, mine and hers…I just don't think I would have coped if I['d] seen her in person, it was easier to block off my feelings into boxes…by not seeing her I mean. I wouldn't have coped I know I wouldn't, and I don't think she would have either.' (Margot)

Moran (2013) describes the 'liminal space' of the visiting room as a place where families temporarily feel the same shame and surveillance experienced by prisoners. Something others have argued results in secondary stigmatisation (Minson, 2018). Karen's children, aged eleven, 12 and 17, only visited the prison once, like Mavis's adult children. Karen, a middle-class professional, had been 'embarrassed' and 'ashamed' when her children visited. She did not want to go through the experience again and wanted to spare her children's shame, despite her youngest child pleading to see her.

> 'I just hated it, I could see Tilly and Oliver just looking around aghast at what they saw and…I know this sounds awful, but at the people in the visiting room, it's just not our world. I think the two older ones were relieved when I said no more visits. I absolutely know Francesca would have come back in a heartbeat because she's a mummy's girl, but I just couldn't allow her. It was too painful, and I don't actually think my husband had any desire to repeat the experience at all. He did not put up a fight when I said no more visits, let's put it that way.'

Rees et al (2017) suggest that several factors affect the 'quality' and 'success' of a visits between mothers and their children. They found that longer visits, with flexibility of movement and the freedom to hug and enjoy physical contact, were unsurprisingly regarded more positively by mothers and children. Not all prisons facilitate these 'Family Days' or 'special' visits[1]. Only two of the Mothers experienced them (Tarian and Rita); however, it was clear that they found this type of visit a much more enjoyable experience than 'normal 'visits. Tarian, who had her extended visit because she was on the MBU, said:

> 'It was mint, we were only supposed to have sandwiches, but I'd told my mum to bring Christmas dinner stuff and the staff didn't care so I just about cooked for us all, loved it I did, I was a proper mam for a day I was.'

---

1. A number of prisons have projects that allow more meaningful visits between mothers and their children—they are often managed by the third sector as opposed to prison staff. They are characterised by being several hours longer, permitting freedom of movement around the room, and physical contact is allowed. Some schemes, like 'Visiting Mum' at HMP Eastwood Park (now closed due to lack of funding) also arranged transport and did not require the presence of caregivers during visits, thereby facilitating a deeper mother/child bonding experience. Some prisons even facilitate overnight contact where mothers are able to, e.g. cook with their children in a separate house in prison grounds.

Rita's special visit was also around Christmas, although it had so nearly not occurred as her application was misplaced. Rita felt it only went ahead in the end because she pushed for it:

'Because I was articulate and strong and passionate about it, if I'd backed down I wouldn't have got it…but I'd told the kids, I could not let them down. In the end we had a lovely day. So much more relaxed than a normal visit, they, by and large were awful and stressful.'

Several Mothers experienced prison moves at short notice (such as is described by Tia earlier), which again impacted on the regularity and possibility of visits. The women felt that their needs as mothers and their children's needs consistently came second to the needs of the 'the system':

'This is my third prison in two months. Just as I have got settled, planned courses, made friends, booked in visits, I'm moved again—visits lost. I haven't seen my kids or grandkids now for five months. I miss them like mad.' (Sandy)

The rules of the institution and whether the prison was open or closed had an impact on the quality of the visit for both Mothers and visitors. The Mothers described how the rules around physical contact and free movement within the visiting space were inconsistent as between prisons, even between those in the same category. Some prisons allowed only a first hug and then no further physical contact. This included the Mothers holding their very young babies or toddlers or allowing them on their knees. In other prisons (or in the special visits described above) this was allowed. In some prisons Mothers were not allowed out of their seats, which they found incredibly frustrating—especially for Mothers of toddlers and younger children because children would go over to the play area (if there was one) to play with other children and the toys provided.

Tia described how on one visit, her four-year-old and another visitor's child made friends and spent the whole visit playing in the play area in the far corner of the room, then sitting themselves down for their 'picnic' on a separate table from their mothers. Tia stated it was awful and frustrating, but she and the other mother felt helpless as they were not allowed out of their seats to interact:

> 'Me and the other mother just looked at each other and shrugged, we were gutted, but what can you do…they were happy.'

The Mothers spent the whole visit watching their children play, from a distance with minimal mother/child interaction, instead spending the precious visit time engaging with the caregiver or professional (foster carer/social worker) who had accompanied the child on the visit:

> 'No I had to stay seated at all times, [the social worker] could move into the play area with my kid, but not me. I wasn't allowed…so for at least an hour of the visit I wouldn't even see her. I used to pray to get seated next to the play area…but usually I wasn't nowhere near it. One time my daughter fell over…I wasn't even allowed out my seat to pick her up…if that had happened outside and I ignored her crying…well then that would be abuse. Another time my daughter wanted to give me a picture…[it was] taken off her, not even allowed to show it me. So before she even got in she was upset already…then she wanted to bring some crayons and paper from the play area to sit with me…which is allowed…but this officer told her no. She went round and took crayons off all the kids. My daughter was broken, the visit got ended because my daughter was heartbroken, the social worker took her out and that was it over. I put a complaint in about that but the IMB[2] never did nowt about it. All I could think about was how sad my daughter would be on her way home.' (Sophie)

Tanisha was frustrated that not being allowed out of her seat prevented her from even 'doing the basics' for her children during visits:

> 'I just wanted to get them the stuff from the café, just to be able to buy their treats. Basic stuff…not even allowed that.'

---

2. Independent Monitoring Boards (IMBs) are statutory entities first established by the Prison Act 1952 to monitor the welfare of prisoners in the UK to ensure that they are properly cared for within Prison and Immigration Centre Rules, whilst in custody and detention.

It was clear that Tanisha saw buying provisions from the snack bar as an act of mothering. These frequent frustrations of their maternal-role affected the Mothers deeply and was one of the reasons cited by them as to why they might have only one, none, or infrequent visits with their children. This had obvious implications for the maintenance and strengthening of family ties and bonds and, ultimately, the Mothers' desistance (Farmer, 2019).

Several Mothers described feeling relieved when visits were over. They were exhausted at having gone through an extensive period of being 'watched' and 'judged' by staff, and sometimes by family or caregivers in their performance as mothers:

'…you knew they [staff] were watching you to see if you were a good mum or not.' (Dee)

Rose (1989) asserts that family life is subject to close scrutiny in the community, and it was felt no differently by the mothers in prison. The additional surveillance of themselves as mothers, and of their children and families, was another reason cited for the cessation or infrequency of visits. Wells (2019: 82) suggests that prison visits have long been a means of regulating mothering behaviour, and that they are a time of increased scrutiny because the mother and the child (or other visitors) are viewed as 'potential vehicles for contraband.'

Some of the Mothers had the additionally challenging experience of closed visits,[3] meaning prisoners and their visitors are separated by glass and are in a small room separate from the main visiting hall. As well as it being traumatic for her and her children, Ursula described how this was 'stigmatising' because 'everyone knew then that you were regarded as suspicious.' She added:

'This is how wicked these people are man. They put me on no contact [closed] visits for three months, they can't hug you, you can't touch them,

---

3. Closed visits (which are not exclusive to closed-prisons) are actioned if the prison staff believe there may be a potential risk, e.g. of smuggling, escape. The prison may impose these either due to previous convictions or suspicious behaviour, or drugs dog indication on previous visits.

just look at them through the glass…I mean…you know what…one time I said then no more I just said don't ever come again.'

However, for some of the Mothers the visits were 'all that kept me going' (Lauren) and were opportunities 'to be a mum, even if only for an hour or two' (Tanisha). Tanisha goes on to say that the 'cuddles' were all she could think of before a visit.

As described earlier, most Mothers felt anxious before a visit, often fearing it would be cancelled, or scared that it would be tense or awkward. Although they were excited to see their children, they were ashamed that they were coming to a prison. Several Mothers described visits as 'emotionally exhausting' or 'draining.' Nevertheless, visits were definitely viewed positively by many of the Mothers (and grandmothers) and provided them with windows of opportunity to show the love and care for their loved ones that they had been craving and missing, 'just to hear their news and just to hold their hands.' (Rayna)

> 'We would almost pretend like we were round the dinner table and it would be like a normal conversation at home, me just being a mum and them just being their normal bickery selves.' (Rita)

Several Mothers were frustrated that the male estate seemed to them to be more advanced in the use of additional technology to facilitate greater contact. They were keen to see an advancement in the women's estate that could only improve their contact with their children. However, 'surveillance' of motherhood in prison is a form of control over mothering practices (Wells, 2019: 77), and Wells suggests that video visits actually have the potential to increase that already present surveillance as the prison staff take on the role of 'watcher.' Wells (ibid :78) argues that this 'forces mothers to perform motherhood under the gaze, influence and judgement of correctional officers, peers and other mothers.' Wells argues that mothering in these circumstances reinforces the stigmatisation and stereotyping of prison mothers as 'bad' mothers, by the very fact that they have to be surveilled. It is not only video calls that are monitored, but telephone calls, and letters, too.

Phone calls and letters

Like all people in prison the Mothers faced practical challenges around other forms of contact such as access to phones, the cost of paper and postage stamps (Booth, 2020). There were inconsistencies between prisons in the support and facilitation of contact with children, again highlighting structural failures to recognise and value the needs of mothers and their children.

Interestingly, in Ireland—where, arguably, motherhood enjoys a greater 'status' and significance, because of the Catholic ethos of 'the family' (O'Malley, 2018)— prisons provide free phone calls home to children, even if they are in multiple homes, and free postage stamps. In contrast, the Mothers were frustrated by the cost of calls (six times the cost of calls outside of prison), by the delays in official approval of phone numbers and of adding them to the personal PIN[4] list, and just by access to phones generally. Mothers described having to choose between buying stamps and buying toiletries. Because most of the Mothers were single parents the impact of frustrated contact with their children added to their maternal guilt and pain.

Confirming previous findings (Barnes and Cunningham Stringer, 2014; Booth, 2018), the Mothers encountered structural frustrations regarding telephone contact. They described having to navigate prison rules and regulations around contact, which they saw as serving to complicate and confound their relationships with their children. Rita, like several other Mothers, spoke of how challenging it was even to access the telephone, particularly when she had been in a closed prison:

'…for a time we were only out half an hour a day and told there would be no phone access, but even on a normal day…we were locked up mostly 23 hours a day, in our cells…we only had access [to phones] between three and four, well my kids weren't at home then how could I phone them?'

4. Personal identification number which allows the prisoner to make calls to either landline or mobile numbers and put phone credits on weekly as needed.

Rita described how this was even more frustrating as there were 'phone sockets in the cells, but no phones, how ridiculous.'[5] However, as with visits, the phone calls home were also sometimes bittersweet, and the Mothers described again their mixed emotions. Some of them found it painful, frustrating and difficult to phone home and some avoided it, feeling that it was less painful for them and for their children.

Like the mothers in Baldwin and Epstein's (2017) study, some of the mothers had multiple caregivers for their children and so they would have to 'choose' which children to ring if they did not have enough phone credit to phone them all. Tia described this as 'Sophie's Choice.'[6] Mothers of teenagers would describe their frustrations; at not being able to get hold of teenage children and the expense of calling mobile phones; this would then be a source of tension for the mothers which might sometimes leak into the next phone call or visit:

> 'I just used to get pissed off I couldn't speak to her; she wouldn't answer if she was with her mates…but then I'd be hurt and mad and grumpy with her next time she called, then it would escalate…in the end it was easier just not to phone at all…we wrote instead.' (Tia)

Grandmothers amongst the Mothers faced similar challenges, as obviously their grandchildren were not all siblings and so not located in one space, so again they were sometimes forced to choose which grandchildren to ring, and then whether to speak to the grandchildren or to the parents. This is something that Pham, Sandra and Mavis cited as an additional source of guilt. Several spoke of an 'emotional transfusion' where they would speak to their children and feel their pain, then their children would recognise their mother's pain, and so deep conversations were sometimes avoided as coping strategy — on both sides. This had an impact on the quality of the mother/child relationships (discussed later) and rendered some of the phone conversations superficial — especially,

---

5.   Some prisons can facilitate in-cell telephones for incoming calls only — this is more common in the male estate than in the female estate.

6.   After a well-known film about the Holocaust and a mother in a Nazi concentration camp who was forced to choose which of her children would live and which would die.

though not exclusively, between older children and adult offspring. For example, Maggie:

'I didn't want to upset her by telling her it was awful, and she didn't want to upset me by telling me she was struggling…so we were both like "[Y]ou okay?"…"[Y]eah, I'm okay, you okay?"…"[Y]eah." It was silly, really, we both knew we weren't…but it was easier that way for both of us to cope.'

Mothers of younger children described how they would adopt a forced cheerfulness to try to mitigate the pain that their younger children were feeling, which again would leave them emotionally exhausted:

'I just used to try to distract her and tell her it was okay, mummy would be home soon and just make it sound nonchalant…but inside I was breaking.' (Sophie)

For some mothers phone calls were an opportunity to engage in active mothering, but from a distance. This was essential to the Mother's own sense of self as a mother and to her ability to retain an affirming or positive maternal identity.

The Mothers endured several home crises that they tried to guide and assist their children through, over the telephone and sometimes in visits. These included school bullying, teenage pregnancies, relationship breakdowns, miscarriage scares, exams, serious illness and bereavement. These were, of course, stressful times for the mothers and grandmothers, yet being involved in decision-making and solutions as they might have been had they been at home was an important factor in their retaining a positive maternal identity and role. As previously stated by Shanice, however, it was often the 'little things' — the everyday things — that they missed most, and they would phone home as often as they could, often daily, to be able to engage in 'normal' everyday conversations and activities:

'We would actually go through the shopping list together on the phone and I would help her decide what meals to cook for the little ones and her dad…then I'd go through how to do it, step by step. I think I enjoyed those phone calls the most as I was just a mum then … just a mum on the other end of the phone.' (Rita)

The Mothers described how they would continue their active mothering via telephone and letters, going through homework with their children, phoning to see how their school day had gone or continuing to parent them by disciplining or just listening to them:

'Yes all of us used to say that … it was so important to still be mum, even to nag them. I would be telling them off down the phone, and they would tell me stuff they wouldn't tell their dad.' (Rita)

Alexandra and Adel both described how they continued in the same disciplinary role that they had undertaken at home, and how this was an important factor in retaining their 'place' in the family. Similarly, Natacha was 'the organized one' in her family and despite her being in prison it was she who organized everything for her son's and daughter's birthday parties: where possible she made the calls herself, but where not possible she posted out lists and tasks for others to complete to her specifications.

Carla and Adel both described how their telephone calls and letters home were opportunities to 'build bridges' and 'mend fences,' which they hoped would stand them in good stead for their release. Both felt that away from the chaos of their pre-prison lives, the telephone calls and letters were a 'calmer' means of communication with their children and families, better than they had had for 'some time.'

Four of the mothers were able to take positives from their incarceration although, as previously stated, this was mostly because they were able to secure help and support that had not been available to them within the community. Prison was described by four Mothers as a 'safe' place where they were able to secure help, and which actually assisted them in reforming and repairing fractured relationships with their children and their wider family (see also Lockwood, 2018 and O'Malley, 2018). These Mothers (Annie, Dee, Shanice and Tarian) felt that opportunities to engage in active mothering via the telephone or during visits was an important part of their time in custody and was 'practice' and an 'opportunity to build up trust' (Dee) and repair relationships before they returned home and to motherhood full-time.

Research has demonstrated that this contact with family is a significant and positive factor in relation to desistance (Farmer, 2017; 2019); more than that, it is vital to the maintenance of family relationships and the wellbeing of prisoners. However, it is not always without tension or strain. The families of prisoners are forced into challenging circumstances as caregivers, in circumstances where they are completely unsupported by the State. It is perhaps not surprising that challenges faced by the Mothers inside and the families outside could result in tension. Some of that 'tension' may previously have been present in family relationships, and relationships dynamics, and they became exacerbated by a Mother's incarceration. For many Mothers who had experienced domestic abuse, this simply continued 'through the bars' and children were used as a means of punishing, gaslighting, and hurting the women *as mothers*, perhaps where their abusers knew they could hurt them most.

Caregivers, Tension, Gatekeeping and Control

Mothers are 'imagined' to be the 'glue that holds families together,' and when mothers go to prison, the dynamics within the family are altered. The importance of maintaining family ties has attracted policy and practice attention (e.g. Farmer, 2017, 2018; JCHR, 2019). Often it is families who take over the mother work, or caregiving role, hopefully (and where appropriate) whilst assisting the mother to maintain an active mothering role from prison. As demonstrated in this book, Mothers' efforts and whether they were allowed to engage in active mothering from behind bars were varied and challenged; most if not all were constantly trying to renegotiate their mothering role and identity in the face of carceral challenges.

Not all of the challenges originated from within the prison. For some of the Mothers, difficulties with family dynamics and caregivers impeded or complicated their ability to continue actively to mother their children and grandchildren, which further contributed to their reducing and spoiling maternal identity and feelings of maternal powerlessness.

Mothers were reliant on caregivers to facilitate contact, and their relationships with caregivers was therefore a significant factor in the shaping of the Mothers' relationships with their children.

The majority of the Mothers' children were cared for by their grandmothers, but a quarter by their fathers, a significantly higher figure than the most often quoted figure of nine per cent, which relates to a 1997 study by Caddle and Crisp. For some of the Mothers this was not a positive factor and some ex-partners who had been abusive and controlling of the Mothers pre-prison simply continued their abuse by restricting and controlling their access to their children.

Six Mothers experienced violent/controlling ex-partners who limited or controlled access to their children, which contributed to their sense of powerlessness as mothers. The abuse and control they had previously endured was simply continued through their children. Taranpreet stated, '…he knew he could hurt me most through the kids.' That the acts were deliberate and direct attacks on them as mothers because it would be the most painful way to 'attack' them, was shared by Annie, Jennifer, Pham, Natacha, and Melanie. Melanie illustrated this:

> 'I don't have much contact with my daughter, my ex has her whilst I'm in here and he don't want me to have contact with her, it's just an excuse to punish me and control me like he always does. He don't care that it punishes her too. God knows what he's saying to her about me.'

Similarly, Annie described how her violent and controlling ex (the father of her child), controlled not only her access to her daughter but also what she was 'allowed' to tell her on the phone:

> 'I didn't speak to my daughter for the first five weeks I was in, I cannot explain the emptiness of that time. We have a good bond my daughter and me and we had been together or spoken every day before that [they had a 50/50 shared custody arrangement]. But he wouldn't let me speak to her, I was literally in pieces literally you know, emotionally and physically. I can't describe the pain because she is and always has been the reason I get out of bed. But he told me what I had to agree to say to her before he would let me

speak to her. I had to say I'd let everyone down. I had to say I'd done wrong and I was ashamed and that I was a bad person and was now where bad people went. He made me promise to say all of that when she rang and if I didn't he said he would cut off the call and not let her ring me back. He only allowed five minute phone calls, that's it five minutes once a week…then he would hang up.'

Annie went on to say how she tried desperately to retain a 'connection' with her daughter between these infrequent and highly controlled phone calls:

'I would write to her and I would send her a picture and she would write back and then by the time she wrote back she had got the next one—so it was like a conversation almost…I wrote to her every day…and she would send, I mean I would send her a picture not coloured in and she would send it back coloured in…that was our thing, our connection.'

Jennifer's ex, who had secured custody of his son when Jennifer was imprisoned, completely blocked her contact with her son, saying it 'wasn't in his best interests.' He then moved 300 miles away to his former home-town, taking their son, changing his school and refusing to provide her with an address even to write to him:

'I was powerless to stop him moving as we had shared care, I begged him not to move him—it was his GCSE year, my son had plans, a future, that must all be wrecked now, and I can't even speak to him to see if he is happy or how he coped with the news. He [the ex] writes to me, almost taunting me, but I can't get to my son…I have begged him. How do I even fight this from in here?' (Jennifer)

Violent ex-partners were not the sole source of control and tension Mothers' contact was restricted by other caregivers who acted like gate-keepers, too. One of the ways in which the Mothers were impeded was by caregivers physically restricting access to the children, either by refusing to accompany them to the prison, or by limiting and controlling access via visits and telephone calls, or sometimes both:

> 'My son and his wife only came once, and they wouldn't bring my grand-children at all. They said it was not "something they wanted in their world," which I can understand, I guess. But it was hard having no contact with them … and teenagers, well they don't like to write these days do they. So no, I had no contact at all with my grandchildren whilst I was in prison … and before I went in I had them every day. It broke my heart. I missed them even more than my own children. That bond you have with grandchildren, well its precious isn't it.' (Mavis)

Similarly, Queenie's daughter would not allow her child to visit her grandmother in prison. Queenie stated:

> 'My daughter categorically said to me, Ria is not allowed. I don't want her to come to those places.'

Both these grandmothers felt that their children were explicitly giving the message to the grandchildren that prisons were a place of shame; this added a whole new layer to their spoiled identities (Gofman, 1963) as mothers. They were also 'spoiled' as grandmothers and it was made clear to the grandchildren in both cases that 'normal grannies don't go to prison' (Queenie).

The significant financial and emotional pressure on caregivers when they are caring for a child of an imprisoned parent can lead to tension, recrimination, anger, frustration and judgement, which the Mothers described would sometimes leak into their communication and contact with caregivers. As the 'gatekeepers' of their charges, other family caregivers sometimes physically restricted or blocked contact with children. Understandably, some tensions between caregivers and the Mothers would leak into the visiting space or phone calls, negatively affecting the Mothers and their maternal identity, even when mothers were sympathetic:

'She had every right to be mad at me…I get that. I fucked up and she had to drop everything to care for my kids, I feel bad about it I do…but I was doing my punishment…I didn't need her punishing me through the kids as well. When she came on a visit with them, I just wanted to be a mam and have a nice time and that…not sit there getting told what a fuckup I am in front of my kids. I'd rather she didn't bring them than it be like that, so I told her not to come and I stopped the visits. It weren't fair on any of us having them [the visits] be like that.' (Tia)

Several Mothers talked about feeling replaced or displaced and, as Dee stated, it was often a feeling that was intensified in the visiting space.

'My mother-in-law would deliberately bring them in clothes she knew I'd hate; she'd just talk about stuff they'd been doing and kind of excluded me from conversations with them…I know life goes on and that. But that was meant to be our time…and she couldn't even let me have that hour…it was all about her and what she was doing with them…made me feel crap man…like she was the mother now and I didn't matter.'

Mothers spoke of children being 'clingy' with caregivers which, although they were grateful from their child's perspective, it still 'hurt' (Rita) as a mother. Rita described how her 18-month-old son became especially close to her oldest daughter, Penny, who had taken over the bulk of his everyday care (Penny was 13). Rita described how in visits Penny would 'mother' him:

'She would say, "Oh he's tired now mum," or "He wants his bottle"…I would be like, yes I know Penny…I am his mum! On the one hand it was nice to see but on the other it really hurt.'

This sense of 'competing' for their children or feeling replaced/ displaced was a common theme of the Mothers. As demonstrated in *Chapter 4*, most of their dependent children were cared for by grandmothers. As most mothers in custody 'retain dreams of a return to active parenting' and indicate that their children are their primary concern, it is then apt to characterise the relationship with grandmother caregivers as a 'co-parenting one.' However, whereas previously a mother may have been the family individual with all of the parenting 'power,' this is substantially reduced once she is incarcerated. Strozier et al (2011) argue that co-parenting with an incarcerated mother is inherently challenging, suggesting that when co-parenting 'alliances' work well, this fosters a healthy environment in which children are reassured, supported well and feel secure — which in turn bodes well for their futures (already disadvantaged simply by having a parent in prison). However, when it does not work so well, children experience 'conflict, strain and resentment,' promoting insecurity and less favourable long-term outcomes. The Mothers experienced both of these types of co-parenting alliances. Taranpreet described her parenting relationship with her mother-in-law of her twin toddlers as a 'tug of war.'

Like several of the Mothers, Taranpreet had mixed emotions about her children being in their grandmother's care. On the one hand she was 'grateful' as her husband 'would not have coped,' but on the other she stated, 'A big part of me feels so bitter towards my mother-in-law, like as if she has taken my place.'

Mothers described being 'visibly, emotionally and physically reminded' during visits that they 'no longer had any real power or control' over their children. Ursula described how 'from the food they were eating, the clothes they were wearing, the words they were using' that it was 'obvious' she had been 'replaced as a mother.' Five of the grandmother caregivers refused to bring the children to the prison for at least part of their mother's sentence and to a greater or lesser extent controlled telephone access too:

> 'I would ring up and ask to speak to the kids and she'd say, oh they're in bed early or out with mates…I could blatantly hear them in the background…but she just didn't want me to speak to them.' (Tanya)

For some of the Mothers, grandmothers restricting access and contact with their children came after periods where the Mothers had been addicted and/or living chaotically, or — in the grandmothers' opinions — had repeatedly 'let their children down':

'I know I'd been a rubbish mam but how was I supposed to make it up to them or prove myself if she wouldn't let me speak to them …It honestly made me hate her. I could understand it, but I hated her. I felt like she was turning my kids against me.' (Carla)

The Mothers' resentments and upsets with caregivers would impact on their relationships during contact and, for some Mothers, they felt this also impacted on their relationships with their children as well as generating tensions between each other. Sometimes the difficulties surrounded 'differences' in parenting styles — 'he makes them do homework, I hate it and I think it should be banned — childhood is for fun … I would not have encouraged them to do it' (Rita). At other times anger, resentment, and frustration related to things happening in their children's lives that wouldn't have happened if they had been 'at home.' Sandra's two teenage daughters both got pregnant whilst she was in prison, which Sandra felt 'would not have happened on my watch.' For Dee, her anger was with her sister who had initially agreed to care for her children but then 'couldn't cope' and so had placed them in the care of the LA:

'She gave my kids up man …how am I meant to forgive her. She could have asked my friends. She didn't have to put them in care …she was their auntie, man.'

Interestingly, the relationships with caregivers and the success of the parenting relationships with caregivers 'outside' closely aligned with the findings of Strozier et al (2011). Healthy, meaningful relationships were found where the parenting was shared and without struggle, where the caregiver and the Mother both accepted and agreed the relationship and, importantly, who would 'lead' or control the relationship, where good communication, teamwork, problem-solving and compromise were all easily achieved and, finally and importantly, where affirmation and empathy existed for both parties:

'I was lucky, we had a good relationship, and he recognised my need to parent from prison and made sure I was involved in all decisions about them and even in their day to day care wherever possible.' (Karen)

Conversely, a negative relationship will exist if communication is poor and influenced by conflict and power struggles; where each party undermines the other with differences in parenting styles and discipline, the mother is disconnected, and experiences an overwhelming sense of despondency, guilt and fear; and/or the mother is 'disconnected': 'I felt redundant, pointless' (Taranpreet). When this occurred, some of the Mothers simply refused to allow visits, partly because they were making protective decisions about their children and partly because they did not have the emotional resilience to maintain those physical links and relationships, or the 'fall out' (Tanisha) from visits.

What was clear was that relationship dynamics whilst the Mothers were incarcerated set in motion other dynamics that persisted post-release. Ultimately, many of the difficulties and challenges faced by the Mothers (and their children and grandchildren) whilst they were separated by prison left an enduring legacy which affected post-prison relationships and family dynamics (as explored in later chapters).

Summary of *Chapter 7*

The Mothers described how the interruption and disruption to their maternal role impacted on their maternal identity and role. Mothers described some of the challenges in relation to contact, and how they were affected by factors outside of their control. They described struggling to maintain any agency and power as mothers, highlighting the importance and significance of relationships with caregivers. Such relationships and whether there were tensions present or instead there was a supportive co-parenting type of relationship had a significant impact on a Mother's own feelings about her role and identity.

The Mothers tried hard wherever possible to maintain an active maternal role by trying to be involved in what they called their mothering tasks or duties—where this was not possible they often remained preoccupied with mothering and/or maternal emotions despite feeling invisible as mothers and removed from mothering.

 Pause for Thought

Imagine for a second what it would feel like to drop your child at school then be taken to prison — knowing you can't contact your child, talk to them easily, you don't even know who will pick up your child — your solicitor told you that you wouldn't be going to prison so you made no provision — How would you feel?

How might that manifest in prison? — What if your child becomes seriously ill while you are inside? — What if your child is weeping on the phone and the credit cuts out and you can't phone back, and they can't phone you? — What would that feel like? — What would it feel like to have your child wrenched screaming from your arms after a prison visit?

How would you explain to your toddler that they can't sit on your knee because it's against the rules? — How would you feel/your child feel after that visit? — What might you decide after that?

159

CHAPTER 8

Regimes, Rules and Relationships

'In open conditions it was so nice, we had the freedom to walk about and mix with who we wanted to, it made a difference and groups with things in common bonded together—like I always bonded with the older mums and grannies, it was funny we were, like a kind of "Mothers United."' (Margot)

We have seen that the Mothers described how they found the experience of entering custody both painful and harmful; they felt that the punitiveness and harm of this was exacerbated and magnified for them as mothers. They all described how they would turn to each other for mothering support, replicating the nurturing they were used to performing as mothers of their children.

The prison environment, especially whether the prison was open or closed, and their relationships with the prison staff bore a relationship to how the Mothers coped and managed their maternal emotions, maternal-role and maternal identity.

Open/Closed Conditions and Maternal Relations

The type of prison to which the Mothers were sent had an impact on their maternal experience and the Mothers' relationships with each other. Women are not always placed strictly by their risk[1] or in local prisons, unlike in the male estate: they are placed based on the requirements of

---

1. In the male prison estate, establishments are categorised A, B, C, or D and prisoners housed based on their risk of harm or escape. Cat A is the highest security category, Cat C and D the lowest. Their individual risk category will match that of their location. In the male estate, those below Cat A will normally go automatically to their local prison—that nearest their home court—and may serve their entire sentence there; or they may be dispersed to one of a correlated category. Male prisoners often move down through the categories as their risk reduces. In the female estate, there may be no 'local' prison, so women can be sent to any UK location depending on available space (in a much smaller number of women's prisons): a suitable location is often 'considered' but prisoners can be sent randomly to an open or closed establishment. At the time of writing, this is under review with evidence from this author in support of positive change.

the prison estate and the availability of spaces; and although efforts are made to place them near to their homes, women are often sent over 100 miles away from home (PRT, 2019). This is yet another example of the CJS mirroring the discrimination and inequalities of wider society (Carlen and Worrall, 2004; Gelsthorpe, 2007). Ten of the 12 women's prisons in the UK are closed-prisons, although some have both open and closed areas within a closed environment. Guidance from the Ministry of Justice Women's Policy Framework (2018: 3: 3.20) states that: 'Women are managed appropriately to their current risk level and complexities of need, with the aim of reducing risk as their sentence progresses. Where possible, and subject to the considerations of security, good order and addressing their offending behaviour, women are held in prisons that best enable them to maintain their family ties.'

Despite this guidance, women are often located many miles from home, are subject to being moved at any time, and are often held in closed conditions despite their offence and risk levels (in terms of harm or escape) not indicating that necessity. Most of the Mothers experienced at least one prison transfer, while some experienced several. Often these moves would take place with only a few hours' notice, and for no reason other than to accommodate the prison estate's needs (as opposed to those of the women). For women who were mothers, such moves could be especially traumatic, as often they would have imminent visits with their children booked in and have no way of informing relatives that they had been moved (as strongly emphasised earlier by Tia).

The Mothers were often moved further away from home and between open and closed prisons 'without rhyme or reason' (Mary). Consequent changes of regime impacted on all aspects of prison life, but especially on Mothers' contact with their children and caregivers and, therefore, their emotional regulation (see also discussion in Baldwin, 2018).

The Mothers described how, when held in open conditions, they would 'at every opportunity' (Maggie) talk about their children and grandchildren and found that motherhood was something that bonded them. Several spoke of how they would gravitate to other mothers 'because we all knew what [were] going through' (Cynthia). Rita spoke about how she and 'a group of other mums ... called ourselves the Mothers Club,' would seek each other out 'just being mums and talking about life and everything…actually it was always about the kids.'

Karen, who by her own admission tended to avoid social interaction with other prisoners, described how when she did speak to other prisoners, they 'tended to be other Mothers' because she felt that:

'Although we might have nothing else in common in our lives, as mothers we were often the same. Thinking the same thoughts, just missing our kids, it wasn't so much being a prisoner we had in common but being mothers.'

Similarly, Rita highlighted the positives of an open regime, whilst expressing her frustration about the inappropriateness of most women being confined in closed conditions:

'We all bonded over motherhood. It felt lovely to be able to talk about our kids, it wasn't all we talked about—but it was mostly…it made us all feel 'normal'…we had nothing in common at all other than we were mothers. We probably wouldn't have spoken outside, yet in prison we walked in the grounds, about three miles a day every day…just walking and talking. Closed conditions you can't do that…it makes it harder…and for what for? For nothing…most women don't need to be in closed conditions…what were we going to do? Shoplift them or fraud them to death?'

Contrastingly, the Mothers spoke of how in closed conditions they would adopt a stance of emotional control and restraint: they would avoid talking about issues that would upset them the most, i.e. their motherhood and/or their children. They did not want to 'burden' other mothers or 'remind them what they were going through' (Marjorie). Crewe et al (2014: 8) described similar observations related to male prisoners; however, in the male estate this 'emotional control' was a means of maintaining a 'masculine' mask or stance as well as a means of coping. The Mothers described it more in terms of emotional regulation and protection over each other as mothers:

'In closed you didn't know them [other mothers] as well, you didn't know if they had their kids in their care, or had had them took off them, or if they had visits…you just didn't know them as well so you'd just keep it light in case they went back to their cells upset like.' (Rita)

Annie, Rita, Ursula, Margot (see the caption at the start of this chapter), and Carla all explicitly stated that being in open conditions made a significant difference to how they spent their time with each other *as mothers*. In a closed-prison the regime is often such that women spend considerably less time out of their cells and have much less freedom then. In a typical open-prison, women are unlocked for most of the day from their rooms, and they are able to walk around the inside sections of the prison freely during their non-lockdown hours, except when at work. They are often unescorted and are allowed to congregate or associate with a chosen peer group. Women in such environments make full use of the outside space and enjoy a sense of freedom within a confined space, thus they create and access their own networks to help them to cope. This network was often made up of other mothers.

The Mothers described how they felt united in a kind of motherhood solidarity. Contrastingly, women in closed prisons are held in much more rigid conditions: their movement will be regimented and escorted, they mostly mix only with other women on their wing, except sometimes at work, and they spend more time behind their cell doors or locked into their wing, which makes it more difficult to form bonds of choice rather than association.

In closed conditions, particularly, the 'cell' became a private space of concentrated pain and or/hope where Mothers desperately tried to create a space where their children were 'present' via photographs and drawings, and to 'make it feel like home' (Kady). It was also a space where Mothers would 'hold' their pain and try desperately to manage their maternal emotions: tragically, when they could not manage, it would be in their private spaces that they would self-harm or attempt suicide (see also Baldwin and Quinlan, 2018). Maggie speaking about being alone in her cell:

'[That] was when I missed my kids the most and it was always then I would cut up—I never felt safe on my own or in my own head…I coped much better when I was with the other girls, they understood.'

As acknowledged by Sykes (1958: 82) the pains of imprisonment can never be completely eliminated by the very definition that it is a prison, 'but if the rigors of confinement cannot be completely removed, they can at least be mitigated by the patterns of social interaction established amongst the inmates themselves.' Sykes suggests that understanding this simple fact is key to understanding the inmate world. This was certainly important for the Mothers specifically as mother inmates. However, their attempts to generate, maintain and sustain relationships with each other as mothers were often frustrated and challenged by the prison space itself and by the rules and regimes within it. Mothers in closed-prisons found accessing supportive relationships with other women challenging, but nonetheless they would actively seek such relationships.

Mothers' acceptance of each other as mothers was not, however, universal. Representing Sykes' (1958: 77) concept of 'outlaws within this group of outlaws,' the Mothers revealed that, although many bonded through shared motherhood, motherhood, or—more accurately—perceived 'good' motherhood was also a source of division and separation. Six of the Mothers spoke of what amounted to a hierarchy of mothers. Enos (2001) alluded to similar findings that negative judgement was directed at the addicted mothers by 'other' mothers. Enos (2001) and Couvrette et al (2016) found that, despite the fact that mothers in prison felt negatively judged themselves and resented it, some would nonetheless judge each other. This phenomenon is replicated in this book, with several Mothers speaking about a hierarchy of good motherhood where a mother's place was judged against the 'traditional' models of motherhood and how far from this widely accepted model each Mother was deemed to be.

Several additional factors influenced where Mothers were placed on this perceived hierarchy: they included offence type, who had care of their children whilst in prison, whether they used substances, whether or not children visited, and whether or not they were likely to have care of her children on release. Mothers who abused children, especially their own, were at the bottom of the hierarchy, and Mothers who had had the care of their children prior to prison and who expected to resume their care from family caregivers (but not from LA care) on release, and who did not misuse substances, were at the top. Mothers who had already lost their children prior to coming to prison were seen as 'the lowest of the low' (Shanice). Such mothers were not well regarded because it was felt that 'if the State didn't think they were good enough to be mothers why should we' (Shanice).

This judgemental stance was different from that observed by other Mothers such as Queenie, who felt they were all 'just mothers who'd made a mistake.' However, most of the Mothers exhibited some form of judgement towards certain 'groups' of mothers. Mothers were openly judgemental of mothers who had misused substances, even though most often they understood that drugs were a means of escapism or of coping, often from abusive histories:

'The child molesters, no I would have nothing to do with them, disgusting a mother being a kiddy fiddler—you just think how? How could she?' (Sophie)

'I really didn't want to associate with those ones, the smackheads the druggies, the pervs and the ones on the game, I just couldn't get my head round it. Kids come first, I know I'm in here, but I had no choice, and I wasn't well…I'm not like them.' (Annie)

'Yeah like I said, the addicts, the prostitutes, the ones that beat their kids, neglected their kids, left their kids to starve, put drugs before their kids, they were like dogs, don't speak to them, don't have nothing to do with them, spit on them even, whatever…because how could you do that to a child. How can you call yourself a mother?' (Shanice)

In other words, mothers who were deemed to be acting outside of the norms and ideals of traditional motherhood were judged the most harshly, which again indicates how the Mothers had deeply absorbed traditional motherhood ideology and imported it into the prison. Mothers who were violent were not necessarily placed lower on the scale — if their offending was in 'defence' of their children, then they were put higher up the scale. For example, Shanice spoke about one mother whom she used as an example when discussing the 'scale':

> 'So there was a woman on my wing and the screws hated her because her offence was vicious, but the bastard she tortured raped her six year old daughter, good on her I say, we [the prisoners] all were like, "Go Tina." We admired her and thought she'd done what any good mother would and should.'

In this instance the Mothers appeared to endorse the behaviour of the mother described because her actions were in keeping with the most basic of motherhood ideals, i.e. to protect. Shanice described how maternal emotions were 'on high alert' in prison and that mothers' responses to what they saw as 'bad examples of mothers' and mothering triggered an emotional response in Mothers 'because we were really feeling not being with our kids.' It is clear that living in the emotional space of prison is challenging for all prisoners.

The above accounts reflect the challenges and coping-strategies employed to manage emotions and behaviour amongst mothers in a setting comprised of rules and regulations, all of which impacts on mothers' experiences, self- and maternal identity and their perception of others. The regime and staff/prisoner relations were important factors in how the Mothers coped with their imprisonment.

Care or Uncare? Rules and Staff Relationships

The Mothers described being 'desperate' (Mavis) to hold on to their maternal identity and role, whilst navigating through a carceral space entrenched in rules and regulations which served to frustrate their efforts at every turn. They described how they felt that the prison environment and their own identity as a prisoner served to disempower them *as mothers* by reducing their maternal agency. Motherhood interacted with accepted notions, as proposed by Foucault (1977) and Goffman (1961) to replicate the power and control relationship of a 'total institution.' Ursula described her perception of her lack of power as a mother, and the lack of visibility of that role, which she felt was afforded to her by prison officers:

'Denying your motherhood...it's a visible tangible demonstration of their power, isn't it? So prison life is all about tip toeing around the power, they hold the power and whether you get out or not, whether you get an easy job, or you don't, whether you see your kids or not...that's the reality. Whether you realise it or articulate it, that actually is the reality. You are in an abusive relationship with that power aren't you—because you don't have a voice...nobody cares. Do you think the public cares what happens to a prisoner? Nobody cares about you...You're just...you're what...you are not even Ursula you're a number...certainly not a mother, that's the last thing you are to them...That's the reality.'

The 'cultural contradiction' (Hays, 1996) of the prison was the dichotomy between Mothers' identities as prisoners and as mothers. To the prison they were prisoners first, and to themselves they were mothers first. The Mothers felt that the rules and regimes of the prison impacted on them more heavily as mothers, not least because their children were affected, too. Which most felt was unfair. For example, Pham described her frustration at the rules around childcare resettlement leave.[2]

'The difficulty that has been the greatest is that the Child Resettlement rules mean that because my youngest has turned 16 I am not able to claim this right, nor I was told does it apply to grandchildren—so even though they are younger, I can't see them either.'

Pham goes on to say, 'these are his most important years,' and 'not being there for him' at such a time fuelled her 'guilt' and 'failure as a

---

2. Childcare Resettlement Leave (CRL) can be granted if the prisoner provides proof that he/she has sole caring responsibility for a child under the age of 16. It permits the primary carer to have contact with their dependants outside of the prison environment—for a day's leave or overnight stay at home (Prison Service Order (PSO) 6300, National Offender Management Service, 2012).

mother.' She was frustrated that her status as a mother was ignored by the prison simply because her children were older:

> 'The enormous guilt and sorrow that being away from your child at such an important time as their GCSEs, especially when you're a person that places great emphasis on education like myself, is so hard to deal with…it's my job to take him to college, to university open days, all of that and I can't do it…I don't understand why more flexibility to allow mothers the opportunity to support their children isn't allowed…it's my punishment not his.'

Although all prisoners are subject to the Incentive and Earned Privileges Scheme, Mothers described how this had at times affected them differently as mothers. Goffman's (1961) concept of 'total institutions' offers a framework in which to understand the IEPS.[3] Although the Joint Human Rights Committee Report (2019) and the female-focussed Farmer Review (2019) advocated against it, prisons have historically regarded visits and contact with children as a privilege rather than a right (Booth, 2017). Threats of losing visits or losing access to phone calls has been an established means of controlling prisoners' behaviour.

Rita described how she had seen it happen 'many times,' in hindsight she was aware it was wrong, but at the time she had not challenged it. Sam had two visits with her mum and her son cancelled, one because she self-harmed, the other because she 'kicked off at staff when I was moved back to basic.' Several Mothers described similar instances, amongst the most troubling were from Mothers who had spent time in a prison MBU:

> 'I remember they used to say all the time about being on the Unit "It's a privilege not a right to be here," man they used to make threats all the time that our babies would be sent out — we had all heard stories of mothers this happened to, and one girl I was in with said it had happened when she first was on the Unit, they sent a baby out because the mum had answered back a few times so then she was a real goody two shoes after that cos she was scared.' (Kady)

---

3. Ways of controlling prisoner behaviour through reward, denial, deprivation or access, e.g. to TV, facilities, goods, services, etc: see *Chapter 2*.

This form of surveillance, regulation and control secured compliance in the women by promoting an atmosphere of fear. The ultimate fear being losing the care of their babies and their space on the MBU. In this context it is not surprising that the MBUs tend to have far fewer adjudications than 'normal' prison locations.

Five Mothers spent time on MBUs, whilst they were able to take some positives from their experience, all would have much preferred to have been 'at home with family—anywhere but a prison with a baby' (Kady). Kady and Carla had both found the MBU experience, and the additional surveillance of them as mothers, stressful, described by Kady as 'like a goldfish bowl.' Erin wrote about her experience of how the surveillance and control could manifest, describing how her refusal to 'comply with an instruction' had led to the removal of her child:

> 'I felt they were always watching me and waiting for excuses to challenge me, I felt it was personal. They had no thought for the wellbeing of my baby or myself after she was removed. They gave my mother less than 2 hours' notice and said if she didn't come to collect her she would be handed over to social services. I could not believe it. My heart is broken and I'm angry.'

Erin went on to say how she felt 'frustrated, angry and powerless,' unable to do anything because of her prisoner status. She felt 'embarrassed and ashamed' moving back to the general prison population after losing her space on the MBU. Sykes (1958) argued that 'deprivations and frustrations' of prison pose threats to the self and to self-esteem. Erin made it clear this was true for her:

> 'Going back to the wing was like a walk of shame, my baby was gone and I know the other mothers and especially the staff would have been thinking "What did she do to risk losing her baby," they would have imagined it was something really bad. I felt embarrassed and ashamed … like the worst mother in the world.'

Erin also spoke of another incident she was aware of where a mother had temporarily lost the care of her twins, again as a 'punishment' for bad behaviour. The twins were later allowed back on the unit, once they had secured the total compliance of the mother. This situation powerfully reflects Moore and Scraton's (2014) argument that prison radiates a power that is tortuous to women, deeply affecting their hearts, minds and souls, and damaging their children in the process.

The sense of powerlessness in prison, as previously described in literature, pervaded many of the Mothers' narratives but was particularly relevant regarding their motherhood. Mothers described feeling that their motherhood was 'at the mercy' (Queenie) of the prison, it's regime and sometimes of individual officers. Rita described her motherhood as being held hostage by the prison, with the prison dictating the terms of its release:

> 'I felt like they held my motherhood and my access to my kids as a hostage, and only if I played the game and did everything they asked did I gain access to my kids, but actually even when I did everything they asked, they still decided not to do what they said...it was all on their terms...my release from incarcerated parenting all up to them. A one way street.'

Similarly, Adel describes her frustration at having no control over her children's lives and struggling with that, 'It's my job to be in control, to know.' Tamika, also described her sense of powerlessness and relating it to her motherhood stated:

> 'You just have everything taken away from you, you have no rights over your children, no contact with your children, nobody cares about it either. They don't look at you as if you are a Mother...they don't care.'

Canton and Dominey (2020: 17) highlight the often contradictory relationship between punishment and care, recognising that 'care' is more easily directed towards 'victims' of crime rather than the perpetrators. This 'selective compassion' (ibid) is even more complicated concerning female 'offenders' as they are often 'victims' of crime too. Law breakers are often only considered 'reductively' and in terms of their criminal behaviour and thus are perceived as 'undeserving' of care (Canton and

Dominey, 2020). For the Mothers, this already disadvantageous position was compounded by their mother status, and they were seen as being even less 'deserving' of care.

Tait (2010: 440) believes that 'care is central to staff prisoner relationships' and argues that exchanges of care in prison are frequent. She suggests that the care officers extend to prisoners is often overlooked and underreported, but nevertheless is an inevitable part of working with traumatised individuals and an aspect of their work that officers find rewarding. It is especially important concerning vulnerable and suicidal prisoners (Crawley, 2004). Tait (2010) suggests that care can be interpreted in different ways. Suggesting that although an officer might not recognise something as necessarily delivering care, it may be interpreted as such by the prisoner; 'just by asking their names, or even acknowledging I was a mum, showed me she cared … she was nice' (Nicola).

Thus, caring is a 'malleable concept' shaped by variables such as personality, perception, individual experiences and location (Canton and Dominey, 2020: 26). Tait (2010: 449) concludes, despite not being necessarily a specific objective of the prison or even an officer's intention 'caring' nonetheless occurs through the actions of individual officers (within the confines of an institution) and must be understood in that context. She condemns the individual behaviour and lack of care she also observed. However, such behaviour highlights not only the 'othering' and 'dehumanising' that can occur in total institutions like prisons, but also the power imbalance between officers and prisoners. Which Goffman calls the 'supervisory' and the 'managed' groups (1961; 10), something which, despite its obviousness and significance, Tait does not appear to address.

There was an inherent power behind the staff/prisoner relations. All of the Mothers described how treatment from prison staff (particularly prison officers) towards them *as mothers* was important. Moreover, how it could impact on their maternal experience and ultimately contribute positively and/or negatively to their maternal identity. Crewe (2011: 455) suggests that prisoner/staff relations are 'at the heart' of the prison. He argues prison staff have changed in more recent years, becoming less physically 'combative and impenetrable.' He argues that officer power has become 'softer,' but still remains significant. He rightly highlights that trust can be an issue for both prisoners and staff in their relations with each other.

Gender plays a role in staff/prisoner interactions as it does in most social interactions (Carlen, 1983). Many of the women in the female prison estate will have issues related to trust because of past abuse by men; although the power imbalance is present in the male estate too, for women it may feel magnified, especially concerning male staff.

Additionally for the Mothers, the fear of negative evaluation *as mothers* also created a barrier between officers and themselves. Mothers spoke about 'expecting' officers to treat them negatively as prisoners but appreciated that not all officers would be the same: 'You get bad bus drivers, you get bad prison officers' (Queenie); but as Mary stated, 'I didn't expect them to treat me as a bad mother ... who are they to judge me on that, they know nothing about me ... or my life.'

Mothers spoke about the level of 'out and out judgement and disapproval' (Rita) they had experienced from some officers concerning their motherhood, and that this had had a definite impact on their mothering self-esteem and maternal identity:

'The way they look at you when they see you are pregnant...the look on their faces...it's disgust, you can see it is...you know they are thinking what kind of mother will you be...I used to hide my belly as much as I could...they made me ashamed...I was already ashamed, but they made it worser.' (Kady)

'On D wing...the officers would say stuff yeah...they made all of us feel like we didn't even deserve to be mothers let alone treat us like mothers...we all said it, we all felt it.' (Rita)

'He actually said to me these exact words, 'What kind of mother are you? You must be really bad to have three kids taken off you?...that nearly broke me you know because he was a decent bloke...that made it worse.' (Nicola)

Crewe (2011) rightly highlights the enduring nature of 'soft power,' particularly when it is written into reports, assessments, or rehabilitative records: these can have a particular significance for mothers. Especially those engaged in childcare proceedings where such records have potentially huge implications if they are included in personal and maternal assessments. Mothers worried what the officers thought of them *as mothers* and worried about what was written down about them.

Mirroring Goffman's (1963: 23) avoidance of interactions between 'normals and stigmatised' individuals, many of the Mothers described how they would actively avoid having any conversations with staff about their children, even if they were preoccupied or stressed with maternal worries, because their perception was that the 'officers didn't care' (Ursula). However, the Mothers described some incredibly powerful and positive interactions with individual officers, and Kady credited the officers in her first night centre[4] as having saved her life. She felt that had it not been for the compassion and observation afforded to her on her first days in custody, she 'would not have made it.' Similarly, Dee, Tarian, Rita, and Sophie all described positive interactions in which they had found particular officers to be compassionate, kind, mindful of them as mothers and supportive and understanding about a mother's situations and circumstances:

'Then I went to [.......... Prison] and there was this fantastic Family Support worker who knew that I had got kids and knew their names. To walk into that on your first day after having—actually, I don't remember anybody ever asking about my kids—an officer or anybody, so to have that it was like a different world.' (Rita)

'Miss Brown said I shouldn't even be in prison; she knew a different kind of help was what I needed, and she said that my sentence was just punishing my little girl...she was really kind.' (Sophie)

Crawley (2004) argues that prisons are 'emotional places' where the relationships between prisoners and staff are 'structured and performed'

---

4. Many prisons have a dedicated First Night Centre and/or Induction Wing where new arrivals are placed, with a separate unit for vulnerable prisoners. In some cases, sharing a cell can offer newly arrived prisoners additional support in their first hours in custody.

through the 'feeling rules' associated with prison. She argues that prison officers are 'people too,' therefore not immune to responding to prisoners on an emotional and human level as well as a professional one. Most Mothers experienced both positive and negative interactions with prison officers and other staff:

'The officers in [......... Prison] were lovely, just their attitude was nicer, kinder, less bossy. But in [.......... Prison] nah just shit, real shitty people.' (Tanya)

Six Mothers mentioned positive experiences with Family Engagement Workers (FEWs), who are staff members employed by third sector organizations such as Barnardo's or Prison Advice and Care Trust (PACT). The Mothers observed that these staff members, although a welcome positive support to their maternal needs, were 'mostly run off their feet ... you couldn't get hold of them, but when you did they were brilliant' (Rayna).

Mothers who had experienced pregnancy in prison were especially grateful to those officers who treated them well, although the Mothers gave the impression this was more to do with individuals acting independently of the rules rather than with a sense of them being accommodated and cared for in any procedurally, structurally organized way:

'If Mr Ball was on then I knew I'd get extra food and milk, but not if he wasn't on ... he wouldn't put the cuffs on at the hospital for my ante-natals, either. If I'd still been in prison when I was in labour I would have wanted him to be there—even though he was a man. He was kinder than all of the women put together.' (Emma)

The four Mothers who gave birth during their sentence also highlighted how important it was to them to have 'good' officers on duty when they were in labour, and how they hoped for one when they would eventually go to the hospital to give birth. This was best summed-up by Kady:

'You just prayed it wasn't one like Mrs White,[5] or the ones that ignored the bell, we all heard the horror stories of giving birth in a cell, one woman I know did and she nearly died, but the thought terrified me so, yeah, I wanted Mr Pink or Miss Blue, they always made me feel supported and didn't judge me…some of them others well they just make me feel shit as a mother, man they really did…but Mr Pink and Miss Blue they used to even take the cuffs off me at the hospital scans…they were kind, man.'

The grandmothers amongst the Mothers did not fare so well in terms of positive prisoner/staff relations. All of them stated that they felt disrespected because of their age, but importantly also because of their grandmother role and status. Echoing Wahidin's (2004) findings, Mothers said they felt officers infantilised them and 'had no respect for my age, what I had previously achieved, my status as a mother, and certainly not as a grandmother…as a grandmother, I was dismissed' (Queenie).

Grandmothers reported how their role was undermined when accessing resources such as phone calls, that their value as grandmothers was deemed less important than that of mothers:

'I was told I was selfish for "hogging" the phone and that I should let the "younger mums with little ones" have the phone, but I loved my grown-up children and my little grandchildren just as much as they love theirs.' (Diane)

Prison staff responses to the Mothers not only impacted on their maternal selves in terms of their positive maternal identity, but also their engagement in prison life and sentence planning, as illustrated by Tanisha:

'Mr Green was so kind when my daughter was being bullied, he knew I wouldn't be able to concentrate in the sentence planning meeting, so he asked for it to be postponed. If it had gone ahead that day I was so distracted I know I would not have joined in or seen the point to it—in fact I think I would have withdrew from the programme…but because he moved it and

---

5. All prison staff names have been changed in this book to preserve confidentiality.

helped me speak to the school and my daughter to sort it out my mind was clear when we did have the meeting. I was happy and they were happy … but without Mr Green understanding it could have gone badly wrong.'

Jaspreet and Tanya particularly spoke of how 'good' officers listened to their worries about losing their maternal-role and encouraged them to be open with their families and children about their fears: both these Mothers did this and described how their children and families reassured them and, as a result, their communication and contact improved. Both women said this then allowed them to engage in the opportunities offered for progression in prison more fully than they had before. Mary also highlighted how conversations with one particular prison officer had prompted her to get back in touch with her children whom she had not seen for 'years' when they had been taken into care. Mary had believed her children 'were better off without her' and had 'put them to the back of my mind' for years, but the officer who spent time with her in what Mary described as a 'non-judgey way,' encouraged her to see that it was 'never too late' and to think about what 'kind of Mary' she would want her sons to see if they did come back into her life. Mary said this motivated her to 'change' and to access the support in prison that she had been unable to secure outside. She wanted to 'be a mother again.'

Sociologists argue that social expectations and reactions are influenced by the norms and values inherent in a given society and culture (see, e.g. Kelly, 1955). As illustrated in *Chapter 3*, the ideology surrounding motherhood is heavily influenced by widely held societal and cultural beliefs. Such beliefs shape and influence mothers and reactions to mothers in the free world, and those beliefs are not left at the prison gates but are imported inside in mothers' own values and beliefs, and also those of the staff. Almost every Mother had experienced an officer or staff member say to her in response to their mentioning their children, or of missing their children, 'You should have thought of your children before you did what you did,' or words to that effect. This had a profound effect on the Mothers and added to their level of mistrust and distance already felt between prisoners and prison officers (Goffman, 1961), also impacting on their maternal self-esteem.

Feminist geographers have identified intersections between gender space and feelings (e.g., Valentine, 1989) which are relevant to the relational experiences of mothers in prison. The Mothers felt othered and stigmatised not only by being in the prison space itself but by the officers and, importantly, *specifically* with regard to their motherhood. This layered and deeply felt 'disapproval' (Tanya) concerning their motherhood was on top of the feelings. They were already 'discredited' individuals because of the very fact that they were prisoners. Goffman (1961: 18) suggests that inmates and staff in total institutions will view each other with hostility and suspicion and through stereotyped lenses of their 'side' — but what the Mothers described was more than this; it was about them *as mothers*. Motherhood was a pivotal aspect of their incarceration experience and, as demonstrated, was often compounded by the prison space and staff interactions, yet mitigated (to some extent) by the Mothers' relationships with other mothers in prison. This remained the case whether the Mothers were mothers of very young children, teenagers or adults, or were grandmothers.

Grandmothering Behind Bars: Reproducing Motherhood

Particularly when viewed through a matricentric lens, it is impossible to ignore the valuable contribution grandmothers often make to the lives of their grandchildren. The significant role they play in the family, even from behind bars, is not to be underestimated. The experiences of older Mothers and grandmothers have been almost invisible in UK-based prison accounts, and this book, I believe, responds to a significant gap in this area of knowledge. Grandmothers amongst the Mothers experienced prison in similar ways to the Mothers themselves and shared many of the Mothers' emotions and descriptions related to their maternal pain. However, for grandmothers, the challenges of the prison experience were often amplified, not least because their experiences and emotions were 'layered,' relating to their own adult children *and* their grandchildren. They not only had to contend with imported beliefs about motherhood, but also those about age and the grandmother role. Mothers of older children, and/or grandmothers described feeling an *additional* sense of shame and judgement *specifically* related to their age and/or their grand-mothering identity. The sense of shame alluded to by most, if not all, of the Mothers was magnified for the grandmothers because of the expectations and ideology of both femininity *and* ageing.

The lack of research around older women in prison represents what Wahidin (2004: 10) calls a 'latent form of agism' highlighting the status of older women in prison, whom she suggests are perceived as 'not worthy of discussion.' She did not specifically explore the experiences of grand-mothers in prison, but several of her participants were grandmothers who spoke of their pain and the challenges they faced as incarcerated grandmothers. Wahidin quotes Petra Puddepha who stated, 'You never stop being a mother, you're a mother till the day you die.' Puddepha goes on to express her frustration that the prison fails to recognise her as a mother, focussing instead on the mothers of younger children (ibid, 2004). Echoing Wahidin's research, grandmothers in this book felt they lost the status that 'automatically comes with or should come with age' (Maggie), but more than this they also felt 'reduced' in terms of their motherhood and grandmother status, feeling an additional layer of shame as older mothers 'who should know better' (Queenie), and invisibility.

Mavis, a retired teacher who struggled with depression in prison, described the stripping away (Goffman, 1961) of her maternal and grand-mother roles as 'uniquely painful.' She said:

'I wasn't a grandmother anymore...that's what it felt like, yet I had looked after my grandchildren every day, but then nothing, it was like I was nothing to them. It's like I am nothing, just nothing.'

Sandra who, as previously stated, felt the officers' judgement of her was exacerbated by her grandmother status, said:

'It was like they just thought we were...I dunno, double wrong, we was last in line for any of the mother stuff...like I said invisible, its wrong really you know, grandkids are just as important to us as our kids.'

Similarly, Mavis was frustrated by the lack of recognition for her role as a grandmother, despite her significant one in her grandchildren's lives:

> 'I used to do all their childcare, in fact because they [her son and his wife] were professionals, I saw my son's children more than he did. I feel so guilty for them, that I'm not there for them, it's bad enough their parents work the long hours they do, at least they had their granny to fill that gap. I should be there for them, for my son and daughter, too, obviously, but especially for my grandchildren. It's what grandmas do isn't it, it's what we are for.'

Many of the grandmothers felt that their maternal needs were neglected and that they were not afforded the same courtesies or access to support as the Mothers with young children. Wahidin (2004) highlighted how failing to meet the needs of older women prisoners constitutes additional punishment, and that was certainly something felt by the grandmothers in this book:

> 'It was so much worse for us grannies and nannas, we got none of the special leave or [release on temporary licence], we missed funerals and things younger mums would get compassionate leave for, it felt like we were either invisible or extra punished.' (Sandra)

Maggie spoke of her frustration at the prison and 'the system' and its failure to recognise grandmothers and grandmothering as important. She described challenging the rules about what was defined as 'close and immediate family' and described how she 'took on the fight' for other grandmothers to help them challenge negative decisions about compassionate or childcare special leave. Maggie's grandchild was diagnosed with leukaemia while she was in prison and she felt that her grandmother role and status was ignored at a time when she was 'most needed,' not only as a grandmother but as a mother to her adult child:

> 'I absolutely had to fight for everything, I absolutely had to fight, in the end I was given permission to see him [her grandson] in hospital, but only because he was so ill they thought he might die! Before all of that there was

his treatments, his appointments, the diagnosis. I should have been with my daughter for all of that and I would have been. Even when they grow up its times like that your kids need you the most, I was her mum and I wasn't there, it honestly nearly killed me and I know it broke my daughter's heart, it so added to the pain for her, doing all of it without her mum, can you imagine that?'

Grandmothers described feeling 'ignored' (Queenie) in activities that focussed on mother/child separation or mothering. This made the grandmothers feel that not only had they lost their status and roles as grandmothers, but even as mothers:

'It was like because we're old, because our "children" were adults we didn't count … yeah there were some things for mothers inside … but mainly for mothers of little kids like family visits and parenting classes … which weren't parenting classes as such, but where the mothers got together to talk about their kids, but because my kids were grown-ups and even my grandchildren aren't babies then I was ignored as a mother, I feel.' (Queenie)

It is important to note that grandmothers' experiences were not all completely negative. Different prisons had different rules; e.g., in one prison where the 'Family Day' visits were run by a third sector organization (PACT),[6] grandmothers are automatically included in the reach of eligible mothers, although mothers with younger children were given priority — which was still a bone of contention for one Mother:

'It's shit … it just gives the message to my grandkids they aren't as important as the other kids … but they are.' (Sandra)

As a grandmother in custody, Ursula was allowed childcare leave to attend the birth of one of her grandchildren, but the sense of benevolence was not lost on her:

---

6. Prison Advice and Care Trust — a charity working with prisoners and their families by delivering services but also advocating for and championing change in the CJS/penal reform.

'I was overwhelmed with gratitude when I was told I could go but imagine that, man, being grateful for being allowed to attend to your daughter, to your grandchild…imagine having to feel grateful…if I had missed the birth I don't think my daughter would ever have forgiven me—I don't think our relationship would have recovered, it was already hard enough because of my sentence. She was angry with me for missing her pregnancy—if I had missed the birth too…well I think that would have been it.'

As has been described, often Mothers were far from home, so for some visits were few and far between, and for others did not occur at all. For Mothers of older or adult offspring, employment reduced visiting opportunities:

'My son would never have taken leave from work to visit, he would not have seen that as a worthy reason to take time off work…and I suppose neither would his employer. Not that he would ever have told his employer where I was. But no, he would not take time off work to come.' (Mavis)

The Mothers of older and adult children described feeling the judgement from their children, which was less of an issue for the Mothers of young and very young children. Diane highlighted that children who were 'emotionally old enough to express their feelings' were able to 'use their words to hurt' and to make choices that younger children could not—like to refuse to visit. Queenie felt the disparities between older and younger mothers and the expectations of motherhood were never more apparent to her than in her adult daughter's judgement of her and, conversely, her lack of judgement for her father:

'Her judgement of me was harsh, she gave me absolute hell, "I should know better, what kind of mother was I?" worse still, "What kind of a grand-mother was I?" Her verbal was worse than prison, her trying to teach me right from wrong. She just dug and dug and dug and dug, "I've never known any woman, a woman in her fifties that's been to prison," blah blah…then "All my life I'm going to be ashamed of you, my own mother"…no sympathy, none…yet you know what? Nothing about the domestic abuse

I went through, nothing about her father. Dad's been to prison, yeah her dad's been to prison for drugs and whatever but nothing about that…she's good with him…but I have let her down being her mother, her children's grandmother and who's been to prison…she doesn't hide the fact he has been to prison, but she does me. It's more normal for a man to go to prison isn't it, more acceptable.'

Ursula also described struggling to deal with the 'judgement, disapproval and disappointment' of her older children:

'The thing I couldn't cope with was like, the emotional…like my daughter saying that I wasn't a good mother. It was like destroying to the core. She was old enough to know her mind man and that's what she thought.'

Ursula went on to say that the earlier mentioned statement from her daughter that she could not consider herself a good mother was more painful than hearing in court that she would be in prison for years and 'than actually being in prison.'

Diane, who also experienced judgement from her older children, described how she 'distracted' herself by focusing on those she felt would not judge her at all—her fellow prisoners. A way for some of the grandmothers to ease the 'profound hurt' (Datesman and Cales, 1983: 142) of being separated from their loved ones and losing their maternal-role, was to replicate motherhood with those prisoners much younger than themselves and who were perceived as in need and receptive of their nurture. Queenie, who was imprisoned over 200 miles away from home, described how rewarding she found her 'grandma persona' in the prison space:

'Every prison I went to I was one of the oldest, sometimes there were only another two or three women fifty plus…so I did adopt grandma persona in prison. For 99 per cent of the time it was like "Oh Queenie will know," "Queenie will sew that for you," "Queenie is a nice lady go see her"…I was pulled into it but I loved it. It made me feel still like a mother. I loved it especially when I was up in […… Prison], I never saw my own family, so my prison family made me feel better—better than my own actually because they didn't judge me.'

The lack of judgement of her *as a mother* was important to Queenie. Judgement felt by adult children was something discussed by all of the Mothers of older or adult offspring.

Diane described herself as a 'more mature lady'; she was serving life for murder, and gained a degree of comfort from 'mothering' the younger women on her wing:

> 'They actually call me mum some of them, or nan the really young ones…I can't believe they are here, poor souls, breaks my heart it does, I just look at them and think they could be my daughter, or my granddaughter and it just makes me want to hug them, which I do. Apparently, I give the best cuddles. The thing is I do it to make them feel better, but the truth is it makes me feel better too. The officers have started asking me to mentor the young ones when they come in now. Because they know I've got a long stretch, all these little ones, they come and go, and well me, I'm here for a long time so they get some consistency with me. I think that's why they've put me in the reception bit…I think they think a kind maternal face will help and apparently I have one, quite funny really when you think what I'm in for!'

These findings extend what Crewe et al (2017) found when they described women 'lifers' as struggling to 'switch off' their mother role and the loss of the act of mothering as an ache that never goes away. Hairston (1991) suggested that the 'stripping' of the mother role was the most traumatic aspect of being a mother in prison. My own findings demonstrate that for those Mothers who were also grandmothers, losing their active role as mothers *and* as grandmothers was especially painful. Mothering other mothers gave the women a sense of purpose while creating a kind of prison family. For the mothers of older or adult offspring or those who were grandmothers, replicating motherhood in prison was a means of coping and also of retaining their maternal identity and role. 'Mothering' the younger women served the purpose of giving the Mothers an 'outlet' for their maternal emotions and their need to nurture, whilst also making positive connections and letting them feel better about themselves:

> 'I mothered the younger ones…because I could, I liked it, it made me feel better, and them feel better why not? so win win really.' (Maggie)

Mavis, a grandmother with a solid middle-class background, surprised herself with how her maternal instincts transcended class barriers; she described in her interviews almost 'needing' to mother as a way of healing her own maternal pain and managing her emotions:

> 'I would not have looked at some of those girls twice outside, in fact I'm ashamed to say I would have avoided them and been suspicious of them. Yet in prison I just wanted to nurture them, I felt sorry for them and I did used to mother them I suppose. I think we needed each other, they needed to be mothered and I needed to mother.'

As previously evidenced, many of the Mothers had negative or poor experiences of mothering in their childhoods and lives before prison, something also evident in O'Malley's (2018) Irish study with mothers in prison. This was relevant to both Mothers who replicated mothering and those who experienced the mothering from older women prisoners:

> 'I guess in some ways it was a chance to redeem myself almost as a mother, I looked after those young girls in some ways better than I ever had my own kids on the outside.' (Carla)

Rayna, whose own mother was sick with cancer and died whilst she was in prison, felt 'desperate' for the nurturing she was missing from her own mother and she took a great deal of comfort from the fact that an older woman in prison had taken on that role for her:

> 'There was this old lady Elsie, I don't know how old she was, I never asked her…but old old, she was a lifer and she just really took me under her wing.

I would be desperate to see her every day, for her to cuddle me in her big fat arms…she was all warm and mamsie looking…and she'd tell me it would be okay…even though it wasn't…okay I mean, she still always made me feel better. I really really loved her…like a mother and I think she saw me as a daughter…in fact she used to call me that, just "daughter"…all the time.'

Rayna went on to say that she felt many of the women were looking for opportunities to mother someone — 'even the staff' — and that she observed it 'making them feel better.' Interestingly, Rayna described how, whilst her own mother was sick, her role as a daughter preoccupied her as much as her mother role. So, for her to have had the opportunity to seek out and find a mother figure in prison was especially important. Sophie and Beth also spoke about older women taking them under their wings, mothering and 'looking out' for them. Both described how they felt this was something they had benefitted from, especially Beth, the youngest Mother who had had to leave behind her three-month-old baby:

'Without Anya [her mother substitute], I don't know how I would have coped, in the end they padded me up with her and she really did just become my mam.'

Summary of *Chapter 8*

Many of the Mothers entered prison with an already reducing maternal self-esteem and spoiling maternal identity. The spoiling continued and was confirmed to the Mothers once in prison. Being a 'prison mother' was seen by the Mothers as the ultimate failure, failure to live up to deeply embedded ideals of what a 'good' mother should look like.

The pain of separation from their children, was profound and traumatic. Mothers experienced a stripping away of their maternal identity and role, resulting in distinct and specific maternal pains of imprisonment. Mothers and grandmothers sought comfort and support in their relationships with each other, demonstrating their maternal skills through nurture or the replication of motherhood. Motherhood and its associations remained Mothers' and grandmothers' primary focus.

The Mothers felt their motherhood and maternal identity mattered most to them, but it seemed to matter least to the prison system. Being in prison compounded the Mothers' already challenging circumstances, and the physical space of prison and the dynamics within interacted with the Mothers' experiences to shape a heavily stigmatised and painful experience of motherhood/grandmotherhood. The prison environment bore some relationship to how the Mothers coped and managed their maternal emotions, maternal-role and maternal identity. Mothers felt surveilled and controlled not only as prisoners but as mothers, and this sometimes had an impact on their relationships with each other, and on contact and relationships with their children and families outside.

The Mothers struggled to manage their maternal emotions whilst navigating through the carceral space. Most of them felt their motherhood and grandmotherhood status was either ignored or judged. In the main they felt their needs *as mothers* were not well accounted for, and where they were met, it was because it suited the prison. As such, the Mothers embodied Sykes' (1958) 'pains of imprisonment,' illustrating how the 'frustrations and deprivations' of prison impacted on their maternal identity and role, and subsequently their interactions with their children, thus setting in motion the persistent pains that would prevail beyond the prison walls on release.

Chapters 9 to *11* explore the experiences of the Mothers and grandmothers post-release, revealing the impact of their incarceration in the months, years and decades following their release; thus revealing the enduring and persistent pains of maternal imprisonment. They move on to examine how the prison system frustrates the maternal-role, as mothers and grandmothers are separated from their 'home world' and the tasks associated therein (Quinlan, 2011), leading to role dispossession.

Pause for Thought

Who is in your support network as a parent? — What if you didn't have access to that network? — In your own life what are the relationships that have had the most influence on you, good or bad?

What would it feel like for you if you were prevented from attending a special event of your child/loved ones? — Imagine what it was like for mothers in prison to not see their children for over a year because of Covid-19? — Or to have to choose which child to ring if your children were in multiple locations and/or you had limited funds? — What if you had no funds at all?

Do you think prison is/should be a place of care?

CHAPTER 9

Renegotiating Motherhood

'It never ends, the guilt the shame, the worry that their mistakes
are because you went to prison, I get good days and bad days … But
even now all these years later it's back in a flash … it is, it's a life
sentence when a mother goes to prison … for all of us.' (Margaret)

Taking up the Mothers' narratives post-release, *Chapters 9* to *11* now demonstrate how the effects of maternal imprisonment are felt far beyond prison walls. They show how the Mothers' imported values and beliefs about motherhood continued to impact and inform maternal self-esteem. Considered alongside the complexities and challenges of post-prison life generally, these lingering effects served to frustrate and undermine the Mothers maternal-roles, their re-entry into their families, and their desistance from crime.

This chapter provides new knowledge about the persisting long-term traumatic effects of maternal imprisonment. Particularly concerning maternal identity, maternal emotions and women's maternal-role already mentioned. Responding to a specific gap in the literature, it identifies the particular ways in which grandmothers and mothers of adult children are affected by imprisonment and how the subsequent 'layers of shame' (Mavis) continue to challenge maternal identity for many years. The chapter explores the 'deprivations and frustrations' (Sykes, 1958) that contribute to the persistent pains of maternal imprisonment as well as the Mothers' attempts to renegotiate and repair their motherhood as they re-entered the lives of their children and families. Further, it reveals how the Mothers strived to come to terms with the collateral damage of their imprisonment in terms of enduring guilt, shame, loss, changed relationships, post-prison supervision and long-lasting trauma.

The Mothers articulated their 'hope' and 'wish' for things to 'get back to normal' (Margot) on release. However, the reality is often very different (see also Eaton, 1993; Enos, 2001; Brown and Bloom, 2009; Leverentz, 2014). Reintegration and reunification into families presented many challenges for the Mothers. The greatest of these lay in the re-establishing of their altered and/or broken relationships with family, but especially with their children and grandchildren. Resuming their maternal-role, was a 'precarious enterprise' (Brown and Bloom, 2009: 313).

All the Mothers found their release and the post-prison period challenging, some in ways they had anticipated— 'I knew it would be a while before they forgave me' (Tanisha)— others in ways they had not anticipated— 'I did not expect to feel like a stranger in my own home' (Rayna). They found that they had to renegotiate their place in their families, their relationships with their children, and their new or altered maternal identity; in short, to renegotiate their motherhood from their now disadvantaged position as a 'spoiled' mother.

Spoiled Maternal Identity

The legacy of their pre-prison and in-prison experiences left the Mothers feeling 'tainted.' In their own eyes most remained 'bad' mothers, not now because they were *in* prison but because they had *been to* prison. The repair to their maternal identity was not immediate if it happened at all. Although most Mothers demonstrated a 'spoiled maternal identity,' several actively resisted the 'spoiling.' They fought against being labelled, and sought to make their experience 'count,' either by utilising it as a catalyst for change (Giordano et al, 2002) or to assist others with similar experiences, and/or by actively challenging and disrupting 'the system' via activism; and/or by simply refusing the label.

> 'I refused to be labelled as just a mother who's been to prison. All the way through [the system] that label is shoved onto you and all the bad that goes with it. But I am much more than this, I am not going to let what I did to myself and my family define me for the rest of my life.' (Rita)

Some Mothers felt angry at the persistent negative emotions they felt and pushed against the negative identity and connotations they felt were imposed on them by others as well as by themselves. For example, Kady stated she was 'not ashamed to be me' and Emma said:

'I know I've been to prison and that makes me a bad mother, but I'm out now so does that mean I can never be good enough? What person hasn't made mistakes?, it's just that we mothers aren't allowed to make mistakes are we?'

Similarly, Cynthia—who felt strongly that her past should be allowed to remain in the past despite the guilt that she lives with 'every day':

'I know most people think I must be a rubbish mum because I went to prison, but I'm not completely, I was but I got better...now I think I'm a better mum than some people I know who haven't even broke the law...who are they to judge me? My son thinks I'm a good mum and that's all that matters to me now.'

Post-prison mothers often encounter challenges, and stigmatisation, and many face the same difficult circumstances that they were living in pre-prison, now compounded by ex-prisoner status, spoiled maternal identity and reduced maternal self-esteem and, sometimes, agency (Carlton and Seagrave, 2013; Leverentz, 2014). The internalised perception of themselves as 'bad mothers' was something the Mothers felt unable to escape from, and they were often reminded of it:

'...there will be a happy family discussion going on, you know just normal round the table chit-chat, then someone will say "Oh Mum, do you remember when such and such happened?"...then there will be the inevitable, "Oh sorry...that was when you were away"'...then the room will fall momentarily silent, it will only last a few seconds...but those seconds feel like a lifetime for me. A lifetime of being a bad mother.'

Several Mothers felt that they had permanently relinquished any previously held 'good mother' identity, in their own eyes, and in the eyes of their family and wider society.

'I'm not sure I will ever be able to think of myself as a good mother now. Going to prison changed that and even if I weren't judging myself I know others would judge me if they knew. It's not something I'm proud of, or am happy for people to know about me, put it that way, even all these years later.' (Karen)

Feeling stigmatised (Goffman, 1963), was familiar to many Mothers and was often related to a fear of negative evaluation by others (Liss et al, 2013). Tamika:

'I hate people knowing that I was pregnant both times I went to prison, it was bad enough being judged in court...I think, well everyone thinks, it's worse being in prison pregnant...so no I don't tell people if I can help it...it's just wrong, innit, and those that I do tell or have told, well they just look down their noses at you...it's like, "How could you?" You can see it in their eyes. It makes them question what kind of person you are.'

Many Mothers experienced discrimination, stigma and judgement in their pre-prison lives as women, as working-class women, as black women, substance misusing women, older women. Often there was an intersectionality to their experiences, and they were deemed triply, or even quadruply deviant. This was replicated post-release. For several Mothers, their age, class, race and culture interacted with their motherhood and their own maternal self-assessment and others' assessment of them.

'My family obviously told me I brought shame on the family, I flip between being shunned by those who know [about prison] and lying to those who don't...obviously, I did know it would be like this. My culture is very judge-mental, especially to women...It's worse because I'm a mother,...even now my mother-in-law gets digs in all the time, she told my husband I was not "morally capable" of guiding them [her children] now and bringing them up. I lost my profession, too, and that doesn't help me feel good about myself at all...that I can't practice anymore, but it is as a mother I feel the most ashamed. For my husband it is both, but for my mother-in-law...to her I am not fit to be a mother.' (Jaspreet)

Kady, a black Mother, was supervised by a black probation officer and on her release was told by the probation officer that she had 'let her race down'; she told Kady that as 'an intelligent black mother you should have been better, you have let us all down.' Kady described how this conversation played over in her head, interacting with her own already reducing self-esteem, specifically her maternal self-esteem. Her guilt and shame was layered:

> 'I have never forgotten it. I was already questioning myself, could I do this, could I be a good role model to my daughter as a mother who'd been to prison? As a mother whose baby was born in prison. I was already questioning, man, and she went and said that … she said that! … so now I have to feel guilty not only as a mum … but as a black mum too.'

Eight years post-release, Kady had yet to tell her daughter she had been to prison. Nor that she was born in prison and had spent the first five months of her life in a prison MBU. She said she had 'put off' telling her daughter 'because I feel like … like there's something just so wicked about it.' She was afraid of her daughter's rejection but also feared others would judge and negatively label her daughter a 'prison baby.' Kady did not think her daughter would 'forgive' her:

> 'I put her there, she didn't ask to be there. I just don't think she will [forgive], and the thing is I wouldn't even blame her if she hates me … but she will always be that child who was born in prison. My shame is her shame, or it will be when she knows, I don't want her tainted like me, why would I want her to know that about herself, about me, she's got the most horrible birth story forever, I did that to her, me.'

Goffman (1963) suggests that mothers, as ex-prisoners generally, now had what he called 'blemishes of character' and would continue to be further stigmatised. As alluded to earlier in this book, just as motherhood held master status in terms of identity (Higgins, 1987), 'ex-prisoner motherhood' occupied a master identity in terms of spoiling. It was Mothers damaged maternal identity that hurt and impacted the Mothers the most. The Mothers spoke of feeling 'forever tainted' (Kady), 'damaged' (Cynthia), and 'tarnished' (Mavis), *specifically* as mothers. Thus illustrating the Mothers' absorption of traditional motherhood ideology.

Maggie described how she felt all positive aspects of her previous mothering and grandmothering were now 'wiped out,' or erased. The expectations of mothers and motherhood and their relationship to guilt was more fully explored in previous chapters, but this aspect further reveals that the shame and guilt mothers continued to feel post-prison remained rooted in traditional expectations of motherhood, maternal-role and identity. Queenie, who had previously described herself as the 'runt' concerning motherhood, repeatedly spoke of her daughters' 'shame' at having 'an ex-prisoner, a criminal as a mother.'

> '…it's years later now, and they are still ashamed of me, so how can I not be ashamed of me too, they don't know anyone else with a mother who's been to prison…it's a big secret, this is. No matter what, her shame [that of her daughter} won't go so how can mine? I want to shed it, but I just can't.'

Arditti and Few (2006) argue that the 'enactment' of mothering alters dramatically during imprisonment, and mothers' identities change as a result of that disruption. This struck a chord with the Mothers. Illustrated by Taranpreet, writing from prison:

> 'I just don't feel like a mother anymore, and if I'm not a mother I don't know what else I am except just a criminal.'

The Mothers' spoiled maternal identity sometimes acted as a paralysing factor regarding reactivating their mothering. Mothers were so traumatised by their experiences that they were simply unable to mother their children because of an overwhelming fear of failing (again):

> 'In the end I couldn't see the point in fighting her…she [their grand-mother] was a better mother to them than I could ever be, and I just didn't want to let them down again.'

The Mothers also felt keenly that the reduction in their maternal self-esteem was heavily underpinned by guilt and shame and was directly related to their fear of negative evaluation and judgement by others (Liss et al, 2013). For Mothers who had previously had issues with addiction, and/or had experienced their children being permanently or temporarily removed from their care, their maternal guilt, shame and fearfulness of an uncertain future, was a trigger for a return to substance misuse as a means of blocking out or coping with their ongoing, all-encompassing maternal emotions. A return to substance misuse often made a return to law-breaking more likely.

'I can't turn the clock back and I know I'll feel shit about it forever, I know it makes me a bad mother, all I can do is try to be better, it shames me, it really does ... it shames me ... it's so difficult not to use [substances] to block out feelings like this ... and that's what I always did in the past ... it was a cycle: block out, use, feel worse, block out, use more.' (Sandra)

Beth, the youngest Mother, had predicted in her interview that a return to drug use or suicide attempts would be likely for her because of her struggle with guilt, shame and sadness. She was utterly traumatised by the enforced separation from her baby (who was three months old when Beth was sentenced), which, alongside her own negative self-evaluation of herself as a mother, was too much for her to bear:

'The bairn had to stop breast feeding cos I was sent down ... that's sick isn't it? Her health for life affected because of me and my mistakes. I felt like a shit mother, the worst in fact ... she went into care because of me, I felt like nothing when I was in prison ... Even now I think what's the point of me. She doesn't know me now ... I try in the contacts[1] like, but she doesn't want me ... when I come out of my contacts, all I want to do is block out the pain with drugs ... that or leave this life altogether ... sometimes both.'

---

1. Supervised regular contact organized by Social Services and usually in a contact centre, with a plan to move gradually to more frequent and unsupervised contact as part of the process of gradual full reunification.

Beth's shame and guilt were layered: not only did she feel stigmatised as an ex-prison mother, but she worried about what her daughter would 'think of her' in the future when she found out she had been in care. Worrying about this fuelled Beth's lack of hope and her uncertainty about what kind of future they 'could have.'

'It's Just Different'

Motherhood and maternal experiences preoccupied Mothers thoughts, and the reduction or altering of their maternal-role had a profound effect on their self-concepts and self-worth (Mireault et al, 2002). Rita, like several Mothers, was torn between feeling 'invisible' and wanting to retreat further into the background of her family and fighting to regain her previous role and matriarch status.

Echoing many of the Mothers' experiences, Rita recognised that she had lost 'power' as a mother. Not just over her toddler son, but all her children. Previously the lynchpin of the family, she went on to describe how she had to renegotiate her relationships with all of her children. She, like several Mothers of teenage children, stated it took her time to recognise that her children had all matured whilst she had been locked away. Her elder children had been pre-teens and teenagers when she went inside—a period of intense change in young people's lives. They had all become more emotionally mature and more independent in her absence and Rita felt they all needed a 'period of adjustment' whilst she fought to re-centre herself in the family and come to terms with the changes in their relationship dynamics. She felt her and her family eventually found and negotiated 'a new normal' they were all happy with, and slowly relationships between her and her children strengthened.

Sadly, this is not always the case. Shanice, who had described feeling like an 'outsider' and 'watching in' whilst in prison, had not expected that feeling to continue once she was released; however, and echoing Brown and Bloom's (2009) findings, she discovered that was in fact magnified and she felt more of an outsider than ever:

'Sometimes I'd watch my mother with the kids and think, that should be me doing that…but at first it was like I was paralysed or something, I just used to watch and not do nothing.'

Similarly, Tia had been heavily addicted to heroin before prison, and by her own admission had 'never been a mother to Meg,' due the chaos they lived in. Now clean and sober, she wanted a better relationship with her daughter, but felt that it was gone:

'…we are not close in that way now. It feels more like we are living together as sisters or something. It doesn't feel like mother and daughter anymore. I'm on eggshells.'

This was compounded because Tia had a younger son, whom she had felt it was not 'too late for.' She described very different relationships with her two children: her youngest had been so young before her sentence that he did not remember much about Tia's 'chaotic pre-prison drug-affected life,' so Tia felt that to him she was untainted. She described her relationship with her son as less scarred by guilt, so to her 'it is easier, more pure.' Paradoxically, she described this 'pure' relationship with her son as also a source of guilt because it triggers anger and jealousy in her daughter:

'He has a clean mother, he doesn't really remember me being in prison or away from him, so he doesn't know any different and we are close, really close, she never had that. I see her watching us and I know what she's thinking, like she's on the outside…I see it and I hate it because I know it's too late for us.'

Four of the Mothers said that their relationships with their children were affected because the children 'chose' not to return to them post-release. With the exception of Tarian who felt that in her family they all 'shared the kids anyway.' The Mothers felt to blame for this situation and saw it as rejection, further reducing their maternal self-esteem. Thus, changing their relationships with their children:

'Now she [their grandmother] has them more than me so when we are all together it's like I have to check with her if it's okay to give them something, like she's the mum now not me, worse is the bairns look to her first to check as well. I hate it.' (Tanya)

Several Mothers described their relationships with their children as 'forever changed.' Some with older or adult children felt those relationships would never be as strong or at least the same again. Particularly if their children had matured into adulthood (Lockwood, 2020). Sandra lamented the changed relationships with her teenage daughters, which she believes was a direct result of her imprisonment:

'We had made headway and put the past behind us ... I thought we were really close, I worried about them every day when I was in prison ... but we are now not close again. I wasn't expecting that.'

Sandra's situation was compounded by the fact that both of her teenage daughters became pregnant during her imprisonment, as did one of Ursula's and one of Queenie's daughters. Marjorie's son became a father whilst she was imprisoned. All of them, as grandmothers-to-be, were deeply affected by this. They all felt their maternal guilt was magnified because they were 'not there' for such a significant event in their children's lives, an event which they as *mothers* were *supposed* to be there for. The Mothers felt that not only did this add to their guilt and shame, but it affected their relationships with their children — either temporarily or permanently — and ultimately then affected their relationships with their grandchildren, too, adding to the layered impact.

Research has demonstrated that having a parent in prison, especially a mother, can sometimes be a factor in subsequent anti-social behaviour and offending in children (Beresford, 2018; Murray and Farrington, 2005). Some of the Mothers felt that their teenage children had 'gone off the rails' (Karen) because of their absence. Their teenagers' behaviours interacted with the Mothers' guilt, which also had an impact on their relationships and the Mothers' parenting decisions (discussed later). Dee described how her teenage daughter now used cannabis, but she felt that she 'just' had to 'let her,' 'because she's just like I was so what right have I got to tell her not to?' She described how she and her daughter had 'actual physical fights' where there would be 'venomous arguments' about Dee's 'neglect' of her daughter, and her decision not to allow her to visit whilst she was in prison.

Opsal (2015) argues that prison rules and policies do not appropriately accommodate mother/child visits and reunification complications are therefore amplified. Some Mothers in the research had taken the 'protective' decision (O'Malley, 2015) to not allow their children to visit at all, thus sacrificing their own needs and wants to see their children whilst 'sparing them' the experience of prison visiting. Dee said she made this decision because she herself had visited her own mother in prison and she had hated it; she remembered being 'terrified of the dogs' and just feeling 'confused and frightened.'

Prolonged Separation

In refusing visits, Mothers were using their maternal agency to make decisions which they felt were in the best interests of their children. Retaining at least some decisions about their children was an important part of retaining a maternal-role (Enos, 2001). Whilst none described regretting that decision, several Mothers felt that the sometimes lengthy periods of no contact had 'changed' their relationships with their children, even if only temporarily:

> 'On my first sentence, I didn't let them come, the baby was too young but my son, well I didn't want him to even know I was in prison … but that meant he was angry when I got out, he thought I'd chosen work over him, so he was angry … and he acted out a lot … at me, always at me.' (Shanice)

Sophie stated simply, 'I didn't want her to think it [prison] was normal so I stopped her coming.' She went on to say that the prolonged separation was painful, but she was reassured and empowered by the fact she had made a positive and selfless decision — ironically this made her feel 'more like a mother.' However, it also meant that when she was released her daughter was 'so different.' Sophie described her daughter as 'unfamiliar' to her, this feeling endured and left an imprint:

'[S]he smelt different, her hair was long, she knew words I hadn't taught her, her…just everything…she even walked different. It's like…when I got out I felt like I didn't know her, I felt like I didn't know my own child, like I didn't know what made her tick, I didn't know what food she liked or owt like that. And that's horrible, my own child and I don't even know this stuff about her. Like now I have caught up with it, her favourite colours, her favourite books, blah de blah…but it made me feel depressed until I did…and I still don't feel I get it right no more.'

When asked how this made her feel as a mum, Sophie replied, 'It didn't make me feel like a mum because mums are supposed to know this stuff, aren't they?'

Given that the maintenance of family ties and bonds is an important consideration in relation to recidivism (Farmer, 2017, 2019; Shammas, 2017; Codd, 2013), the implications of mothers making the painful decision not to see their children, whether they were 'protective' or not, are huge for both. Particularly when, as argued by Sykes (1958), the more deeply felt and extensive the pains of imprisonment are, the greater is the likelihood of reoffending. Despite making what they felt were positive maternal choices, the Mothers acknowledged that not seeing their children affected their adjustment post-release and impacted on their relationships with their children. Karen, sentenced for a serious driving offence, had no prior contact with the criminal justice system 'or people like that.' After one 'awful' visit she did not want her children to experience prison again, as it was 'not something I ever thought would be or wanted to be part of their world'; so she refused to allow further visits. She described her children as feeling angry with her post-release, and she felt 'distanced' from them as a result:

'Oh, they were all angry. My middle daughter had started her periods whilst I was inside, but she didn't tell me this when I phoned home, I only found out when I was home, and even then only because she asked me to buy sanitary products. I asked her why she hadn't told me, she said it was because she didn't want the prison guards to hear at my end or her brothers at her end, but I know having to go through that on her own...without me has changed how we are. I still don't know who bought her first sanitary towels. I worry we will never be as close as we were. Same with the other two really, they grew up so much when I was away, I was away at such important developmental phases in their lives, it's hard for me to know them, really know them...like I did before. Same for them with me, I think they feel like I've changed. I'm not the mum they knew anymore. We have all changed and because of that our relationships with each other have, too. It's sad.'

Sophie stated that *not only* had her daughter 'grown up' whilst she was incarcerated, but she felt that *she* had too. She felt more independent and less needy, both as a daughter and as a young mother; this caused tension in her relationship with her own mother:

'It caused real tension between us — me just wanting to be a mum, she was used to me asking her everything and I think she felt redundant...but I developed a much better bond with my daughter because I was actually being her mum, so in the end I think I'm a better mum to my daughter now.'

Several Mothers felt their relationships with their children had changed because they themselves had. Ursula said, 'I've changed, I know I have; the kids say I'm colder now.' Some Mothers, particularly those whose children had been separated from each other and cared for by different family members, found their mother/child relationships had fractured. Tarian, whose eldest daughter (aged 14) had lived between her father and both her paternal and maternal grandmothers during her mother's sentence, continued to do the same when Tarian was released:

'I don't feel I know her now, not like I used to, she doesn't want to come home, I thought she'd want to be just with me, but she's got used to her freedom, I think she uses her moving about as a way to get away with stuff — how can I tell her off for being late if I don't know which house she's meant to be in, it's gone. We won't ever be the same.'

Several Mothers described their different relationships with individual children, something perhaps all mothers have, but in Tia and Tarian's cases, their relationships were directly impacted by their prison sentence. Tarian found out she was pregnant on admission to prison and had her youngest son with her on an MBU throughout her whole sentence, which resulted in a closer bond for her and her new baby. She said:

> '...for a bit I wasn't as close to the others no, with him [the baby], it was like it was a chance to do it properly, be a proper mum, being pregnant with him in there, it was like it was just me and him in our own bubble. Plus I was clean and sober for this pregnancy, so I was focussed, especially because I didn't see the others much. Then when he came, god I loved him. Still do, he's my baby, he'll always be my special baby.'

Tia's pre-teen daughter hated visiting the prison, and so Tia would go for long periods without seeing her; she also 'wasn't great on the phone.' Tia went on to say:

> 'So for over a year [on the phone] we barely had a conversation beyond you okay? yeah, I'm okay, you okay?...it was like getting blood from a stone, but visits with her were worse, like a long drawn-out hospital visit. She was embarrassed, I think, always worried she'd see someone she knew, that made me feel ashamed, in the end I stopped making her come—she hated it, I hated it, so what was the point. I know it was the right thing to do, but that changed us as well...I don't think we will ever again have a brilliant relationship, too much has gone on...we are not like mother and daughter now, more like sisters really...but my son and me, we are as close as close.'

Tanya's children 'chose' to stay with their grandmother when their mother was released: their roles were completely reversed, with Tanya now being the weekend parent and her mother being the children's primary carer. This had a profound effect on their relationships, and she felt 'unable' to take back her full maternal-role or even her maternal identity. Resonating with previous studies (Arditti and Few, 2006; Codd, 2013; Leverentz, 2014; Baldwin and Epstein, 2017; O'Malley, 2018; Masson,

2019; Booth, 2020), the Mothers' changed relationships with their children impacted on their re-entry experiences. Mothers had lost confidence in their maternal-roles and felt a reduction in their maternal self-esteem and fuelling their guilt.

The guilt and shame the post-prison Mothers and grandmothers felt manifested in several ways, not least of which was the need to 'make it up' to family and all that that entailed whilst trying to cope with crippling, self-flagellating internal blame and shame, which Mothers often accepted as their new normal, and as their penance.

Penance and Making-up

As well as the pitfalls and consequences the Mothers faced in society as ex-prison mothers, they were also to some extent authors of their own penance.[2] They would either do all they could to 'make it up' to their children and families, or they would absorb and focus on their own perceptions of their 'blame,' or a combination of both.

In direct contrast to Masson's research (2019: 58–9), which found 'admitting' feelings of guilt was 'rarely discussed' or that the 'burden they had imposed on others outside' was not something disclosed by the mothers in her study, the Mothers in spoke frequently about their guilt and shame and the impact offending and imprisonment had on their children and wider families. Echoing other studies (see Enos, 2001; Sharpe, 2015; Baldwin and Epstein, 2017; O'Malley, 2018; Lockwood, 2020), the Mothers' narratives and post-prison maternal experiences were absolutely underpinned by guilt and shame.

Influenced by their internalised guilt, the Mothers described 'spoiling' their children upon release to 'make up' for lost time and their absence. Most of them expressed their need and desire to 'make it up' (Lauren) to their children by 'making up for lost time' (Mary), or by 'spoiling' them (Annie), or 'ruining' them (in the Northern sense of the word—which equates to spoiling). Spoiling children to 'make it up to them,' was

---

2. Meaning punishment inflicted on oneself as an outward expression of repentance or wrong-doing—*Oxford English Dictionary.*

something almost all of the Mothers of younger children described they would do and was often linked to shame and guilt. Tamika stated:

'...I felt disgraced...like I didn't love him enough...like other people would think I didn't love him enough. That's probably why I spoil him. To this day I still do. I still feel like I've got making up to do, I am constantly trying to make up, constantly trying to play catch up.'

Cynthia, who had served nine sentences, most when her son was younger, had felt she had 'much to make up' to her son:

'David used to see his mum [Cynthia] drunk on a lot of occasions and then his mum goes to prison, I was so guilty and so ashamed that's why I always used to spoil him and buy him lots of things. My sister used to say I spoilt him, but who cares, I don't, but he's my son, if I want to spoil him I will, he's been through a lot.'

Similarly, Annie, described how in the early days of her release she would 'basically give her anything she wanted.' Annie, now a few years further down the line, reflected how her need to 'make it up' to her daughter almost drove her into a spiral of debt that could have gone disastrously wrong for her. She had missed her daughter's birthday whilst in prison and so when it came to her next one, Annie wanted to 'go all out,' spending an inordinate amount of money on an 'outrageous' party that she could ill-afford. Annie stated the debt she got into for the party, had she not been supported by friends, would have led her to reoffending, triggered her mental health issues and potentially further imprisonment. Her feelings of guilt and how they manifested could easily have led her back into a further separation — creating a spiral not difficult to imagine. This 'risk' caused friction with Annie's family, resulting in enduring strained family relationships. She is annoyed and frustrated that her family do not understand her need, and her family were frustrated and 'embarrassed' by the cost of the party. Furthermore, they had issues with Annie's new parenting style, which they described as unduly lenient or 'soft,' something they felt would potentially have a negative impact on Annie's daughter in the future. Similarly, Queenie described how she was:

> '…desperate to make it up to my daughter…So, now I drop everything if she asks me to do anything, I really think it's a conscious effort to make up for what I missed. I know with her next baby I will be on her like a rash. I just so want to make up that lost time with Belle [the baby], through the next one.'

This need to 'make it up' to their children also affected the Mothers' ability or willingness to discipline their children.

'It's a Bit Rich…'

Mothers felt that their discipline related challenges impacted directly on the children themselves. Maggie felt that her indulgence as a parent (borne out of guilt) had been a significant factor in her son 'going off the rails' and becoming an offender himself, a potentially under-explored contributory factor to what is already known about intergenerational offending (Farmer, 2017):

> 'I felt guilty because I hadn't been there, so I gave him everything…too much, so he didn't learn he couldn't have everything he wanted, and now he's in prison. I blame myself; I really do.'

Maggie was not the only Mother whose child offended and who blamed herself. She reflected that her 'reluctance' to discipline her son, alongside her need to 'make it up' to him, may have contributed to his waywardness. Several Mothers described struggling to discipline their children because they felt 'hypocritical,' but also because of their conflict with the need to 'make it up' to their children. Kady, even though her daughter did not know her mother had ever been in prison, stated:

> 'Since the day she was born, I've promised myself I'll make it up to her. Sometimes if I'm shouting at her or if she does something wrong…I'll

catch myself. I do put her in time out, I do … but all the time I'm thinking, do I have the right to do this, should I be shouting at her considering what I've put her through?'

Tia described how, when she was previously heroin-addicted, she was 'less bothered' about discipline. There had been no rules or sanctions in her home as she was constantly under the influence of substances. Now clean and sober, Tia wanted 'to be a good mother,' part of which she saw as being a disciplinarian where appropriate; however, both she and her daughter struggled with the change. Tia was torn between 'just wanting her to have whatever she wanted, because of what I've put her through,' and knowing that she 'should' discipline her.

'The discipline I just found so difficult, because for her she thinks, why am I like this all of a sudden, like I say to her help me run the house or clean your room and stuff like that—all stuff I wasn't bothered about before. I see the confusion on her face and that just makes me think, oh I should do it all for her anyway—that might make up for how I was before and in prison, but then I'm not doing her any favours for the future by doing that am I? It's so hard.'

The Mothers felt their 'maternal authority' had been reduced by 'conviction, incarceration and absence' (Brown and Bloom, 2009: 326) because they have been publicly discredited as persons and, by default, as mothers. This further complicated the issue of maternal discipline. Mothers of teenagers felt this particularly, with several saying their children 'threw it back in my face that I was the criminal' (Karen). Mothers struggled with losing the 'moral high ground' they are 'expected' (Tanisha) to have as mothers—further chiming with Brown and Bloom's (2009) US-based findings. Many of the Mothers felt the reduction in their maternal-role and maternal power was their own fault, 'I've only got myself to blame for all of this haven't I?' (Rayna)

Shame and Blame

As illustrated in *Chapter 3,* most mothers internalise mother-blaming attitudes, often for things that may be completely out of their control (Sutherland, 2010). Wider societal tendencies to blame mothers for their children's negative outcomes (Jackson and Mannix, 2004) are in fact mirrored by the Mothers themselves. For post-prison Mothers, their ex-prisoner status provided the hook on which to hang their own internal blame and shame. The range of outcomes Mothers accepted or wore the blame for were almost infinite. Rita, speaking about persistent thoughts of guilt and blame, simply stated:

> '…you feel to blame for everything. Every time they do something that's out of character or they play up, you question is it all because I went to prison?'

Three Mothers whose teenage daughters became pregnant during their sentences felt this would not have happened had they been at home. They blamed themselves for the early pregnancies and all of the potential negative outcomes of a teenage pregnancy — 'Her future is limited now' (Diane). Ursula questioned whether her daughter having a child at such a young age would also limit her future, and she felt that her daughter's choices of partners and life-path had been negatively affected by her prison sentence, saying, 'I feel responsible, all the time.'

> 'I know it was all my fault, I dunno maybe I've internalised from prison, you know, like it's your fault, you've got to do something about it…You know, actually there's a socio-political-economic context in which offending takes place but, you know, it's your fault, your responsibility, to fix it, do you know what I mean? I don't know, it's shit.'

Ursula's son offended whilst she was still in custody, something she insists would not have happened had she been home; revealing her deepseated guilt about this, 'He has that label now, ex-offender, because of me. I have to find a way to make it up to him.'

Mary blamed herself for the fact that her sons were now described as 'career criminals,' which she felt was rooted in them being taken into care 'because' of her. Echoing Lockwood's (2020) research, the Mothers of teenagers felt responsible for any disputes in the family home where siblings were fighting each other. This generated additional worry for the Mothers and was a source of discontentment when they were reuniting:

> 'I'm like a sodding referee…there is so much tension and resentment in my house now…it wasn't like this before. It's like we all have our own private hurt from that time, and we focus on that instead of supporting each other like one family…we are fractured now, broken.' (Karen)

Mothers blamed themselves that some sibling groups had been 'spread' amongst relatives and so had not lived together during their mothers' incarceration. As a result, relationships between the separated siblings had altered, causing additional stress, tension and resentment through the families. Echoing other studies (Booth, 2020; Baldwin and Epstein, 2017), Tia's two children, who had been separated and rarely seen each other during their mother's imprisonment (because the two caregivers 'did not get on'), were described by Tia as 'nowhere near as close.'

The Mothers blamed themselves for their children being bullied at school, for their changed behaviours, changed relationships, offending behaviour, disconnection with education and a myriad of other outcomes. Rayna felt that her mother's cancer had 'spread faster' because of the stress of Rayna's prison sentence (as, indeed, some of her family believed). Maggie went as far as to blame herself for the fact her grandchild went on to develop cancer:

> '[W]hen Ryan got cancer, all I could think was that cancer is related to stress isn't it—the stress of me being inside, us being separated, that's what caused it—I know it. It doesn't matter what anyone says, I just know it was the trigger and I have to live with that now.'

This self-blame did not ease as the children grew older; many of the older Mothers blamed themselves for outcomes in their mature adult children and their children's children. Both Mary and Maggie felt that their sons had trouble bonding with their own children *because* the bond with their own mothers had been broken by imprisonment.

> 'He struggled as a parent, he couldn't show them affection, but then it's not surprising really, is it — he hadn't been mothered, not properly and not by me anyway, so how was he meant to know how to be a parent when he hadn't been parented … something else that is my fault.' (Mary)

The Mothers spoke about how there was 'no end' (Tanisha) to their penance when it comes to their children: 'It's a life sentence for a mum' (Ursula). Ursula went on to say that she prays to 'be released' from her life sentence of questioning and examining her children's outcomes and looking for positives as 'evidence' that they were not irrevocably affected by her imprisonment.

Cynthia blamed herself for her son's anorexia: 'My son was anorexic … and I thought … I've done that to my child … my boy … because he was pining for his mother.' Her son was an adult when he developed anorexia and she had been out of prison for 24 years, having been sentenced to custody for arson after setting fire to herself. She had a long history of horrific abuse, sexual violence, substance misuse, and mental health issues; she had been repeatedly failed by mental health services and was unsupported at the time of her 'offence.' The judge had apparently 'not wanted' to send Cynthia to prison, but 'there were no probation beds' (approved premises will not take those accused of arson) or secure hospital beds available at that time. Despite the significant and relevant external factors over which Cynthia had had little control, she maintained it was she and she alone who was to blame for her son's illness. Beth stated:

> 'I did this, me, I chose to take the drugs, yes it was the only way I could cope, but I chose that path, what kind of mother does that[?]'

Tragically, such was the level of Beth's trauma, pain and self-blame surrounding her separation from her baby daughter, and the subsequent painful process of gradual and surveilled reunification, she, as she had predicted, inflicted on herself the ultimate penance, and took her own life just before her 21st birthday.

Most if not all of the Mothers absorbed the blame, and often the responsibility, not only for their own crimes but for the circumstances around them too. Those who misused substances, as a means of 'blocking out' or coping with abuse, only ever blamed themselves for their addictions, not their abusers nor society that had failed them by its lack of resources to support them financially, practically or emotionally.

Influenced by discriminatory policies and legislation and cultural ideology, the widespread failure to support 'troubled' women plays out through all of society's 'systems' (Clarke and Chadwick, 2018: 64), yet it is the women themselves who most feel the guilt of their failure (O'Reilly, 2016; Sutherland, 2010). Feminist criminology (Carlen, 2002; Renzetti, 2013) argues that this kind of 'individualist thinking' is influenced by criminal justice policy makers and sentencers, which give strong messages to criminalised women that their circumstances are solely of their own making; it perpetuates the belief that women need only make better 'choices' to 'turn their lives around' (Clarke and Chadwick, 2018: 208).

The reality is that the responsibility for the outcomes of criminalised women is, at the very least, shared: to have effective criminal justice, there must be social justice and, rather than focusing on individual pathways into and out of 'offending,' there must be a forceful challenge to the institutional and structural inequalities, discrimination, and under-resourcing of gendered support that contributes heavily to women's criminalisation.

Layers of shame — Grandmothering post-prison

The deep sense of shame felt by the post-imprisoned Mothers was magnified in the grandmothers, not least because of the cultural ideas, ideals and expectations around age, gender, motherhood, and grandmotherhood (Wahidin, 2004; Baldwin, 2020). Mavis described it as 'like an onion of shame.' Grandmothers felt their shame was related to not only their maternal identity but also specifically to their grandmother identity, 'It's ridiculous really a grandmother in prison' (Mavis). Another factor adding to the 'layers' of shame for post-prison grandmothers related to secrecy and enduring shame. For several of the grandmothers, their status as ex-prisoners was a 'family secret' that had been kept from grandchildren.

'It's the elephant in the room—my grandchildren know nothing of it, imagine them bringing it up, god forbid, oh my granny was in prison, it's not right is it, I should have known better.' (Queenie)

Margaret felt she could never truly relax or be herself in front of her grandchildren, despite being 46 years post-release:

'Sometimes I feel really on edge with them [the grandchildren] if I'm not in control of a conversation, just in case it goes down an avenue that will lead to prison talk … in some ways its meant I've had to keep some distance, I'm not totally relaxed with them … it's actually very stressful, you know, even now … carrying all that about … it wears you down.'

The grandmothers 'lived in fear' (Margaret) of their secrets coming out, the secrecy, fear of judgement and negative evaluation, and the unknown added to their shame (Liss et al, 2013; Warr, 2016; Goffman, 1963). For Margaret this was compounded by the fact that her own daughter was now in prison, and she became the caregiver for her daughter's children. Margaret not only felt 'to blame' for her daughter's criminality but was also fearful of her grandchildren discovering her past. Fearing their blame and rejection, Margaret found her maternal identity and maternal self-esteem vulnerable and precarious (Sharpe, 2015):

'The thing is now I don't feel I can ever tell my grandkids about me being in prison in case they think it's normal … I'd feel like I'd let my family down all over again if they knew … but it's just layers of deceit, isn't it? I just feel guilty all the time, it never goes … It's bad enough my children knowing I went to jail, but if my grandkids found out … well … it's just … shameful isn't it?'

Despite her own children being not yet born when she was imprisoned and her now being 46 years post-prison, Margaret still spoke of
her ongoing guilt as a mother and grandmother. She revealed an additional 'secret,' a baby she had given up for adoption soon after her prison
sentence. She called her prison sentence 'a dirty secret,' so ashamed about
her ex-prisoner status that she rarely even used the word 'prison,' instead
preferring to refer to it as when she was 'away.'

> 'There are so many situations where I have to tell white lies to cover up for
> that period I was away. Just the other day my granddaughter asked me what
> I did for my 21st, well it was a kick to the stomach because I was away for
> my 21st. I just feel so guilty for lying but I'm too ashamed for them to know.
> Imagine telling them their granny was a common criminal.'

Sandra described how the shame was layered regarding her grandchildren, and she did not want her grandchildren to view her in the same
ways that her children had. Sandra 'accepted' that she was spoiled as a
mother but did not want to be spoiled as a grandmother, too. This chimes
with Bachman et al's (2016: 225) research which found that 'second chance
grandparenting' could be directly related to desistance.

> 'I can't undo what I did, I know me going to prison ruined their childhoods
> and it's almost too late for them to see me as a good mum … but for the
> grandkids, well maybe it can be different.' (Sandra)

Several grandmothers described how the perceptions and judgements
of their adult children now shaped their relationships, not only with
them but also with their grandchildren. Queenie, previously the main
childcare provider for one daughter, was told that her 'services' were
'no longer required' (discussed later), conversely she felt she was being
used for 'unlimited childcare' by another daughter. Queenie felt she
was 'sort of being blackmailed' to 'do whatever she needs in terms of
childcare and see her on demand … because I owe her.' She felt that the
childcare service she was now providing for that daughter, and which
was her route to forgiveness, impacted negatively on her relationships

with her other children who resented how much she did for 'the most judgemental one... but if I don't, she digs and digs... and her knife is quite deep when she digs.' Since leaving prison, Queenie had tried to 'turn a negative into a positive' and set-up a business for women leaving prison: it had garnered attention in the media. She recounted when she was telephoned by the BBC to discuss her venture:

> 'I phoned my daughter to tell her, all proud and that, and I told her and nothing...complete silence on the end of the phone. She turned around and just said, "Do you think that's a good thing, bringing all this attention, do you ever think about me in this?" And that's it really, that's how we've changed with each other—she can't be proud of me and I can't talk to her.'

Mavis, who had previously been the main childcare provider for her grandchildren, was all but rejected by her adult, middle-class children:

> 'I thought I'd raised my children to be less judgemental than this, so you could have knocked me down with a feather when he reacted like this...I've looked after my grandchildren for years so he and his wife could be the highflyers they are. I made one mistake, and now it seems I've lost them all, I feel sick at the thought that my grandchildren are embarrassed, and I miss them desperately. I effectively brought them up. As for my son, well I don't know what to say, I feel I've failed as a mother because he's so unforgiving, but I love him and hate the thought that he's ashamed. It's like there are just layers of guilt and layers of shame, it consumes me. I just miss them, desperately, all of them.'

She not only took on the shame of being a grandmother who had been to prison, but also of what she felt had been a fault of her parenting—that her son was not able to be more empathic with her.

Sandra highlighted how, through her grandchildren, she was seeking to 'do a better job' than she felt she had as a mother. She described how becoming a grandmother, despite the fact that she blamed herself for both her teenage daughters' pregnancies ('If I had been home it would never have happened'), was a motivating factor in her desistance (Kerrison and Bachman, 2016):

> 'I want to do well for them…nannas are meant to be warm and kind and the "go to" person, not in prison, not a criminal—that's not the nanna I want to be. I don't take anything anymore. I think I would have stopped anyway, outgrown it—but I'm definitely clean for them. I don't want them to have no drunk and druggie nanna, imagine the shame of that.'

However, Sandra's newfound motivation and desire to be seen as a 'good nanna' was a source of tension with her daughters who, although pleased their mother was doing so well, felt frustrated and angry that she 'had not done the same for them.' This compounded her layered shame and she stated how she would 'torture' herself:

> 'I know they are pleased I'm better, but I torture myself with knowing they feel shit because I didn't do this for them. Our Molly actually asked me why they weren't enough, isn't that awful that that's how she feels. But the fact is I suppose they weren't, I was too into the drugs, too selfish, in too much pain, really, to stay off them, I couldn't have done it then. But you get stronger as you get older don't you, you think more I guess. Maybe I just grew up. I'm ashamed of that old me…but I can be a good nanna, it's not too late for that.'

Summary of *Chapter 9*

This chapter reveals how, for post-prison Mothers and grandmothers the often already challenging experience of re-entry into family life is further compounded by their maternal experiences, maternal-role and maternal emotions. It has begun to demonstrate the importance of supporting all mothers in their re-entry and renegotiation of their motherhood. As part of their re-entry, all of the Mothers were subject to forms of supervision or State surveillance. The Mothers revealed how their motherhood and mothering role was often frustrated, complicated—and occasionally supported — by the agents of the State, and also by their families, and how their experiences were marred by issues of trust.

Pause for Thought

Imagine for a second being away from your home for a significant period of time — maybe a year, maybe more, maybe less — What would it feel like to come home to find everything had changed? — To find your primary school child is now a teenager with no time for you?

How would it make you feel if your toddler seemed not to remember you well and now preferred their granny for comfort? — And how might this make you feel if you previously used substances as a coping mechanism?

What if you had just got your kids back? — Would you be afraid to tell them off? — What if you were struggling, would you be nervous to ask for help? — Would you want to just try to cope alone and not draw attention?

What would it feel like if you thought/your children told you they were ashamed of you?

CHAPTER 10

Trust and Surveillance

'Trust is a very difficult thing isn't it. It was broken in my personal life. I didn't come into prison as a person who trusted ... and when you get out, well it's even worse, trust no one! — Because the stakes are higher, you can lose your kids — at the drop of a hat. If they think you are not good enough, not proving yourself, then they are gone — you have to be a better mum than all mums, whiter than white.' (Ursula)

Trust has important implications for the engagement of mothers with statutory services post-release from imprisonment. Harris and Fallot (2013: 26) posit that when a traumatic experience occurs, trust is broken, as 'trauma violates our beliefs that the world is a safe place': for the now additionally traumatised Mothers, engaging with services that have the potential to 'hurt' them further was often challenging. Not least because Mothers found it difficult to trust that services were there to 'help' and support them, rather than to punish them further.

Earlier chapters revealed the extent to which all mothers come under scrutiny and surveillance and are measured against widely accepted ideals in ways which do not necessarily transfer to fathers (Jackson and Mannix, 2004). The Mothers felt that their post-prison mothering was subject to increased scrutiny and judgement, describing how they felt that others' trust in them had reduced not only because of their 'ex-prisoner' status, which Goffman (1961) referred to as a common phenomenon in individuals perceived to be of 'blemished character,' but additionally and specifically as mothers who were 'obviously' now not 'good mothers' (Tamika). This in turn was experienced by some of the Mothers as a lack of trust in them as mothers.

This chapter explores how issues of trust, surveillance and support interacted with motherhood to affect and inform the Mothers' post-prison experiences in both the short-term and long-term, impacting on their relationships with 'agents of the State' such as Social Services and the Probation Service, and also with their families and children.

State Surveillance: Social Services

Hays (2008) argues that support for post-release mothers is vital to their success but that mothers are often reluctant to ask for help for fear of negative assessment (formal and informal) and of ultimately losing their children. Empathy and genuine concern for criminalised mothers can be lacking and, as Lockwood (2018) identifies, criminalised mothers are not always afforded the same level of empathy as mothers who have experienced child death or their removal in other circumstances. Opsal (2015) identified that women's experience of post-prison supervision is underexplored: her study with women, although not specifically focussed on mothers, offered important insights to women's experiences of 'surveillance.' The Mothers' experiences of probation supervision is discussed later but several Mothers experienced additional surveillance from Social Services, either because their children had been taken into care or because they were subject to reunification processes.

Even for those Mothers whose children had long ago been taken into care, managing their maternal pain remained a challenging aspect of their post-prison life and was intertwined with all aspects of their post-release rehabilitation and desistance.

Untrustworthy Motherhood

The previous chapter evidenced how criminalised mothers feel the gaze, evaluation and observation of others extremely, whether formal or informal. Trust is particularly important for criminalised women, whose lives have often been characterised by abuse of power. The Mothers described the impact of feeling 'untrustworthy' (Annie) and 'watched' (Tanisha). As Ursula had stated, the threat and fear of losing their children was significant and most of the Mothers had anxiety about this, especially if Social Services were actively involved. This fear and lack of trust in professionals, particularly felt by mothers of younger children

(Sharpe, 2015), was something mentioned by several Mothers, as verbalised by Tanya:

> 'You have to be careful about trust after prison, it is certainly something to be really careful about, you keep your guard up.'

Issues of trust 'went both ways,' i.e. Mothers felt wary of trusting others, especially professionals, but they also felt as though professionals had an automatic mistrust of them, over and above the 'expected' mistrust directed towards ex-prisoners (Goffman, 1963). The Mothers felt it as *mothers*. Six Mothers had lost the care of their children to their LA (Beth, Mary, Nicola, Dee, Lauren, Tanisha), either permanently or temporarily, as a result of their sentencing, but several more Mothers had social work involvement in their post-prison lives (mainly for pre-existing substance-misuse or mental health issues).

Sophie, whose daughter had been taken into foster care, felt a palpable level of mistrust directed towards her from Social Services concerning her resuming the care of her daughter, despite there being no concerns about her ability to be a successful and suitable parent *prior* to her incarceration. The sole reason why Sophie's daughter was placed with foster parents was because there was no 'suitable' adult to care for her when Sophie was imprisoned. Sophie felt that, because of her status as an ex-prisoner mum, she had to mother to a higher standard than 'normal mums' in order to prove that she was capable of having her daughter returned to her, stating, 'If they had their way they would have kept her and had her adopted.' She felt that Social Services were 'waiting' for her to fail and made her feel that she 'couldn't be trusted with my own daughter.' Sophie went on to say:

> 'I felt under surveillance…is that the word? Spied on…I think if it was legal they'd have put a camera in my house to watch me when I had my home contacts.'

Before her death, Beth had described how only seeing her baby through supervised contact visits[1] made her feel 'not a real mum,' saying she felt like she could not be 'trusted even with my own baby.' It is not unreasonable to assume that the culmination of these feelings, the weight of the perceptions of others and the continued surveillance of her reunification with her daughter were pressures that contributed to her decision to end her life.

The Mothers, especially the younger ones, spoke of a constant feeling of 'being watched,' which they associated with an expectation of failure and a lack of trust. They described how others' lack of trust in them made them doubt themselves and increased their own levels of anxiety and paranoia; in some cases, these feelings were relevant to their relapse into substance misuse (and ergo offending to fund it).

Beth's and Sophie's experiences chime with Sharpe's research (2015: 1) with young post-prison mothers whom she found had experienced judgement, 'gendered surveillance social censure and stigma,' long after they left prison and regardless of whether they were currently engaged in criminal activity.

Mothers lack of trust in professionals also contributed to the Mothers' reluctance to ask for help:

> 'If I said I was finding it tough, I knew they'd assume I was back on the drink, then they'd be all over me like a rash. I would have lost my kids forever this time…so I just kept quiet and managed…it nearly killed me, but I managed.' (Shanice)

Shanice went on to describe how she struggled with her autistic son post-release. She described coping with his behaviour on her own, reluctant to ask for help for fear of unwanted attention. She had therefore not been able to access support and guidance in managing his behaviour and ensuring their safety:

---

1. Visits with children that are pre-booked, often in a Social Services contact centre, are either observed via two-way mirrors or are physically supervised by a social or family worker; they are often part of a prolonged process of reunification and may progress to being unsupervised, and then overnight contacts sessions, before full reunification.

'My son was kicking off, I thought he was going to hit me...but I didn't want to call the police or ask for help because then they'd assume I couldn't cope and mark me as at risk of drinking again...but the last time I had no choice, he was really kicking off so I had to call them, he's so much bigger than me now, but also to protect him...the police asked if there were any other children in the house, I was terrified of saying so because I'd had to sit in my car to protect myself from him...but my daughter was upstairs in bed...she slept through it all thank goodness...but now I'm just waiting, waiting for them to come and say that that wasn't good enough, they already think I'm a shit mum because I went to prison so this will just confirm it in their eyes.'

Several Mothers had experienced violent and toxic relationships that had at different times in their lives brought them to the attention of Social Services. Despite rarely being the perpetrators of domestic abuse or violence towards their children, it is often the mothers who will come under scrutiny for their 'failure to protect' (Barnes, 2015). Mothers felt this scrutiny particularly keenly post-release. Several Mothers felt their previous traumatic experiences (although obviously not their 'fault'), and their imprisonment was 'held against' them (Carla).

'They, the SS I like to call them, kept talking about all these risk factors being part of their assessment—apparently the fact I was raped and abused by a sick bastard is a risk factor for me being able to be a good enough Mother...how the fuck that can be right?...none of it was my fault what happened to me and was directly related to why I lost my way and went to prison...so instead of helping me, they punish me through my kids and tell me I can't be trusted to look after my kids...and apparently "getting myself locked up" proved that to them!...I honestly wanted to scream...WELL FUCKING HELP ME, THEN!'

The Mothers felt their prison sentences served to confirm to Social Services that they were bad mothers making them fearful of engaging with support agencies—however, this also often served to compound their situation. Mary, who had been in a violent relationship and struggled

221

with mental health issues and alcohol-misuse, lost the care of her sons after her second custodial sentence. She illustrates how reluctance to seek help and fear of negative intervention, and/or negative evaluation, had a devastating and long-lasting impact on her and her sons.

> 'They said that because I didn't "engage with services," whatever that means, that I hadn't proved I wanted to change enough…but I was in a lose-lose situation. They had already made their minds up I was a terrible mother. If I had asked for help and told them I'd taken him back, was not coping and drinking again, well they would have taken the boys into care, so I just made the most of it while I had them…and guess what? They took them anyway.'

Kady was feeling isolated and nervous after the recent birth of her second child, eight years post-release, yet was 'afraid' to ask for support from the usual networks (e.g. health visitors, midwives, Social Services). She felt that, if she asked for help with her 'troubled past' — as a mother who'd been to prison — she would be inviting unwanted attention into her life, stating, 'once they [social workers] get their claws into you they don't let go, they watch you like a hawk, ready to pounce and take your kids.'

The Mothers' lack of trust in professionals and their fear of negative interventions (Baldwin, 2015) resulted in many missed opportunities to access the support they needed. Several Mothers felt they would have benefitted from input regarding ongoing issues of domestic abuse, addiction, housing, and mental health, but did not want to draw attention to themselves for fear of being seen as failing, inadequate or neglectful mothers. Mothers who felt unable to access support were therefore vulnerable to many of the same pre-custody challenges that had led them onto an offending pathway in the first instance. Their fear of accessing support, as mothers, had the potential to affect their rehabilitation and desistance pathways (Garcia-Hallett, 2019).

Creating an atmosphere of 'emotional safety' (Baldwin, 2015) for mothers so that they can share their concerns with professionals is vital for services engaged in work with mothers, particularly when working with criminalised mothers. Leaving mothers to cope alone increases the risk of a return to previous unhealthy coping-strategies, which may include substance misuse (O'Malley, 2018), to cope with maternal emotions and the enduring stress of post-prison life. This can be accompanied with a return to offending to fund the substance misuse—which can ultimately lead to a return to prison or permanent loss of children.

Invisible Motherhood

The Mothers who did not have care of their children remained preoccupied with their motherhood. Nicola described feeling desperate to hold onto her mother identity despite no longer having the care of her son. Parallels are drawn with Morris's research (2018), which explores the experiences of mothers who live through state-ordered child removal, which Morris calls 'haunted motherhood' (ibid: 816). Compounding their existing stigma and shame as ex-prison mothers, Mothers whose children were taken permanently into care felt additional layers of stigma and shame. Losing their children gave the explicit message that they could no longer be trusted to care for their children themselves, that they were deemed to be 'not good enough' mothers (Winnicott, 1987).

Yet the Mothers who had lost their children to care still very much felt like mothers. Their maternal emotions remained relevant to their wellbeing, their successful re-entry and their desistance. Nicola, whose three-year-old child was taken into care during her sentence stated:

> 'Just because I don't live with my child and my child doesn't live with me, doesn't mean I'm not a mother, I still feel like a mother, I think like a mother—I worry about the world he's growing up in, where he is and what he's doing. I remember his birthday and think of him at school, in fact now I'm clean, even though I don't have him, I'm more of a mother than I was before, I was too chaotic to think of all that stuff then … it's sad though that he doesn't get to see this mother, I'm invisible [to him], that pain for me is my worst enemy because it makes me want to use.'

Their children's loss was a source of great shame and embarrassment and contributed to the Mothers' enduring spoiled identity. Mothers internalised the 'blame,' sometimes having a devastating impact on their wellbeing and maternal self-esteem. Which was already reduced by imprisonment. Coupled with the critical gaze and the surveillance of the state, proved 'overwhelming' for the Mothers. Morris's (2018: 816) suggested haunted mothers feel 'forced' into silence about their experiences for fear of the judgement of others:

> 'It's not something you can easily tell people, "Oh I was a mum, but they took him off me"'…not to mention the two they took before him. It's like one of those huge birthday badges, but instead of happy birthday it says, "bad mother." It's too much really.' (Nicola)

Nicola and Mary had both felt so 'ashamed' of having their children removed from their care that they often lied about having children at all. Which served only to add to their layers of shame and maternal guilt:

> 'When my boys were in care I thought of them every day, even as the years went on I did…but it got to the point where if anyone asked if I had kids I'd just say no, it was easier than explaining everything that had went on, me going to prison and losing them and all that…but doing that, denying them, made me feel ashamed.' (Mary)

Being criminalised Mothers was felt as an additional layer of this already heavy shame and was perceived by the Mothers as additional outward 'proof' that they were bad mothers or, as Morris puts it, 'a deeply flawed mother' (2018: 816). Mothers felt the loss of their children was their 'own fault.' Morris (2018) described how separated mothers lived in what she called a haunted future, an imagined future where mothers were reunited with their children, or where their children would come and 'find' them, Mary described this exactly.

> 'Before my boys did come to find me I thought of them every day at first, it used to make me drink again because it hurt so much that I'd lost them, the hurt and the guilt…but I wanted them to find me, it was all I thought

about, I used to imagine hugging them and us just being so happy…like on Cilla Black's "Surprise! Surprise!"[2]

As well as living in the future, the Mothers would obsessively focus on their past and the circumstances in which they lost their children—absorbing all of the 'blame' for their circumstances with little or no recognition that services had failed them (Clark and Chadwick, 2018):

'[L]et's face it, I wasn't the best mother anyway before I got to prison, what could I offer, we were always skint, I'd had fucked up relationships where he'd seen violence, heard screaming, I couldn't even give him brothers and sisters because of my fucked-up insides from the abuse, no dad, a crap flat and a useless mum.' (Nicola)

All of the Mothers who had children removed from their care described feeling powerless or 'at the mercy' (Lauren) of Social Services/social workers. This added to their sense of invisibility and further reduced their maternal self-esteem and maternal identity as well as their maternal-role and maternal capital. Dee's son was placed with gay foster parents, which was something she really struggled with:

'He went into care for three years with a same sex couple that was a big choice for me…I wouldn't say I was homophobic, but I grew up in a Rastafarian culture and I am like, NO, my son is going to be gay—arggh!'

Dee was told that if she did not agree to her children being placed with a same-sex couple then her children would be separated, so she felt 'forced' to 'compromise' her own 'cultural and religious' beliefs and agree to the foster placement. Losing custody of one's children is seen by the Mothers themselves, and by wider society, as 'the ultimate failure.' This had the potential to send the Mothers into a downward spiral. Mary stated that because she had lost her sons, she saw 'no point' in either 'trying to be good and stay off the drink,' or in fact to leave her violent

---

2. A popular TV show of the 1980s hosted by Cilla Black in which long-lost family members were located and reunited by way of a live on-screen surprise.

partner of that time, both factors were relevant to her ongoing offending which resulted in many more prison sentences.

Emma, who died a short time post-release (from pneumonia), had written and spoken about how, after her child was 'stolen' from her and placed for adoption, she felt she had 'nothing much to live for.' She gave birth one week after getting out of prison, and described how losing a second new-born daughter (her first daughter was in the custody of her father) triggered exactly the downward spiral described by Stone (2016):

> 'The memory of them coming in the hospital with the car-seat, I had thought I was taking her home, but as soon as I saw that car-seat I knew they were taking her. I remember hearing someone screaming and screaming and then I realised it was me screaming. I discharged myself from hospital and went and got off my face. I didn't know what else to do.' (Emma)

Emma served multiple sentences all centred around her substance misuse. Which was triggered by her traumatic history and the loss of her daughters, and for which she had received no support. Effectively, Emma's trauma — including her maternal trauma — was criminalised (Clarke and Chadwick, 2018).

Several Mothers who had served more than one sentence (Carla, Mary, Sandra, Shanice, Dee, Tanya and Cynthia) described how their guilt, as well as their shame as mothers, snowballed. They felt that the guilt and shame would multiply with each sentence. Dee, who had lost more than one child to the care system, stated, 'as a mother there's no worse feeling than feeling you've failed your child is there? ... well imagine that feeling again and again and again.'

For the Mothers who lost care of their children, either temporarily or permanently, their children remained a 'primary focus' and 'in my mind' (Dee); however they often felt muted or 'too ashamed' (Carla) to talk about it. Mary, Nicola and Dee all fought unsuccessfully to get their children back from LA care (Dee regained care of some of her children but not all) and they remain/remained preoccupied for many years with hopeful fantasies about reunification. This chimes with Morris's (2018) research with mothers, not necessarily criminalised mothers, whose children were subject to State ordered removal. She, too, found that mothers fighting to reunite with their children would 'exist in a state of haunted motherhood, paralysed in anticipation of an imagined future' (ibid: 816). She describes mothers who lose their children as 'abject figures … silenced through the stigma and shame of being judged as a deeply flawed mother.' Mary stated that the fear of having future children removed was the single most relevant factor in her choosing not to have any more children. As she said:

> 'What would have been the point, they would have taken them anyway they had already decided I was a bad mother; I couldn't have handled losing another.'

Morris also found that mothers who had lost a child to LA care feared that all future children would be taken away too (see also Barnes in Baldwin, 2015, and Broadhurst et al, 2015). Criminalised mothers who lose the care of their children are vulnerable to having more than one child removed from their care either because of their offending and their 'chaotic lives' or directly as a result of their prison sentence. Four Mothers (Dee, Nicola, Emma and Mary) had more than one child removed.

It was evident in the Mothers' narratives that there had been many missed opportunities to support them before, during, and after prison. Once their children had been removed from their care, none of the Mothers were offered support to assist them in understanding or dealing with the issues that had led to their child's removal or the removal itself. Therefore, they now had the culmination of previous trauma and experiences, their imprisonment and the additional trauma of losing their child. The lack of timely and appropriate support contributed to Mothers' already challenging circumstances and to the loss of their child/ren into care and so a cycle perpetuates.

As previously noted, it is not the services who failed the mothers who are held to account, or the Government that failed to adequately fund the resources to support them; it is the women and children who are directly punished by being separated, sometimes permanently, and with a consequence of altering the trajectories of all their lives. The lack of trust in the women as mothers, and the scrutiny the Mothers felt subject to, came from both professionals or agents of the state and Mothers' own families and friends, their children, grandchildren and caregivers, too. It was not only Social Services who would deny Mothers access to their children, or who caused issues for Mothers post-release — the tensions that sometimes began during a Mother's imprisonment continued between caregivers and Mothers, sometimes worsening post-release.

Family Eyes

Changes in family dynamics and strained relationships occurring because of the Mothers' imprisonment were often influenced by issues of trust. Queenie, who as mentioned earlier was now no longer 'trusted' to take care of her grandchildren, stated:

> 'Apparently, I am no longer good enough to care for grandchildren, my daughter finds me unsuitable to care for her children now, I don't know what she thinks I'll actually do but she just sees me as a criminal now and not much else.'

Sandra and Tanisha's sisters questioned them and their ability to be consistent in their mothering. For example, Sandra's older sister suggested that she should 'keep the younger ones, to make it easier.' Sandra refused. This placed an additional strain on their already fragile relationship. Sandra's sister felt that Sandra's prison sentence was 'proof' that she was 'not the best mother.' Tanisha stated her sister and mother visited much more frequently than they had prior to her arrest. She did not feel this was rooted in support but was because her sister and mother did not trust her to not start drinking again and were 'keeping an eye' on her.

Barnes and Cunningham-Stringer (2014) suggest that incarcerated mothers often chose grandparent carers hoping this would minimise their subsequent loss of control and input into their children's lives, however, as this research illustrates, such arrangements are not without issues.

As discussed earlier in *Part II,* tensions between imprisoned mothers and caregivers may have begun whilst the mothers were still incarcerated

(Booth, 2020; Masson, 2019). Some of the issues that Mothers raised were simply around different opinions in child rearing practices which may well have occurred regardless of their imprisonment. For example, it is not uncommon for new mothers and grandmothers to have some tensions between them about generational changes in mothering practice. However, Mothers raised several issues which could be regarded as *specific to mothers* who had previously been incarcerated.

Several Mothers, despite having legal custody of their children, felt 'prevented' from either having full access to or care of their children, either temporarily or permanently. Two Mothers had grandmother carers who 'refused' to return the children to their mothers' care, and a further three grandmothers insisted on being involved in their grandchildren's care either formally (directed by Social Services) or informally; other Mothers mentioned feeling 'monitored.'

Tia's children had been cared for by her ex-husband and the children's grandmother whilst she was imprisoned; she now had her children back in her own care, but her ex-husband was initially reluctant to return his son permanently and Tia felt he wanted to maintain 'unreasonable' levels of access to the children to 'check' on her (rather than to just see his children). Similarly, Tamika revealed that, despite Social Services agreeing that her children could all be returned to her, her mother refuses to trust her to care for them. Allowing only the eldest child home and insisting the two youngest remain with her. Tamika visits her children daily and is angry and frustrated with her mother, but feels powerless to challenge her for fear of recrimination:

> '…she says if I kick off [about the arrangement] she will tell social services, so I have no choice…that's the worst thing after prison, no one ever trusts you again.'

Some of the Mothers, especially those who had used substances in the past, felt that some of the mistrust in them was 'understandable' (Tia), and rooted in their previously chaotic lifestyles. Sandra remembers her mother telling her in prison that she had been vindicated in keeping the children from her:

'I used to try to fight my mother and convince her I could manage the kids, even with my habit, I thought I was okay…I thought I was that like a functioning addict…but when I went to jail my mother was like, well you are not functioning now, are you!'

However, Sandra felt that her 'hard work to get clean and deal with my issues' warranted a second chance; that her mother had 'actively discouraged' her son from coming back home once she was released. He had in the end refused to come home and Sandra was forced to accept this:

'I guess I have to accept that whatever my view of how I lived and why is one thing, but he went through his own experience and I understand how hard it is for him to trust me still, and actually I suppose for my mother to trust me. I know I won't relapse again, but I guess they don't, do they, maybe one day they will, this is the longest I've gone…but they need longer I guess.'

Mothers found it challenging to ask for or obtain support for motherhood-related issues. Finding their maternal identity and role was all but ignored in their post-release supervision.

Supervision and 'Support'

Probation supervision fundamentally expects and reproduces hegemonic, culturally influenced ideals about what is good citizenship (Bosworth, 2000; Opsal, 2015). Such constructions are gendered (although arguably the Probation Service requirements are most often not) and therefore have consequences for women who are subject to supervision (Jordan, 2013). Probation supervision requires individuals to abide by a set of conditions that are designed to regulate their behaviour, to maintain desistance and to rehabilitate.

Mothers described leaving prison feeling 'disoriented' and degraded' (Eaton, 1993: 56), 'Anxious' and 'suspicious' about the additional surveillance and judgement they expected to face via post-release supervision:

'I didn't have high expectations of probation to be honest, I hate all that watching you stuff…all I wanted was to get my kids back.' (Carla)

Feminist scholarship identifies a twofold lack of support for mothers post-release—support for their mothering, and for the factors which led to their imprisonment in the first instance. This has significant relevance for how well mothers will re-enter into their families and society. Hays (2008) found that once the initial 'honeymoon' period of reunification had passed, some 'old' issues resurfaced for mothers, which had often been compounded by incarceration.

Some Mothers returned to or began substance misuse as a mean of coping with their maternal emotions and maternal post-release experiences. Mothers who were identified as vulnerable to this and who received support not surprisingly fared better than those who did not. Somewhat ironically, motherhood did not feature in formal supervision for most of the Mothers, either during their supervisory relationship or in-prison, despite motherhood being their primary focus and being the source of scrutiny outside of supervision. Despite *all* of the Mothers describing at least some negative impact of their incarceration on them as mothers, most stated they were 'never asked' (Taranpreet) about their motherhood, whatever their circumstances (i.e. reunification or permanent loss of children).

Ursula stated that my interview with her was in fact the first time she had been asked about her imprisonment and its effects on her as a mother, something she said she would be 'eternally grateful for.' Ursula was conflicted in her feelings about probation 'support':

'…it's incredibly difficult. They didn't ask about my kids at probation, but even if they had I would have said everything was okay, why would I be stupid enough to say if I was struggling? Probation have the potential to breach you so how am I going to say I'm struggling to somebody who's got the potential to send me back to prison, and the potential to flag me to Social Services as a mother not coping.'

Echoing Masson's (2019) findings, most Mothers experienced some form of 'collateral damage,' such as loss of homes, loss of employment, relations or education opportunities; however, the Mothers felt most concerned at the losses or harms that directly impacted on their maternal identity and/or role, losses for which many felt they had not received adequate support. Moreover, the Mothers felt that, even if they did ask probation for support, 'real' support would not have been offered:

> 'But what are you actually going to do? …They never even came to visit my home or visit my children or visit …I never had a home visit. Nobody ever came to see me. I lied for the whole four years. I genuinely did …On my licence I was supposed to live at my [place] …I wasn't allowed to go back to my family home because they said Denzel [her dad: a pseudonym] was a risk because the offence occurred with him. And remember he lived in the house with the kids. They said I couldn't go back to my house with my kids. So they licensed me to my daughter's house, Kenise's house. I went back and lived at my house for four years and just lied. I needed to be a mother to my children, to be in our home, so I lied.' (Ursula)

Such was Ursula's need to be with her children to focus on repairing and renegotiating her maternal identity and role she was prepared to risk being breached. This added to her post-release stress but was a decision she does not regret. In fact, she wonders what her relationships might have been like if she had complied with her licence conditions and concludes, 'I don't think I'd have a relationship with them, the state would have destroyed my motherhood.'

Wright (2017: 21), whose research with women who 'persistently offend' also found that on the whole women had negative experiences of post-prison supervision. She found that the women reported that women's needs, in terms of practical support and relational bonds, came secondary to the goal of probation, i.e. a 'reduction in offending.' Although Wright's research was not specifically with mothers, she did identify issues with supervision that affected mothers (and their children). For example, mothers being housed away from children and in accommodation not suitable for children.

Like Ursula, Beth said that her motherhood simply was not discussed during her probation supervision:

> 'At the first appointment she said something like…"Oh, I know there is social services involvement with your daughter so we'll leave that to them, and we will just deal with your offending and your drugs here." So after that we never even spoke about it, I don't think she even asked me once how it was gannin with the bairn after that…shitty really.'

Beth went on to say that supervision for her offending and her drug use constituted simply being asked if she was offending and if she was 'using' or 'drinking,' to both of which Beth would reply 'no,' 'and basically that was it really.'

Several Mothers, when asked about the Probation Service response to their motherhood, said words to the effect of 'They don't care.' Also observed by Canton and Dominey (2020:z 31), although questions have long been asked about whether the primary mission in the role of probation is care, or control, or both, there has been little attention given to how it is experienced by those under its supervision.

Canton and Dominey suggest that indifference to this enquiry or such accounts is in itself a 'failure to care.' The Mothers' experiences of post-prison supervision were enriched when Mothers felt their supervisors demonstrated 'genuine concern' or care (McIvor et al, 2009). The most effective supervision relationships were gendered, tailored. They should be formed around supervisory or supporting relationships that began whilst the women were still in prison (ibid). Four mothers (Ursula, Shanice, Rayna and Kady) explicitly stated that they saw probation as simply an extension of prison:

> '…prison is not a caring environment and that just continued outside. I know that people want to portray it as such, it really isn't. Or if it is I didn't actually ever see it or experience it. In four years in prison and four years on probation, I never once felt as if anybody actually cared.' (Ursula)

Rayna stated that she was not prepared for her release and did not really understand what would be required of her outside. She felt that planning for release and 'getting me ready for it' was an element of her relatively long sentence (three years and six months) that was neglected, 'especially as a mother,' which contributed to what for her was an 'extremely hard' period of adjustment post-release. Several Mothers felt they were 'just let out' (Emma), with little support in the areas they felt they needed it most, and one of those areas was their motherhood.

Throughcare and planning for resettlement[3] is relational to successful post-release outcomes, especially for mothers. Significantly, some of the Mothers who had been free for longer had experienced the Probation Service in an era where individuals would meet their 'outside' probation officer whilst still in prison. Previously the probation officer who wrote the pre-sentence report (PSR) might be the officer who was assigned to an individual throughout prison and release. Mary highlights how important this can be; in present times more women than ever are released homeless, many of them being mothers (PRT, 2015):

> 'On one sentence yeah I met my probation officer a couple of months before I got out...it helped knowing who I was going to see and she made sure I had somewhere to go to when I was released, she thought I might be able to get my kids back see...that was the only time it happened though...it didn't work for me because social services wouldn't let me have them anyway, but some of the girls who are mothers if they were let out with no home, how were they supposed to get their kids back?'

This level of throughcare has always been harder to achieve for women as they are more geographically distanced, but historically, in such instances probation areas would often fund a probation officer to travel to meet their client in prison from between six and three months before their release with the aim of establishing their needs and to form

---

3. The term 'resettlement' is of relatively recent origin, first appearing in a Home Office consultation paper in 1998 as the preferred term for what had previously been called 'throughcare' or 'aftercare' (see Bateman et al, 2013: 8)

a relationship with them.[4] In more recent years throughcare, if it exists at all, has been undertaken by third sector organizations — but their funding and tenure in a prison is often precarious. However, where it has existed, the third sector workers have often provided an important link between the prison and the community supervisors. Many mothers' efforts to successfully re-enter society are challenged by practical losses such as loss of homes and loss of employment, and by ongoing difficulties in regaining either.

The Mothers encountered the same difficulties described by Masson (2019), and often felt their probation supervision did little to alleviate their situation:

'I lost my house when I went in, all my stuff, kids clothes, photos, photos of me dad, everything…my whole life was in that house gone…I was broken, man, broken. What did probation say? "Oh we can't help with housing; you need to go the council"…how was I supposed to get my kids back without a house for them to live in…but they [Probation] were literally not interested.' (Carla)

Supervisory relationships are important (Jordan, 2013; McIvor et al, 2009). The Mothers' responses evidenced the value and need of understanding and accounting for mothering status and emotions, doing so improved engagement:

'I had a good one yeah and I thank god for that, she helped me she really did, and it was through her help and the course I did that I got my kids back. She knew that was most important, but she helped me see I had a road to go down to get there and she helped me get there, without her I'd be back inside, she helped teach me I deserved better and that my kids needed me.' (Tanisha)

---

4. This author qualified as a probation officer, and that is how I was initially directed to practice. When the then 42 probation areas were merged to become the National Probation Service (2000), and the New Choreography for probation meant National Standards with enforcement and supervision becoming the highest priority. Funds for travelling for the purposes of resettlement were all but removed.

Similarly, Sophie described how her officer:

'...just made me open my eyes and see that my bad decisions and partners were affecting my daughter and I didn't even see it, he was good yeah, he knew she [daughter] was most important to me and so he focussed on that to help me learn.'

Some Mothers had experience of community orders as well as prison, or had served more than one sentence and so had experienced help from multiple officers:

'I had some half decent probation officers, you can tell the ones who actually care because they get to know you and want to know you...but some of the others I wouldn't piss on if they were on fire, they didn't care, they didn't understand and they didn't try to...you just didn't go to those appointments.' (Mary)

It is clear most women have similar complex needs on exiting prison to those they had on entering prison. Rehabilitation, especially for women, often pays too little attention to the root causes or pathways into crime, or to the fact that, all too often, women's routes into crime are marred by abuse, poverty, mental health difficulties and substance misuse. However, women's pathways out of crime are often filled with strikingly similar 'landmines in the road' as before, importantly which are then compounded by motherhood. 'When I got out...same shit, different day' (Dee).

Despite being described as 'complex,' many felt that few of their additional needs were met. This had the effect on the Mothers of making them feel that it was 'pointless' to discuss any of their maternal challenges or emotions with supervisors. Although it is still relatively underexplored, especially in the UK, there is an increasing awareness that desisting pathways can be 'shaped by motherhood.' Negotiating post-prison motherhood and attempting to re-establish a maternal-role whilst trying to repair a reduced maternal identity, presents significant challenges for mothers in their desistance journey. As Dee stated:

'Yeah, it was a challenge to stay clean and straight, it was stressful coming back to being a full-time mum after prison and still having all the same shit to deal with as before but now worse…and fighting to get my other kids back.'

The Mothers revealed that the relationship between motherhood and desistance can be complicated and sometimes is paradoxical. It must be understood as a journey—it is not fixed. For example, Mary, Nicola and others all identified how the loss of their mother role, before and after prison, set them on a path of reoffending because they felt they 'had nothing left to lose' (Mary).

Returning to the complex and challenging circumstances in which many of them had lived pre-prison, alongside the now considerable added burden of a spoiled maternal identity and change in maternal-role (as discussed earlier), made it challenging for the Mothers to not be drawn back into the situations that had led them to offend in the first instance.

Ten of the Mothers (Shanice, Cynthia, Dee, Mary, Emma, Sam, Jennifer, Sandra, Nicola, and Carla) all explicitly stated that their status as ex-prison mothers and all that entailed was a factor in their return to substance misuse and subsequent repeat offending. A number of other Mothers admitted that they had used illegal substances, or over-relied on alcohol 'to cope' (Beth) following their release, and also to cope with their enduring trauma:

'I had so many nightmares about prison…I used to dream I couldn't get to Susie [her daughter]…Anyway, I could see her but there was like…I dunno some kind of forcefield and I just couldn't get to her…I had it all the time, so I'd take my mate's sleepers and drink wine when it was bad…I still have to do it sometimes even now.' (Tanya)

Stone (2016: 1959) identifies that, particularly in the case of mothers who misuse substances, the 'powerful and stigmatising master narrative' of addiction challenges mothers' abilities to release themselves from their offending pasts and to move successfully into law-abiding futures. O'Malley and Devaney (2016) and Baldwin et al (2015) found that for addicted mothers, the 'shame' of their perceived previously 'failed' motherhoods compounded the trauma that led to their addiction in the first instance. This contributed to Mothers' abilities (or inabilities) to abstain from drugs and/or alcohol and ergo from the offending they undertook to fund their addiction (and often the addictions of their male partners). Some Mothers felt that once they had 'failed' at motherhood they 'had nothing to go straight for' (Mary).

However, Mary later described how her motherhood became her motivation to seek support and that it was the most important factor in her desistance, because she wanted her sons to be proud of her. This motivation was set in motion by an individual officer who acknowledged her motherhood, using it as a hook for Mary to harness. This again highlights the significance and importance of understanding the maternal emotions and roles of criminalised mothers (whether they have the care of their children or not), and of the importance of good quality, compassionate, gendered and tailored supervisory relationships (Dominey and Gelsthorpe, 2020; Canton and Dominey, 2020).

Reassuming the maternal-role can have a transformative effect on mothers' desistance (Brown and Bloom, 2009; Giordano et al, 2002). Many of the Mothers sought to demonstrate this through the pursuit of an idealised motherhood. Several wished they 'could just be a good mother' (Tamika), equally as important was *being seen* to be good mothers. When/if this was ever achieved, then the Mothers felt that their 'good' mother status could override their ex-prisoner status. They described how achieving or returning to a place of perceived good or good enough motherhood would assist them in their abstinence from substance misuse (and therefore from re-offending) and from crime. Because *as mothers* they became reluctant to 'give up' their hard-won, newfound feelings of increased maternal self-esteem, respectability, and acceptance (in their own eyes, and those of their children and wider society). These findings echo and illustrate previous findings on desistance (Maruna and Mann, 2019) and motherhood and desistance (Bachman et al, 2016):

> 'Eventually I just changed my shit. I worked hard to leave that life behind me and the longer I was just a mum, and a good mum and not using and

stuff, the further I felt away from the shit mother who didn't think of her kids … well, I did but everyone said I didn't. So … I didn't want to go back, to that life, to prison, to any of it. I just wanted to be a mum to my kids, to be a good mum.' (Tamika)

Conversely, if mothers did not achieve this place of 'good enough' mothering (Winnicott, 1987), either by their own or others' evaluation, then the impact on the Mothers was, as Beth's death tragically illustrates, devastating. However, even once the Mothers had moved on, and were successfully moving forwards and living a life uncomplicated by offending or substance misuse, it was important to note that, to them, their positive or affirming maternal identity still often felt precarious (Sharpe, 2015).

Tamika (above) went on to say that, despite where she felt she was now, 'it will never take a lot to put me back there through … I can't hide what I was.' She said that her 'shameful' past still haunted her and, despite the fact most people in her 'new life' did not know that she had been in prison, she still felt ashamed of 'who I used to be,' fearing the judgement of her children most of all — 'more than anything, I don't want them to be ashamed of their mam.'

Thus the Mothers demonstrated that, although they might be seen as 'reformed' characters and may be now externally judged as 'good' mothers, internally they retained an enduring maternal shame which was and is often rooted in their permanently spoiled maternal identity. They universally felt that what would have assisted them in their post-prison journeys and would continue to assist them long past their release — was the feeling that someone 'cared' about their journeys *as mothers*. They felt that by their motherhood being ignored during their imprisonment and supervision not only were they often left struggling and floundering, but that their motherhood, their maternal roles and their maternal identity 'didn't matter' (Rayna). Given that it was often the most important aspect of their identity to them, this gave them the message that they themselves did not matter. Furthermore, not addressing the in-prison and post-prison needs of mothers left the Mothers vulnerable to the effects of deep-rooted and ongoing trauma.

Pause for Thought

Imagine being a mother coming out of prison — What would your focus be/If you had lost your children or things were not going well? — How easy would it be to engage with professionals who ignored your motherhood? — Imagine if you had previously lost children to the local authority — How easy would it be to ask for help if you were struggling? — If you were a practitioner would you factor in motherhood in your work with women — If so how would you do this?

If you are approaching the subject academically, think 'reflexively' about the impact of your own research interviews — How do you know/ensure that you leave women in a good mental state? — Have you demonstrated ethical care in your methodology?

Summary of *Chapter 10*

The chapter described how easily suspicions of the imprisoned Mothers might arise due to a sense that they were being 'watched over' whether in the true sense of surveillance and oversight or as an in-built part of the procedures of prison officers, probation staff or other authority figures. This might also happen back home because, e.g. family members or neighbours knew they had been to prison or simply because they had been criminalised. This in turn made establishing trust harder whether in prison or in the community, when a sense that, e.g. the risk of losing their children, home or being recalled to prison was often present. This provides lessons for practitioners and others seeking to engage with vulnerable women, additionally because many incarcerated women have already experienced broken trust and relationships in their lives and communities before they were sent to prison (thereby increasing the risk of worry, anxiety, trauma, etc.).

CHAPTER 11

Trauma and Pain

'Recognizing the centrality of women's roles as mothers provides an opportunity for criminal justice, medical, mental health, legal and social service agencies to include this role as an integral part of program and treatment interventions for women.' (Covington, 2007: 78)

Covington, a leader in the movement for trauma-informed practice within the CJS, advocates for wide-ranging therapeutic responses rather than penal responses to criminalised women. There has been an increasing awareness of the need for a trauma-informed approach (TIA) in criminology and criminal justice processes (see, e.g. Durr, 2020; Jewkes et al, 2019; Bradley, 2017; Ellison and Munro, 2017; Covington, 2007) which Durr (ibid) further argues should be gendered. The TIA seeks to recognise and respond with understanding and compassion to the ways in which trauma can manifest in and influence the lives and behaviour of individuals. It has steadfastly informed policy and practice, especially related to criminalised women, since the early-2000s.

However, most enquiries examining the relationship between prison and trauma focus on the trauma that the prisoner brings into the prison. It is accepted wisdom that both male and female (especially female) prisoners have experienced multiple traumatic events prior to coming to prison (Bradley, 2017). However, significantly less is known about the association between incarceration and subsequent trauma or post-traumatic stress disorder (PTSD).[1] Significantly, Masson (2019: 146) found that mothers experienced 'enduring psychological harm.' Understanding the full psychological impact of imprisonment is vital to improving outcomes for ex-prisoners. Although Piper and Berles' (2019) research into post-prison PTSD focuses on the after effects of potentially traumatic events (PTEs) in prison, such as violent assaults, they raise important and transferable questions about the significance and prevalence of PTSD in ex-prisoners who, as previously noted, are often already struggling with trauma from their pre-prison lives, and who will be additionally traumatised by prison.

'It's Like PTSD'

Most Mothers had traumatic histories, and many are victims of crime as well as being criminalised. Ellison and Munro (2017) highlight the potential for additional trauma to be caused to those who are involved in the processes of criminal justice, and women have the potential to be doubly harmed by those processes, both as victims and 'perpetrators,' even though many do not report the crimes inflicted upon them (Carlen and Worrall, 2004). Most of the Mothers had previously been victims of violence and/or sexual abuse and were already dealing with the traumatic after effects as victims of such crimes; they were potentially undiagnosed as suffering from PTSD in relation to those offences (Ellison and Munro, 2017).

However, most Mothers were clear that their imprisonment was an *additional* traumatic experience for them; notwithstanding any PTEs, simply the prison experience itself was traumatic. The trauma of the continued separation from their children (or in some cases the loss of

---

1. PTSD is an anxiety disorder characterised by a traumatic stressor leaving the sufferer to continuously have negative thoughts about some past experience. Symptoms often appear within three months after a traumatic event but may be delayed by months or even years (American Psychiatric Association, 2000). The severity, proximity, and duration of a person's exposure to that event are the best predictors for determining who is most likely to develop PTSD (ibid). PTSD was first acknowledged as a mental illness in 1980, when it was included in the Diagnostic and Statistical Manual of Mental Disorders, Third Edition (DSM-III). The DSM is a handbook of the association used by mental health professionals to diagnosis mental illness; http://ilfvcc.org/assets/pdf/ResearchReports/PTSD_Female_Prisoners_Report_1110.pdf

their children), and their subsequent experience of mothering from prison with all that that entailed, left them deeply and profoundly traumatised. More than one described moving on from prison and living with these after effects as PTSD:

'I get what I can only call flashbacks of that awful visit…of my children leaving and of the first steps I took into the prison yard…just seeing the prison in front of me. I get nightmares and I feel anxious all the time…I wasn't like that before, it's like…it's like PTSD…that's the only way I can describe it.' (Karen)

However, even when Mothers did not explicitly mention PTSD, or themselves label their experiences as 'traumatic,' it was painfully clear that they were speaking about trauma triggered by maternal prison experience:

'The effects of that place haunt me, the physical scars on my arms only remind me of the pain and heartache I felt when I was in there. Just not being with my kids, man…but worse for me are the mental scars that no one sees, everyone thinks I'm over it…no one knows, but I'm wrecked really. I still have nightmares from that place you know…nothing will take that away.' (Dee)

Some of the Mothers did mention 'potentially traumatic events' (PTEs) as described by Piper and Berle (2016), which did indeed have a lasting traumatic effect; experiences that included witnessing a suicide attempt, the aftermath of suicide, witnessing mothers' 'last' visits in the visiting hall before children were placed for adoption, witnessing a cell birth. Strikingly, many of the PTEs described were intertwined with their and others' mothering emotions and experiences. Ursula described 'walking in on this … I dunno 60-year-old officer fondling some young girl.' She went on to say how 'traumatised' she was not only by witnessing this happening at all, but the fact that she 'walked away,' going on to say that:

'I should have said something, shouldn't I, because it's abuse. Like that's abusive, she's vulnerable and he shouldn't be doing that, but he holds the power.'

What was equally traumatising to Ursula was that, in being aware of the power that officers, and the prison had over her, she 'knew' that if she spoke up she was likely to be moved to another prison, and she was fearful then that she would not be able to see her children. She felt traumatised by the choice she made to put her own mothering needs before 'an abused girl who could have been my daughter.' The impact of this event, and Ursula's response to it, was obviously a source of significant pain and trauma to her. To deal with her prison trauma, she felt she had to learn to 'contain it,' something she and her children felt had left her 'cold.' She added:

'You have to prevent yourself from being emotional about anything just to survive, don't you. You desensitise yourself to the pain, you squash the emotions, learn to depress the emotions, to keep control of them, to push them away from you. So I think I was quite numb...still am...like my children say I'm cold now...yeah they think I'm really cold. But sometimes that's because when I'm faced with emotional demands, emotional memories, I retract into quite...like an analytical mode...like I don't engage with emotional stuff very well even now...it's how you cope with the trauma.'

Ursula described how she tries to avoid thinking about the period of separation from her children because it is 'just too hard.' Carla described how she felt she 'deserved' to live with her trauma and that she had the 'impression' that most CJS practitioners she had come across felt she should, too: she was told she was 'responsible for your own pain.'

Pain of Separation

The Mothers felt that the trauma of being separated from their children, and the memory of that was their most significant, persistent, long-lasting pain of imprisonment. It was the enduring memory that traumatised them most, triggering symptoms that meet the criteria for a diagnosis of PTSD which is characterised by a number of recognisable 'symptoms,' including flashbacks, nightmares, feelings of isolation, guilt, difficulty in sleeping and coping which are often severe enough and persistent enough to interfere in a person's day-to-day life (NHS guidelines).[2] For some Mothers, it was the actual moment of separation, or the realisation that it was coming, that was worse, for others it was the prolonged separation; for yet others, all of it. Rita, who had known she would be going to prison in advance of being sentenced, stated:

> 'During the day...I mean on a conscious level I can't actually remember physically saying goodbye to my children...it's like I can't let myself remember...but at night I have nightmares and it all comes back...it was horrendous, absolutely horrendous.'

Maggie, who also knew before court that she was 'most likely' to get a custodial sentence, remembers saying goodbye to her children:

> 'I hadn't seen my son cry for years and years...he was a man really, but to me he's my boy, he was broken...he literally just sobbed in my arms...I wish I could forget it I really do...but it's burned on to my brain like...what do you call it?...a branding that's it...it's branded. And my daughter, well I thought she'd be the most upset, but she just was so brave and just said "Mum I'll look after them"...well that finished me off...it was the worst day of my life...the worst moment of my life.'

Similarly, revealing the lack of compassion and thought sometimes demonstrated in police arrests where the needs of the service are placed above the needs of mothers and children (Baldwin et al, 2015), Tia experienced a particularly traumatic arrest in front of her nine-year-old daughter at the school gates as she was picking her up from school. At five years post-release, she considered herself to be 'mostly okay,' yet described the persistent invasive and traumatic memory of her arrest:

---

2. See also 68 Symptoms of PTSD: https://www.nhs.uk/conditions/post-traumatic-stress-disorder-ptsd/symptoms/

'I got arrested outside her school, she was in primary school and I was picking her up from school. The police were watching me, so they could have pulled me over at any time, but they didn't, they waited until I was getting her from school. There was a riot van outside, everyone's parents picking up their kids, and they put me in the van in handcuffs. I was shouting saying, "No, no my daughter is coming out of school, I live ten miles away" and when she came out I had to shout at the woman parked next to me, I shouted at Meg [her daughter] first, but she put her hands in front of her face and she just turned round so as not to look at me. How can I talk to her if she won't look at me, she obviously doesn't want to see … or to see me like this … [sobs] … so I'm shouting at this woman to take her to my Mum's. This lady just wrapped her in her arms and Meg started sobbing. I was shouting, please take her to my Mum's, please. I didn't know what else to do. I was in handcuffs. The lady took her to my mothers.'

Tia was also charged with resisting arrest because she tried to finish shouting to someone to look after her daughter before she was forced into the police van. She described how this memory would occur as a 'flashback,' at 'random' moments, knocking her off guard and taking her back to the trauma. It would trigger guilt, over-protectiveness towards her daughter, anxiety and worry. It was the main reason why Tia had considered taking anti-depressants, which in the end she decided against as she had previously been drug-dependant. She therefore continued to struggle on, unmedicated, to manage the ongoing trauma of this memory.

For the Mothers, their ongoing trauma was more than a result of their sense of powerlessness, or their lack of control, lack of agency or the reduction in their maternal-role and maternal self-esteem whilst incarcerated — it was all of that. Their narratives were clear: the biggest source of their trauma and persistent pain was the actual agony of being physically apart from their children. Several Mothers described experiencing nightmares, flashbacks, difficulty coping and an almost obsessive 'reliving' of parts or all of their imprisonment experience and the imprisonment process:

'I just ached for my children; I can't begin to describe the trauma of what it felt like to just not be physically with them … it occupied my every thought … I thought when I got out at least that ache would go, and I know this won't make any sense … but now I have an empty ache … that sounds stupid doesn't it … but like the hurt has left a hole and it won't go. I still think about being in prison every day.' (Jaspreet)

Beth, who was still breastfeeding her three-month-old baby, spoke of how the baby had to be wrenched from her arms by social workers; she remembers giving her 'one last feed before they took her,' adding:

'I was feeding her, and she was looking up at me with these totally innocent eyes … she had no idea what was coming and honestly my tears were just dripping all over her face, but she had no idea … no idea … just innocent. I was broken … I still am.'

Two other Mothers, Dee and Shanice, spoke of how they tried to flee to stop their children being taken into care. Shanice, who was arrested at home, remembers the police coming and knocking at the door, and she ran out of her back door to a neighbour to hand over her baby daughter so that she would not be taken into care. Similarly, Dee, who recalls how, as soon as she realised that the magistrate hearing her case was about to sentence her to immediate custody, she absconded from court to take her children to her sister's so they would not be taken into care. 'All I could think about was getting there and getting them to my sister's … it was mad but I had to.' She also described how this memory of her running would often trouble her dreams, where she would just be running and running but never getting anywhere.

Pain of Memories

It was clear that both Dee and Shanice were traumatised by memories of their imprisonment and the imprisonment processes, and for some Mothers it was these traumatic memories that trapped them in the cycles of substance misuse and reimprisonment:

'...honestly, I was mentally scarred by having Dwayne in prison...I used to obsess over it. It was stupid but I couldn't put it behind me...so I drank to cope but that just made things worser and I ended up back in again...its crazy, I know...it doesn't make sense, but it was all part of the same thing.' (Tanisha)

Kady described how she often has nightmares from aspects of her imprisonment and felt that her anger issues were a symptom of her not 'being able to process the memories of that place.' She described how she was 'made' to return to 'education' in the prison when her baby was very young:

'They made me leave her at six weeks...six weeks, man!...and go to education, I had to listen to her screaming and not be able to go to her, how fucked up is that? I can feel myself getting angry thinking about it all now, it doesn't need to be like that. I mean why was it essential I go to a classroom and colour in! That's [what] I was doing you know.'

Kady 'accepts responsibility' for her offence and the consequences but feels that the 'system' further harmed her and her daughter; she stated that if she had been a drug user she knows she would have used drugs to cope with the trauma of her experiences; instead, she drank, not to excess but 'to cope' with her emotions.

Several Mothers who were now free from substance misuse described how the hardest thing for them now was having to deal with their emotions as a result of past trauma, not only the original trauma that had triggered their substance misuse but also the trauma from the process of their imprisonment. Dee recalled:

'[T]he hardest thing I have ever gone through is getting clean...and that's because clean I have memories, I remember running from the court, not seeing my kids...it hurts, man...it's trauma, isn't it...every time a feeling or a memory would come up my head would be saying, "just use something"...I wasn't consciously thinking I was using drugs to bury my pain...but I was...it would be like, here's a feeling—my head would start going off…whoa fuck this and use…now I have to stay with the pain. And fucking hell, it cripples me, especially as a mum it makes you more ashamed, not ashamed, I dunno scarred maybe?…but I won't let it consume me…I have therapy now.'

Many, if not most, of the Mothers spoke of how they would be 'dragged back' (Margaret) to prison every day in their thoughts:

'Literally every day when my daughter goes to school I see the panic in her face in case I'm not here when she gets in…every day I'm reminded of what it was like being without her.' (Margot)

Some Mothers, especially those whose children were younger when they were separated, felt their trauma was triggered and retriggered by their children's ongoing trauma from their separation.

'…yes she hates being away from me…she cries if I leave her and I know that's because of what happened [prison]…seeing her traumatised reminds me so much of how traumatised I felt in prison being away from her…we need to get past it, we both do…but it still just feels so raw.' (Lauren)

Despite the fact that most Mothers spoke about their experiences as 'traumatic,' not all of them recognised their subsequent feelings or emotions as 'trauma': some described it as an experience they simply had to survive. Mothers described enduring states of feeling 'overwhelmed' (Carla), 'emotionally unstable' (Jaspreet), and 'exposed' (Mavis). Many described feelings of disorientation and panic once released, as previously observed by Eaton (1993); Masson (2019); Leverntz (2014); and Moore and Scraton (2014) as associated with post-prison women generally. However this book reveals (or at the least emphasises) the enduring nature of trauma, and impact related to ongoing post-release trauma and its interconnectedness to motherhood.

'I have good days and bad days, the weekend was bad, I just couldn't control my emotions, I just wanted to cry and cry. I can't explain it to anyone, and

I know no-one understands, they just think, I'm out now, I should put it behind me and move on, but I can't…it's not behind me, it's with me every day…the memory of leaving them outside, their faces, I can't bear it.' (Jaspreet)

Sometimes years after release, several Mothers recalled or described just 'bursting into tears' (Tanya), mostly triggered by a reminder of their time in prison as mothers, or when recalling the separation from their children; but sometimes 'for no apparent reason, whilst feeling a constant knot in my stomach on some days, like I'm worried about something, but I don't know what' (Lauren).

Pain of Fearful Anticipation

Rayna described how she struggled to sleep at night, stating she had a constant feeling of foreboding, a fearful anticipation that someone was going to come and return her to prison and thus separate her again from her children. Her experience was something several Mothers described and was felt particularly keenly whilst still on licence (see later discussion). Most of the Mothers described having ongoing nightmares and obsessive thoughts, sometimes decades post-release, where they would be unable to 'get to' (Tamika) their children, separated by some sort of physical barrier (Maggie). Mary described a 'growling bear' separating her from her children; Sandra described a wall in front of her children and every time she reached the top the wall would 'grow.'

Most of the Mothers described what are known and accepted as signs and symptoms of PTSD such as detachment, intrusive thoughts, depression, anxiety, sleep disturbance, and flashbacks.[3] The Mothers described how they would 're-live,' or 'play over and over' (Tanisha) in their minds, various traumatic aspects of their sentence or arrest, i.e. the process of imprisonment. Maggie described her anxiety, emotions and feelings to her counsellor, who subsequently diagnosed her as living with PTSD. Her experience was not unique, suggesting that parallels could be drawn

---

3. Post-Traumatic Stress: https://www.nhs.uk/conditions/post-traumatic-stress-disorder-ptsd/symptoms/

of her PTSD diagnosis with most of the Mothers, despite the fact that, prior to custody, many had been living in what could be classed as traumatic situations:

> 'It wasn't like life was rosy before prison, but I thought it would be all alright once I was out and back with them, it didn't occur to me I'd spend hours of days just re-living being apart from them. I'll be sitting watching TV then all of a sudden I'll be thinking about when she was leaving after visiting, or when they said to take me down in court and I knew I wouldn't see them that night. It just haunts me, and the weird thing is in some ways it stops me enjoying being with them now...because I can't stop thinking about not being able to see them...crazy.' (Shanice)

For several of the older Mothers, this haunting feeling of threatened separation was something that persisted throughout mothering and into grandmothering. Cynthia tried to avoid being separated from her son at all costs, to avoid it triggering painful memories; 'Being apart from my son even now kills me, it kills me...and he's 32.' Maggie described how her fear of separation not only applied to her children, but also to her grandchildren to the point where she was unable to book holidays for longer than a week as she could not 'bear' to be away from them.

> 'I couldn't shake the fear that something awful would happen to them if I didn't see them for more than a week, I know it was irrational but I kind of thought they would go off me if I didn't see them...Like they would forget to love me or something. Ridiculous I know, I haven't admitted that before.'

The Mothers described how they would avoid certain people and situations where these feelings seemed to be triggered: for some of the Mothers their anxiety seemed most triggered when they felt they were being watched or observed by people who 'just wouldn't get it' (Lauren). Rayna spoke of a similar fear, which although she said she recognised was 'irrational,' it nonetheless stopped her living a 'normal' life:

'I hated going out in my community, not only because of the shame but because I thought someone would take them from me, what is the word—abduct them, crazy crazy, crazy.'

This fearful anticipation goes over and above Goffman's (1963: 23) suggested wariness and anticipation about encounters between 'stigmatised' (mother) and 'normals' (everyone else), in which he suggests that the stigmatised might seek to avoid normals, and that encountering normals may trigger anxiety. This was specifically related instead to fear, and uncertainty related to their children, their motherhood and their mothering futures (Baldwin, 2015).

Pain of 'Ifs and Maybes'

Maggie described how she is traumatised not only by the prison experience and the separation itself, but by 'missed memories' in her children's and grandchildren's lives. Her grandson was diagnosed with cancer and Maggie was refused ROTL to attend his hospital appointments to help support her daughter. She became visibly upset at the memory of this:

'Sometimes I just torture myself with the "what ifs"…what if he'd died when I was still inside…then that makes me think what if my kids had got run over…or my husband died and they had no-one…I drive myself mad with what ifs.'

Many of the Mothers obsessed over what could have happened whilst they were in prison. Margaret had been pregnant during her prison sentence—she described how she was so traumatised by her prison experience that she had felt totally unable to bond with her baby during her pregnancy, feeling so ashamed that she had been in prison that she felt like an 'unfit mother.' As a result, she made the decision to place her child for adoption, which now haunted her:

'…all the time, what if I'd just had him, kept him I mean, or what if I'd not gone to prison, it's all…what ifs and ands and pots and pans my mother used to say, it's all what ifs, but I do think if I had kept him I would have been closer to my [other children] but I guess we'll never know.'

Similarly, Cynthia, who was described to me by a women's centre worker as 'completely and utterly traumatised,' also described how she would obsess and 'torture herself with guilt' over an imagined life 'if only things had been different.'

'I know I drank because of all the abuse, and that wasn't my fault, maybe if I'd had help or been believed it wouldn't have happened, maybe none of the rest would have happened, the violence, the wife beaters, all of it, my mental health, I think I would have been a good mum. So even though I know they are all to blame, and even the social and probation in a way for not helping me, even though I know that the guilt eats me up, all I missed, I obsess over it—how can I let that go? I'll feel guilty till the day I die, and I should.'

Margaret described feeling so traumatised by the separation and the memory of her child being taken that, when she did go on to have more children, she found it difficult to 'let myself love them.' She felt that only now as a grandmother was she able to find that maternal love, and to love 'in a motherly way.'

The 'physical pain' of an enduring separation, described by Datesman and Cales (1983) as 'profound hurt,' deeply traumatised the women whether Mothers were visited by their children or not—it was more than simply a prolonged period of not seeing the children, it was the physical separation from them and the loss of their maternal-role. Society puts great pressure on mothers, positioning motherhood and mothering at the forefront of their lives; there are innumerate expectations of mothers, not least that they should love their children beyond measure, which in most instances they do. This occurs not because patriarchal society tells them they should, or because biology 'makes' them, but because mostly 'motherhood matters' to women (O'Reilly, 2016: 1). It is hardly surprising, therefore, that the process of imprisonment—the physical separation of mothers from their children—is profoundly traumatic or that the period of separation haunts mothers.

253

As previously highlighted, the Mothers blamed themselves and their imprisonment for their children's negative outcomes, but they would also spend time wondering what if they had not gone to prison: would their children's lives have had the same outcomes? Queenie, despite admitting that her relationship with one of her daughters had always been 'difficult,' wondered whether it would be different if she had not gone to prison: 'Maybe if I hadn't been to prison we would be closer.' Margot, whose 14-year-old daughter had been badly bullied during her mother's imprisonment, stated:

> 'If I hadn't have gone to prison maybe she wouldn't have been bullied at all, but she certainly might have been more able to stand up for herself if she knew I was at home and life was normal.'

Paradoxically, despite the aforementioned widespread 'knowledge' and acceptance of the importance of motherhood, and the role of motherhood in terms of 'producing' well-adjusted, socially acceptable children and adults, mothers and motherhood are essentially ignored and/or neglected in the process and experience of imprisonment. Given all that we 'know' about mothers, motherhood and the mother/child relationship, it is illogical to think that forcibly separating mothers from their children — thus restricting contact and the mother's ability to mother her child — will not have a traumatic effect on both mothers and their children. Trauma, which may be an unintended outcome of maternal imprisonment is nonetheless a significant, additional and disproportionate punishment, and was, it could be argued an obvious outcome.

Piper and Berle (2019) and Liebling (2009) argued for greater understanding of the impact of trauma on prisoners' lives, and how previous trauma interacts with additional trauma both in and after prison. It is clear from the Mothers' accounts that the imprisonment process has distinct and specific implications for mothers, especially those resulting separation from their children and the reduction or powerlessness in their maternal values and beliefs about motherhood, which are, to some extent, shaped and influenced by wider society.

There is greater acceptance of traumatised 'victims' who are seen as more deserving of care and understanding than traumatised law breakers, yet the impact on both can be significant and enduring. The processes of imprisonment, i.e. the whole criminal justice process from arrest through imprisonment, to release and resettlement, must 'take trauma seriously' (Ellison and Munro, 2017: 56), and must be pursued more meaningfully if we are to have a fair and just system. Not only for those easily identified as 'victims' but also for law breakers, who have experienced their own forms of victimisation. It was striking in the Mothers' narratives to observe the frequency with which they sought to make their trauma and experiences 'count for something' (Tarian). They felt they could manage and transform their own traumas by supporting other women going through similar experiences within the CJS, hoping their own could inform the comfort and support of others — sometimes in ways they had not had themselves.

Wounded Healing

The concept of the 'wounded healer' is born from an archetype that suggests that healing power is amassed and emerges from a healer's own woundedness (Zerubavel and Wright, 2012: 482). The desire to 'help others' was frequently expressed by at least 12 of the Mothers. They felt uniquely placed to offer support and would often seek out opportunities to do so whilst in prison. Moreover, eight of them had or have formally pursued this on release (Ursula, Dee, Rita, Queenie, Mary, Tia, Jaspreet, Maggie), with five more stating that they intended to pursue their goal in the future (Kady, Tarian, Karen, Sandra, Shanice). Goffman (1963) suggests that groups of 'tainted individuals' (see *Chapter 2*) such as ex-prisoners, become 'stigmatised,' and those who have not experienced imprisonment are the 'normals.' Illustrating O'Reilly's stance that 'motherhood matters' and that mothering is often a primary concern for mothers, it was not surprising that the division between 'individuals' per se was also felt deeply in the women *as mothers*. Such a division can result in feelings of inferiority, generated by perception of the superiority of 'normals' (Goffman, 1963) and can result in the avoidance of certain social situations, such as the school gates (Tia), playgroup (Sophie), or a wedding (Queenie). They feared being rejected, ostracised and vilified not *just* as ex-prisoners but as ex-prisoners who are also mothers.

Some Mothers coped with their pain of rejection as them as 'good mothers' by trying to dismiss it: 'It's just life, isn't it'(Diane); some developed what Goffman (1963: 29) called a 'hostile bravado,' summed-up succinctly by Cynthia: 'Fuck them all, what do I care,' which similarly Sam called her 'fuck it approach.' Nonetheless, several Mothers described feeling a keen sense of 'difference' between themselves and mothers who had not experienced incarceration, and that was something that 'hurt' (Taranpreet). As a consequence, several of them arranged their lives so as to minimise painful situations and contacts in which their past might be exposed or judged, but described the managing of the underpinning shame and guilt as 'exhausting' (Karen):

> 'I was high alert all the time [when out], I can't keep weight on me anymore and I'm sure it is nervous energy. I just feel so ashamed of being a mum who has been to prison, but honestly living with it is literally exhausting.' (Karen)

As Goffman highlighted (1963: 27), even when the 'normals' are not even noticing the stigmatised person or are not concerned with the root of the stigma, the 'stigmatised person' will nonetheless 'feel that to present amongst normals nakedly exposes [that person].' Goffman (ibid: 31) suggests that the stigmatised person 'stands as a discredited person facing an unacceptable world,' and that it is perhaps obvious that individuals seek to be in the company of 'sympathetic others,' the first set of whom are those who share the same stigma.

Thus not only is pursuing 'work' and company with those who share one's experiences therapeutic, it can be a significant source of identity repair. Several Mothers sought to reshape their own trauma and to 'manage' it by supporting and helping others in similar circumstances, something which Motz et al (2020) suggests can be an important part of recovering from trauma. For several of the Mothers this had begun during their incarceration, and they had sought roles like 'prison listener'[4] to be able to do this.

> 'I'm a prison listener now and I love it. It takes your mind off your own problems when you are helping others, doesn't it[?] It stops me thinking about the kids so much, especially at night.' (Sandy)

As discussed in *Chapter 6*, older Mothers particularly sought to utilise their maternal skills (Kitzinger, 1992), and would mother others, especially younger Mothers. This gave the older Mothers and grandmothers opportunities to mother but was also a means of managing their own pain and trauma as criminalised and imprisoned mothers. It gave them a purpose and for some planted seeds of hope about their future:

> 'You know what?...mothering them little ones...I loved it; I knew they needed it yeah...but you know what it helped my pain as well. I was distracted from it...it made it easier for me to cope...and that was where I got the idea I should do it when I got out. I made a promise to myself to help other girls like me. I thought if I could help one girl not to go to prison and suffer like this, then my life will have meant something...you know what I mean?' (Mary)

Baldwin ((Michele) (2000)) highlights the significance of the relational aspect between two human beings in any therapeutic exchange. Although speaking about a formal therapeutic relationship such as that with a psychologist or counsellor and their client, it is easy to apply her argument to the Mothers. It was clear that the bonds and relationships they formed with other mothers in prison were supportive, even therapeutic, simultaneously boosting the self-esteem of both.

In the process of renegotiating a positive maternal identity, some of the Mothers tried to assimilate their experience and turn their imprisonment into a positive by focusing on supporting others and assisting others to believe in the possibility of a 'better' future:

---

4. Listener schemes are a form of peer support; prisoners work together as a team. Local Samaritans' branches select and train prisoners to be Listeners and provide ongoing training.

'It sounds stupid I know but being there for them young lasses like, well it kept me feeling like a mam, like I could still do good, you know what I mean? Still be like a mam. I just used to sit and listen to them and they knew I was going through the same. One girl had her baby taken by social services like me and I knew what she was going through. She used to say that she did, I mean that I knew how she felt but that none of the others did — and I'm thinking speaking to someone who did know helped her, but really it did help me, too, because I had to try to believe what I was telling her, that it would get better, that we could have more kids and be better, that we could get it right. I was giving me hope as much as I was her.' (Emma)

Bradley et al (2021) highlight the value and significance of 'lived experience'[5] when working with people, especially those who have experienced trauma and particularly women. They note that the shift towards a trauma-informed approach throughout the CJS (Bradley, 2017: Jewkes et al, 2019; MOJ, 2018) demonstrates an increasing recognition of the trauma trajectories behind many of those who find themselves in the CJS. Bradley et al (ibid) argue that people who share the same experiences as those they are supporting are able to facilitate deep trust and meaningful relationships: they call this 'relational healing.' Bradley et al recognise that shared experiences can promote feelings of safety and a feeling of 'not being alone,' in a similar vein to Goffman (1963: 32), who identified that sharing space with those with the same lived experience not only generates 'moral support' but also the 'comfort of feeling at home':

'I volunteer here [a women's centre] with the young mums because it makes me feel worthwhile again. At first I can see them thinking, "What would she know?" but when I tell them I went to prison too then they listen, they know I get them, and they get me.' (Maggie)

Similarly, Queenie, who had described feeling 'just an ongoing pain' about being a Mother and grandmother who had been to prison, also

---

5. Personal knowledge about something gained through direct first-hand involvement.

wanted to 'turn my pain into good,' both through her church work and also through a business she set-up to work with ex-prison mothers:

'I'm not going to lie, working with other prison mums is the only place I don't feel judged—escaping from the judgement of my kids and my church…I can still do the good my church expects of me but I do it where I'm not reminded all the time what a bad person I am, especially what a bad mother I am because I went to prison.'

Rita, who initially had wanted to do something specifically for mothers in and after prison, set-up a community space for women to meet, either just to visit or as a place where they can learn skills to assist them in earning money by selling items they can make at the centre:

'I wanted to do something for all mothers who were struggling, initially yeah it was only going to be for mums who'd been to prison only but then I thought, why should I carry on that finger pointing—that's what we are trying to escape, that's the same shaming, so yes the centre helps mums who have been to prison but also mums who haven't and they all work side by side and no-one knows who's been where unless they choose to tell each other…in my view that's what a women's centre should be, for all women.' (Rita)

Like several of the Mothers, Rita stated definitively that it was her motherhood that provided her with the motivation to 'move forward and succeed.' Becoming a successful entrepreneur was an important aspect to Rita's identity repair and maternal healing—she knows her children 'feel proud' of her and she feels like her 'new identity' also 'compensates' for the fact that she went to prison as a mother; although profoundly affected by the separation from her children, Rita feels that 'helping others has helped me to move forward with less shame' (Rita).

What was apparent and significant amongst the Mothers in relation to their maternal trauma and pain was that it was, and continued to be, ignored in the post- release support agency responses. This represented a continuation and replication of a failure to meet the needs of mothers more broadly in social policy and practice.

Munro (2018) argues that the 'complex burdens associated with trauma' require a broad-based commitment to care and concern in wider society generally, but especially amongst statutory agencies tasked to respond to trauma survivors (whether they are law breakers or not). Most, but tragically not all of the Mothers did survive the trauma of maternal imprisonment. Those who survived live with their pain, and manage to mother and mother well, but they do so mainly as a result of their own resilience and sheer determination rather than because they were able to access gendered and structured support.

Summary of *Chapter 11*

Most of the Mothers entered prison multiply affected by social injustice. Structural barriers, state surveillance and a lack of support interacted with impossibly high personal maternal standards and continued to complicate the Mothers' efforts to maintain or resume their maternal-roles post-release. Sykes (1958) suggests that most, if not all, prisoners experience 'pains of imprisonment.' Similarly, Goffman (1963: 12) presents a convincing argument that most, if not all, prisoners become 'reduced,' 'spoiled' and stigmatised due to the stripping away of roles and 'prisonisation.' Extending these valuable concepts, this chapter has I think amply evidenced the distinct and specific ways in which the 'accepted wisdom' of the spoiled identity and pains of imprisonment notions applied to post-prison mothers, and thus constituted persistent pains of maternal imprisonment. The anticipated 'spoiled identity' of an ex-prisoner status was magnified and compounded for women who are also mothers and grandmothers.

The chapter evidences that the central features and primary concerns of post-release Mothers remain their maternal identity and role, their maternal emotions and their children — regardless of whether they have them in their care or not. It revealed how Mothers' release from prison did not result in the expected 'return to normal' for the Mothers and grandmothers, but instead presented new challenges specific to their motherhood status.

The chapter highlighted the frequency with which criminalised mothers continued to be consistently challenged and disadvantaged by structural inequality and limited access to services and support. This was additionally frustrated by changes in relationships and relationship dynamics. The now traumatised Mothers struggled to repair and renegotiate their maternal-roles and their maternal-self-esteem was now even more precarious, which had the effect of reducing their self-worth, maternal-role and maternal capital. They continued to be measured (and measured themselves), against not only the expectations of society as law-abiding citizens but also specifically against a motherhood ideal (formally and informally).

Further, it identified how notions of control, trust and surveillance interacted with the post-prison maternal experience to reveal the pervading gaze of the state on mothers and the family (Rose, 1999). The chapter reveals how continued missed opportunities to offer support and understanding, care and compassion related to their motherhood impacted on Mothers wellbeing and desistance. Support, which if offered and available might have prevented further criminalisation and reimprisonment and the subsequent enduring harms described.

Although most Mothers shared similarly challenging histories, they also shared a strength and resilience that enabled them to survive not only their multiple realities but also a system that, by and large, does not understand or meet their needs. The personal cost to Mothers and their children has been significant. In recognising this, several of the Mothers voiced a desire to work with women in the CJS or the third sector, either on a paid or voluntary basis, which in line with matricentric and feminist principles of agency and empowerment should be supported and encouraged.

Pause for Thought

As a parent how do you deal with regrets, ifs and maybes? — What if your 'mistakes' had led you to prison? — How might that impact on your parenting? — Mothers who go to prison are often already living with trauma from past experiences — How can this additional trauma impact mothers further?

What are the implications of what you have read for work/engagement with criminalised women/mothers?

How can post-prison services (public, private or voluntary) ensure they recognise layers (and additional layers) of trauma? — How might these manifest?

Why do you think so many of the Mothers in this book wanted to work with criminalised women? — Do you think this is a good idea?

Having presented the evidence I discovered and I hope new understanding of the significant and enduring impact of maternal imprisonment, the book now turns in *Part III* to my concluding thoughts, the impact of my findings and my recommendations.

PART III
CONCLUSIONS AND RECOMMENDATIONS

CHAPTER 12

Drawing Together the Evidence

The Mothers' voices and the experiences they described to me demonstrate the inherent disproportionality of punishment when a mother is criminalised and imprisoned. Here I set out my final thoughts leading up to a number of personal recommendations based not just on the what I learned when preparing this book but many years of working with imprisoned mothers and their families.

I would summarise my main thoughts as follows (some of which apply to mothers in general but all of which impact on criminalised mothers):

- motherhood (and mothering) are defined and experienced within broader structural, patriarchally influenced ideologies but are nevertheless experiences treasured by most women choosing to take on this role;

- significant, widespread and sometimes life-threatening harm is caused to the identity and role of imprisoned mothers;

- we should nevertheless acknowledge the strength and resilience of mothers who continue to mother, often 'against the odds,' in a society that judges them (especially in and after prison);

- prison continues to be used readily for women and mothers because reactions to crime are fuelled by 'moral emotions' (see, e.g. Canton, 2015: 59);

- reactions and responses to crime and 'criminals' do not always reflect the harm they cause and this can be especially so if women who offend are categorised as 'deviant' (or worse);

- we need to recognise and understand how far removed criminalised women are from the accepted norms and values of society, which Canton frames in the terms of 'sanctity and degradation' (ibid);

- mothers committing crimes are deemed to be acting outside not only society's norms, but also outside the social, emotional and moral framework of motherhood and this represents a perceived deviation from maternal 'duties;' and

- ultimately enduring inequality, disadvantage, discrimination and institutional thoughtlessness concerning motherhood combine to have a long and lasting impact on criminalised mothers.

It is clear there were many missed and lost opportunities to support the Mothers whose stories appear in *Part II* of this book, long before prison and often dating back to their childhoods. Furthermore, they all felt that being 'in' prison impacted and influenced their post-prison experiences. They confirmed how thoughtlessness of rules and systems compounded their already pain filled situation.

For example, last minute prison moves, often occurring for systemic rather than individual reasons frequently caused significant pain and disruption — not least when this impacted on planned, even booked visits by children. When it occurred, this had a devastating impact on the Mothers and no doubt on their children too. A simple rule of never moving a mother with visits booked unless absolutely necessary would go a long way towards addressing this aspect of institutional thoughtlessness.

The Mothers described how they were already dealing with their own internal guilt, shame and self-recrimination at being an imprisoned mother; only to experience additional external and explicit judgement and shaming from the system itself and the words and deeds of professionals involved in their care. I did not meet a single Mother in the course of gathering the material for this book who had not experienced at least one person telling them 'You should have thought of your children before offending or you wouldn't be here' — or words to that effect. If only life were that simple. The Mothers were all to an extent mothering in a circle of circumstances that challenged such black and white thinking. Consider their often raw explanations and maybe ask yourself what you might well have done in their situation.

Several Mothers described how they offended in the context of poverty, *precisely because* they were thinking of their children. Mothers like Dee and Ursula described actions that placed themselves at greater risk but that they undertook because their children's wellbeing was paramount in their minds. Dee, when she realised she was about to be remanded in custody immediately, absconded from court to get her children to her sisters to make sure they were safe and would not be taken into care. As she herself stated, 'All I could think of was my children.' Once her children were safe she handed herself in. Imagine her desperation taking that risk.

Similarly, Ursula was not supposed to reside in the family home for her licence period (four more long years!) because her children's father was also convicted of offences. Yes, she risked recall because after four years in prison she couldn't bear the thought of staying apart form her children a moment longer — and most importantly to Ursula, her children were desperate to have her home. Imagine living with that fear of recall for four years — but at the same time 'knowing' it was worth that risk to be with your children.

These examples (and other within the book) are not of mothers who were not thinking of their children — they were mothers trapped in a system that forced them to make difficult, sometimes heart-rending and risky decisions because the system doesn't acknowledge or respond adequately to the needs of mothers. For which they were further punished, criminalised, hurt, traumatised and damaged.

The Mothers described how they faced judgement and condemnation from all quarters because of their imprisonment. Often, they themselves were their harshest critics. They revealed how their motherhood provided an additional layer of complexity to the intersectionalities of race, class and culture affecting criminalised women. Mothering through poverty and trauma before prison, often unsupported, is where the tarnishing of the Mothers maternal identity began. Most of them felt they were already failing to 'live up to' widely accepted standardised norms of motherhood, sometimes worrying even before prison that they were not 'good enough' mothers This endured through and after prison.

The Mothers felt they were judged more harshly by society, by the courts and agents of the state. They also judged themselves more harshly *as mothers*. In addition to feeling angry and frustrated that they were judged as bad mothers, often for things that were outside their control, the Mothers internalised the blame and shame for their circumstances and criminalisation. The book demonstrates how easily the Mothers 'issues' became individualised. Rather than looking more broadly at the role played by successive Governments concerning the lack of supportive polices for women (see also Burrows, 2001; O'Reilly, 2016; Clarke and Chadwick, 2018), the Mothers were perceived as *solely* responsible for their criminalisation and imprisonment because of their own actions and 'choices.'

Underfunded, poorly resourced statutory agencies repeatedly struggled or failed to meet the needs of Mothers — importantly in ways that might have prevented the becoming criminalised at all. Instead of recognising a widespread systemic failure to address this context, they were criminalised, judged, blamed and made accountable for its failings. Mothers were deemed bad mothers for making 'bad' or 'poor' choices, when, in reality, there were often few alternative choices on offer. This affected the Mothers maternal identity and self-esteem, consequently impacting their engagement with rehabilitative support, their relationships and sometimes, desistance. They carried the weight of guilt, powerlessness and sometimes hopelessness with them through prison and beyond.

For many of the Mothers, guilt was a life threatening emotion, and when coupled with the hopelessness felt, e.g. by Beth, it was simply too much and she took her own life at the tragically young age of 21, leaving her daughter to become a motherless statistic in the care system. Beth and other mothers like her are driven by maternal trauma into self-harm and suicide as a means of coping or a response to their absolute despair. Despair that is often not recognised or supported by the system and structures mothers find themselves in.

The Mothers described how their maternal trauma haunted and followed them post release. *Part II* demonstrates that the impact and pains of maternal imprisonment persist far longer and I believe reach wider than previously documented. As I note at the start of this summary those harms are persistent and enduring, for many years post-release, seemingly for much longer than previously known or documented; and the evidence that maternal imprisonment triggers enduring trauma, sometimes to the extent of PTSD is I am sure underexplored. These harms affect the lives of post-prison mothers of dependant children, grandmothers and older mothers and their relationships for decades, often intergenerationally.

The Mothers described how post release they felt 'tarnished,' 'reduced' or 'less than' as mothers because of their imprisonment. Kady summed it up when she described herself a 'tainted mother.' For the grandmothers this was a layered experience, and the Mothers' feelings of shame and stigma intersected with judgements associated with age and gender. They felt judged by their children and grandchildren—or where grandchildren did know of their imprisonment the grandmothers were so fearful of them finding out about their 'dirty secret' that they denied themselves the pleasure of fully engaging with their grandchildren, or them with her because of this hidden barrier.

Decades post-release, some Mothers described how their trauma would be reignited at unexpected moments—derailing or de-stabilising them. How they would be catapulted back to the time of the painful separation and loss-triggering a range of psychological and physiological reactions—which many of the Mothers described as PTSD. Mothers whose children had become adults and to all intents and purposes were 'at peace' with the events of the past, described how the difficulties would return as their 'children' became parents themselves. Particularly as daughters became mothers, the post-prison Mothers found themselves being judged by their daughters through the eyes of their own motherhood (which as noted earlier above is influenced by the ideas and ideals of motherhood thinking). Questions were asked; 'How could you have done that to us? ... Now I'm a mother I know I wouldn't have risked that with my children.' Thus, relationships that were previously settled and peaceful were once again disrupted, fractured and tainted by stigma, shame and judgement. Leading Ursula to state, 'Any sentence for a mother is a life sentence really.'

The Mothers' experiences

What has been learned about this aspect of the Mothers' lives before, during and after prison? Motherhood is a fascinating paradox in which they often feel oppressed, exhausted, judged and invisible, whilst simultaneously feeling joyful, powerful and fulfilled. This paradox is magnified for mothers in and after prison, because as shown in this book being a criminalised mother is a source of sadness, lasting pain and trauma, yet motherhood often also remained and remains a source of joy and hope.

Maternal identity

The Mothers demonstrated the significance of life and motherhood experiences pre-imprisonment, revealing that for many of them the 'spoiling' of their maternal identity began before prison. This was confirmed in prison and endured long after it. In addition to the direct *process of imprisonment*, it was experiences pre-criminalisation and beyond release which caused harm and impact to maternal identity, maternal emotions and maternal role.

The Mothers detailed how their challenging pre-prison circumstances interacted with their motherhood, revealing how their absorption of traditional motherhood ideology influenced their maternal self-esteem, maternal identity and role. Their accounts provide new and nuanced understanding about the specific relevance of being poorly mothered as children and how this then informed or shaped the Mothers own adult experiences and views on 'good and bad' motherhood. Which in turn informed their own maternal identity.

Chapters 2 and *3* provided a foundation for understanding why the criminalised Mothers absorbed the expectations and ideology around motherhood and mothering, rendering them subject to internal and external blame and liability, especially in relation to outcomes for their children. They clearly articulated the additional pain and trauma they experienced *as mothers*. The most often cited pain of imprisonment described was the enforced separation from their children. This was often coupled with feelings of fear, loss, anxiety about the future and a reduction in feelings of worth as a mother. The Mothers were hit particularly hard in relation to their maternal-role. They described how being deprived of their autonomy as mothers made them feel less worthy or, as Enos (2001: 63) describes it, 'less like mothers.' The lack of ability to take an active role in mothering and the resulting negative impact on imprisoned mothers (and their children) bore significantly on the Mothers' wellbeing, sense of self and crucially on their maternal identity.

Present in all of the Mothers narratives of their CJS experience (and from a range of other sources quoted in the text) was moral condemnation, not only as criminals but specifically as *criminal mothers*. The Mothers powerfully described the difference it made to them when someone in authority demonstrated 'care,' 'kindness,' understanding or compassion concerning their maternal identity and role. Several described how simply being asked about their children or their motherhood being acknowledged 'saved' them, for some it literally was a matter of life and death.

It was challenging to separate maternal identity and role for the Mothers, as where one was reduced and the other was impacted. The Mothers practical and physical mothering practices were limited by incarceration, further diminishing their maternal identity and maternal self-esteem. Once imprisoned, they described how they felt less like mothers, in that their motherhood was removed from their identity or subsumed by their prisoner identity. More than that, it was the pain of not 'being,' of not doing, pain of losing a sense of who they were. Of losing what they described as the most important part of themselves, i.e. their motherhood and/or grandmotherhood. This was accelerated by the structure, organization and regimes within the prison. Which impacted on Mothers ability and willingness to engage in rehabilitation as well as their wellbeing and relationships with children and caregivers.

The Mothers sought comfort in their relationships with each other and with older mothers and grandmothers, where the prison regime permitted. This helped them retain a sense of maternal identity and had a positive impact on the Mothers and grandmothers wellbeing. Mothers in open prisons were more able to support each other and were often united in their motherhood. However, in closed prisons Mothers were less able to engage in this support, which had a detrimental impact on their mental wellbeing and maternal identity.

The effects of the Mothers spoiled identity lasted long after prison, with Mothers describing how their reduced maternal self-esteem persisted post-release, in some cases, for decades. They also described an internal shame, over and above their ex-prisoner status (Goffman, 1963). The ongoing pains and shame of imprisonment (Sykes, 1958) related specifically to their mother status. Mothers described feeling 'tainted,' forever labelled and perceived as 'bad mothers' because they had been imprisoned *as mothers*.

Feeling worthless or hopeless left many of the Mothers vulnerable to self-harm and/or suicide. Several Mothers described how losing their maternal identity made them feel like 'nothing.' During incarceration and afterwards, their spoiled maternal identity made some Mothers question whether they ought to remain in their children's lives at all (some didn't). Others withdrew from their children's lives and refused or reduced visits/contact, sometimes for their own wellbeing, but usually because they perceived their children as 'better off' without them. Thus, the impact of maternal imprisonment on maternal identity had enduring, often lifelong and sometimes intergenerational impact.

Maternal role

As previously described, many of the Mothers became criminalised in the midst of multiple challenges to their mothering role. This included past and current trauma, addiction, mental health issues, domestic abuse and substance misuse. Yet most of were involved in the care of their children before prison and were steadfast in their efforts to continue to mother to the best of their ability. For some, their maternal role was a source of agency and power, for some their only source, meaning it was all the more valuable to them. Not managed to retain a full maternal role pre or post-prison. Several Mothers shared their mothering role with additional caregivers, however, maintaining their maternal identity and hopes of an improved future maternal role was often their primary concern.

The book confirms that motherhood intersected powerfully with the Mothers prison experience, which added to the Mothers' 'pains of imprisonment' (Sykes, 1958). As soon as Mothers entered the prison space they experienced a stripping away of their maternal agency, maternal identity and especially their maternal role (Goffman, 1961). Their efforts to continue to mother from a distance were frustrated and disrupted by the carceral space and the rules and regulations therein.

Many of the challenges mothers in prison faced reflected the focus of the penal system and prison estate on male prisoners. Prison officer training is centred around the male estate, and officers do not currently receive more than a couple of training sessions specifically devoted to working with women prisoners. Only because of the my involvement with them for this book have some received specific training for working with mothers at all (provided by myself). Thus, the Mothers felt their motherhood and maternal role was either essentially ignored by CJS staff, or a source of judgement, mistrust, surveillance and control, which impacted on their engagement and maternal self-esteem.

The Mothers ability to maintain a healthy maternal identity and an affirming maternal self-esteem and active mothering role were affected, both positively and negatively, by the prison space, rules, regimes and relationships. Maternal emotion and active mothering was of central importance to Mothers during their incarceration and beyond, whether or not they had the care of their children or were expecting to on release.

As a matricentric-feminist investigation, my remit was to recognise the experiences of *all* mothers, crucially to include grandmothers and mothers of adult children. Grandmothers described feeling discounted in institutional considerations, even those that recognised the maternal role (such as family visits and ROTL). Grandchildren and older adult children were rendered secondary and/or invisible to their younger counterparts, making it challenging for grandmothers to retain an active grandmothering role. This as revealed through the Mothers' stories in *Part II* shows that for grandmothers their pains of maternal imprisonment were also persistent post-release. Furthermore, they were layered and often experienced via their adult children as well as their grandchildren. Failure to account for the needs of grandmother prisoners and post-prison grandmothers was not only neglectful and unjust but resulted in missed opportunities to support families to heal and to reduce the likelihood of intergenerational offending and enduring trauma.

The legacy of maternal imprisonment and the impact on maternal role was significant. Some Mothers lost their maternal-role altogether, for others it was reduced. Mothers whose children were in the care of the local authority were consumed with thoughts either of fighting for their return or trying to accept their maternal loss. The Mothers were not supported with these needs and emotions, which had an impact on their maternal wellbeing, engagement and sometimes their desistance.

For some Mothers, their maternal role was diminished because caregivers were reluctant to return their children to them or heavily scrutinised the mothers in their mothering. Mothers continued to be subject to the formal gaze of the state (Rose, 1999) as well as the informal gaze of family, and crucially, none of the mothers experienced any post-release support focussed on rebuilding family relationships.

The Mothers described how their internalised shame and blame left them feeling like they were in penance and needing to compensate in their post-release mothering. Some were overzealous in disciplining their children, where others relaxed rules as a means to seek forgiveness and favour from their children. Thus, for many, maternal imprisonment not only interrupted and disrupted mothering and maternal-role, it changed it completely. The disregard of Mothers' maternal-role from custodians and supervisors means that opportunities are being missed not only for families to be supported in these changes, but also to try to ensure that any changes that do occur return positive outcomes.

Enduring Harm

Despite extensive existing research around women and imprisonment, there had been a failure, especially in the UK, to fully investigate or deeply understand the experiences of mothers in and after imprisonment, especially by way of a feminist lens and particularly beyond five years post-release. I have tried in this book to significantly adds to understanding and knowledge in this still under-researched area.

As the previous two sections have identified the criminalised Mothers most often felt reduced, tainted, judged and traumatised as a result of their criminalisation and imprisonment. The enduring harm of maternal imprisonment was powerfully described by the Mothers, and all aspects of their post-prison lives were affected. In addition to the collateral damage often experienced by women leaving prison (Masson, 2019, Minson, 2020), the Mothers described lasting effects of shame and guilt regarding their imprisonment, meaning they were not now and perhaps never would be again, perceived as, or feel like 'good mothers.'

Mother's experiences prior to prison reflected a state which had abdicated responsibility for the Mothers as children and continued its failure into their adulthood. This was manifest in missed opportunities that could potentially have prevented Mother's criminalisation, and the consequential enduring harm. Yet, it was the Mothers themselves and arguably, their children, who were held to account and who suffered the consequences of this lack of support. Painfully illustrated by Cynthia, who after repeatedly asking for help and none being forthcoming, set herself on fire in a blatant cry for help. She was subsequently imprisoned for arson when the Judge found 'there was nowhere else' to send her. Cynthia and her child live with the lifelong consequences and enduring harm of her offending and imprisonment. Cynthia took responsibility for her 'crimes' and paid the price, yet for the services who failed her, there was no accountability. Similarly, Mary, who felt so worthless as a mother, and was completely unsupported in that role, made the decision to completely remove herself from her children's lives. Tragically her children then grew up in care, later to become 'career criminals.' As a result, Mothers were absent from their own children's lives. This powerfully reveals the intergenerational impact of maternal imprisonment and highlights the importance of early and consistent support and interventions for mothers and their children.

Mothers were often unprepared for the challenges they would continue to face post-release. Many had simply assumed that things would go back to 'normal.' Yet, the Mothers' narratives revealed significant challenges in renegotiating their place in their family and their maternal role. Or adjusting to life without their children. Mothers were unprepared for the roller coaster of emotions and turbulent times they faced with their children, grandchildren and wider families post-release. Or how long the difficulties would last. Additionally, Mothers described experiences of trauma—an issue previously under researched. Which endured and was attributed to the memory of the separation from their children. Indeed, some Mothers were formally diagnosed with PTSD directly stemming from their maternal harm as a result of imprisonment. Others exhibited most of the symptoms of PTSD, but simply learned to 'live with it.' Those who remained in their children's lives described how they felt 'tainted,' 'watched,' 'judged' and 'permanently changed' by their imprisonment. For grandmothers, the effects were often magnified, producing what grandmothers described as 'layers of shame.' This reflected the 'institutional thoughtlessness' (Crawley 2005) concerning motherhood that occurred at all stages of the CJS. This must be addressed if we are to mitigate the enduring harms described by the Mothers and grandmothers.

In-part due to earlier failures to support women and mothers, and whilst recognising prison as an institution of patriarchally influenced pain (Moore and Scraton 2014); it cannot be ignored that the Mothers sometimes experienced prison a place of safety and refuge (O'Malley 2018). A place where some Mothers were finally able to access support related to substance misuse, domestic abuse, mental health issues. Nonetheless, it must also be acknowledged that with regard to the Mothers who did mention there had been some safety, solace and support for them in prison, *all* felt that the support *should* have been available to them in the community. Importantly, that if it had been, they would in all likelihood have not 'ended up' in prison at all.

'Factoring' Motherhood Into Sentence Plans and Supervision

My findings directly contrast with those of Loper (2006: 93) who suggests it is 'no more difficult to be a mother in prison than it is to be a non-mother,' instead aligning with numerous previous studies (see Enos, 2001; Lockwood, 2014; O'Malley, 2018; Masson, 2019; Easterling et al, 2019; Minson 2020; Booth, 2020). They showed the distinct and specific maternal pains, frustrations and deprivation of maternal-imprisonment. Furthermore, they revealed tensions between what the Mothers said they needed in terms of in-prison and post-release support, and what they experienced. Their narratives described how current approaches and support provisions failed to take account of the persisting trauma caused by criminalisation, maternal interruption and separation.

The damage to maternal identity and their mothering-role was not often regarded as something that fell under the remit of custodians or supervisors and as such it was often ignored. The Mothers revealed that trying to repair and renegotiate their identity and role in and after-prison was often of central importance to them. Or as O'Reilly (2016) put it 'motherhood matters.' Whether they had their children in their care when sentenced or not. Or whether they were to be reunited with children post-release. The Mothers were preoccupied with all matters maternal whilst trying to navigate their challenging maternal circumstances pre-prison, through prison and post-release.

However, the Mothers reported their maternal matters and emotions, though of primary importance to them, were not viewed as important *enough* by the courts, prison or probation services (other than as an additional means of judgement, control and punishment). Which the Mothers perceived as a lack of 'care.' They described how this and failure to recognise the challenges they faced *as mothers* made it difficult, if not impossible, for them to focus on rehabilitation or supervision, which ultimately had implications for their wellbeing and desistance.

Care-focussed approaches in the CJS are of significant importance (Dominey and Gelsthorpe, 2020: 40), both morally (Canton and Dominey, 2017) and because it fundamentally underpins good practice and effective outcomes, fostering a trusting relationship. The lack of 'care' experienced by the Mothers contributed to them feeling that the only role of their custodians or supervisors was to control and subject them to punitive surveillance, particularly in relation to their motherhood. With a few individual exceptions, the Mothers felt that 'what was really going on' in their lives was regarded as not important, or not within the role of the supervisory relationship. Instead, they felt 'watched' and 'surveilled.' The Mothers found the additional surveillance challenging *as mothers* and most described an 'abject terror' of recall and a further period of separation from their children. This had implications for the Mothers in terms of asking for and receiving adequate and appropriate support.

Significantly, where Mothers were supervised via a women's centre, they described receiving a gendered form of supervision in which their emotional and maternal needs were understood and responded to. Indicating that this is the most effective means of supervising women. However, even in these spaces, motherhood in terms of needs and impact remains to a degree underexplored and under-supported. Thus, we are missing opportunities to factor in motherhood into the desistance and rehabilitation journeys of criminalised mothers.

Several Mothers had been supervised by probation multiple times over quite a long time span and noted the shift in the type of supervision they received. Nicola felt that probation officers no longer seemed to 'care' as part of their role. In the UK, following a politically-led tide of change, there has been a shift over the last 30 years which has seen probation or parole moving further away from welfare-focussed values and ideology (Canton, 2015). Subsequently, in the New labour 'Tough on Crime' era following the implementation of National Standards and the 'New Choreography'[1] in the work of probation, the importance and flexibility of the one-to-one 'supervisory relationship' became secondary to the rigid enforcement and supervisory directives that some of the Mothers encountered. Such philosophical shifts have had far-reaching implications for supervisors and custodians and how they undertake their role. The Mothers' accounts demonstrate the detrimental impact of the political shifts in relation to the quality of supervision and custodial care for mothers. Primarily, because without wider aspects of 'welfare' being deemed of importance, supervision for post-release women has become all about avoiding re-offending, managing the threat of being returned to prison and the increased surveillance of their lives (Opsal, 2009).

Dominey and Gelsthorpe (2020) argue that the absence of individual care in probation practice, and arguably also throughout the whole CJS, is what leads inevitably to shifting priorities that are influenced by political imperatives. This is reflected in deficient funding streams, ultimately potentially leading to the poor or ineffective practice that some of the Mothers experienced. However, and importantly, rather than it being the fault of individual officers or agents of the State, the matricentric-feminist lens supports the view that this points to institutional failure at the highest levels. Failure to provide adequate funding, resources and structures that would facilitate staff in meeting the needs of women in the CJS has consequences. The Mothers demonstrated how this structural and systemic lack of care, alongside services not being adequately funded, made it challenging for their post-release needs to be successfully met.

---

1. National Probation Service (2001), *A New Choreography: An Integrated Strategy for The National Probation Service for England & Wales*, London: NPS archived. Home Office.

Several studies, while not explicitly exploring the experiences of post-prison mothers, have identified a relationship between motherhood and desistance. Finding that motherhood sometimes serves 'as a prosocial bond' that may assist women in their desistance journeys (see Giordano et al, 2002; Bachman et al, 2016; Garcia Hallett, 2019). Bachman et al, (ibid: 215) argue that, given mothers do of course enter prison, then it is not motherhood per se that will influence women to desist from offending; however, they argue, that at some point a mother may become ready to adopt 'a prosocial identity by reclaiming [her] role as a mother.' A view shared by Opsal (2011).

Maruna and Mann (2019) suggest security and stable family relation-ships alongside an individual perception of themselves as 'changed,' hopefulness and an affirming self-esteem are important factors in the desistance journey. For post-release Mothers, motherhood was an impor-tant part of self-esteem and self-worth, often the most important part, and as such, it was highly relevant to their desistance.

Michaelson (2011) highlighted the importance that post-release mothers attached to their love for their children and saw this as a signif-icant factor in their desistance. However, they also found that, mothers facing multiple disadvantage and continued substance misuse sometimes re-offended to simply survive. Similarly, Masson (2019) and Brown and Bloom (2009) found that being a mother was a motivating factor for desistance, but for some, the realities of continued poverty, addiction, lack of housing, financial and therapeutic instability disrupted mothers attempts to desist. Which was also evidenced in the Mothers' accounts.

I found that for some post-release Mothers, the guilt and shame they felt as criminal mothers, intertwined with the loss of children or disrupted mothering, became overwhelming. The additional trauma caused by imprisonment and separation from, or removal of their children, led some to feel their only coping strategy was a return to substance misuse. Which often meant a return to criminal activity as a consequence.

In the case of Beth, the lack of support, or a reluctance/inability to ask for mothering-related support led to tragic consequences. This clearly indicates a need for motherhood to be factored into supervision and sentence planning. Furthermore, an acknowledgement that engaging criminalised Mothers in supportive relationships requires understanding, compassion and resources.

The Mothers described finding it challenging to access or ask for support because of the fear of inviting additional unwanted surveillance and attention, which ultimately could potentially result in recall and/or the loss of their children. For some, this had devastating, enduring and intergenerational consequences.

It is important to note, some Mothers did ask for help, especially whilst in prison but were disappointed when the support accessed did not continue post-release. Which O'Malley (2018) identified as a key factor in post-prison relapse and recall. The Mother's accounts echo those findings and highlights the significance of and need for effective matricentric throughcare and post-prison support.

Clearly, it is essential that resettlement work starts within and continues through the prison gates and must involve supporting mothers and families using a matricentric-feminist approach. To meet mothers' needs more effectively in the challenging period of post-prison re-integration and resettlement would involve women's centres. Failure to do so will impact their ability to engage in rehabilitative supervision, which ultimately will further impact desistance, their children and wider society. This book fully demonstrates the 'ripple effect' of imprisoning mothers, as an enduring and long-term harm, with family and community wide impacts. Nevertheless, there is a need for further in-depth research concerning the relationship between motherhood and desistance.

The Mother's accounts provide evidence to support the view that there is merit in 'factoring-in' motherhood and maternal emotion when engaged in the rehabilitation and/or supervision of criminalised mothers. They reinforce Canton's (2015) argument that emotions have a role to play concerning the individual desistance of offenders, in this instance particularly maternal emotion. I believe the book also shows how the emotional literacy of criminal justice professionals plays a key role in the purposeful and effective support of mothers. By understanding the emotions associated with motherhood and maternal imprisonment, some custodians and supervisors contributed significantly to the effective rehabilitation of post-prison mothers. Where this was not present, Mothers' trauma and support needs were unmet, which in some instances resulted in a return to substance misuse and/or offending.

Facilitating the resources, time and space for mothers to explore the impact of their sentence in terms of their trauma and their resilience, would enable supervisors to better support mothers through their reintegration. It is particularly important to recognise, as evidenced by the Mothers' stories, how the impact of imprisonment on mothers can leave a specific and distinct trauma footprint, one which has an impact on their rehabilitation.

Currently the 'community' is lacking in terms of funding and resources, especially related to addictions, so that many women 'end up' in prison when it could have been avoided with timely and appropriate early intervention. However, whilst most studies exploring the imprisonment of mothers focus on the negative aspects of maternal incarceration, several studies identify that for some women it can provide a sense of respite. Most women in prison have 'trauma histories.' O'Malley (2018; 2020), O'Malley and Devaney (2015) and Soffer and Ajzenstadt (2010) found that, particularly for mothers whose pre-prison lives were marred by chaos, addiction and domestic abuse, prison could be a 'safe haven.' Soffer and Ajzenstadt (ibid) have described prison for such women as an 'opportunity' to repair themselves, to address the root causes of their offending and, without the responsibility of children, to gain access to therapeutic and practical support, which they argue mitigates some aspects of the anticipated pains of imprisonment. They cautiously described prison for the mothers in their study (ibid: 13) as a 'far better alternative to their former dire lives.' However, they also highlight that prison is an environment that is not one-dimensional and that, especially for mothers, the emotional response to and experience of prison, can be complex and contradictory.

Moore and Wahidin (2018) find it disturbing that prison is put forward as an appropriate response or solution to the many challenges that women face and that lead them to being criminalised. They state:

> 'To suggest that prison can resolve the significant problems that women can experience—prior to, during and after imprisonment—is to downplay its

punitive function, and to underestimate the pain and deprivation which lies at the heart of the incarceration process.' (ibid: 25)

Existing literature has contributed to our understanding of the gendered pains of imprisonment. Continuing this discussion, this book has explored and demonstrated how those pains persist for many years post-release. It has revealed the enduring impact of maternal imprisonment experienced by both mothers and their children, not least via their feelings of stigma and shame, resulting in mothers feeling diminished and children feeling tainted and stigmatised for having had a mother in prison.

Recommendations for Policy, Practice and Research

A broad umbrella recommendation is that criminal justice for women and how it is approached must be fundamentally reconsidered. In the face of significant and consistent failure to meet the needs of women and mothers, a commitment to improved social justice is required to address the issues and experiences I have described. Prison is a feminist issue of matricentric concern, not least because for women, especially mothers, the effects of criminalisation and imprisonment are experienced in a wider context of patriarchy, oppression, discrimination and disadvantage.

Prison replicates the outside-inside and as this book shows the effects of maternal imprisonment persist for decades, if not for life. As feminists we must challenge and replace the term 'female offender' with the more considered term 'criminalised women' or in the case of mothers 'criminalised mothers.' Doing so challenges the perception that once an offender always an offender, but also and importantly it leaves room for criticality in the discussion about how the woman/mother became criminalised in the first instance. We need to ask 'Was it right and just that she was criminalised and what was the role of the State, or the relevance of our social structures more broadly in her criminalisation?' Based on what I have already summarised my specific recommendations are:

1. Commitment to Social Justice

First and foremost, there must be a commitment to minimising opportunities for women to become criminalised, facilitated via improved social justice and early support. As this book reveals, there were many missed opportunities to support mothers much earlier as well as the impact of this. This requires supporting families and actively tackling inequalities, like food poverty, improving access to mental health and addiction/trauma support. Maintaining partnership working and early intervention for families requires a continued commitment from the Government in terms of resources and funding, which would reduce the risks of offending for mothers and its implications. The matricentric-feminist criminological lens I have employed has provided understanding for how multiply disadvantaged mothers often become criminalised quite unnecessarily. Thus, alongside improved social-justice, early support and diversion away from the CJS is essential. There must be a commitment to support and replicating the many successful, but still nationally varied Diversion and Deferred Caution/Charge Schemes[2] so reducing the numbers of criminalised women entering the system at all.

2. The Courts

Turning attention to the courts, magistrates (and it is most often magistrates who sentence women), *must* adhere to current guidelines (The Bangkok Rules) far more consistently than they currently do. There needs to be accountability of sentencers when they do fail to adhere to guidelines. The Mothers described horrendous experiences from the courts where inappropriate comments were made and guidelines were not followed. In order for the Courts to have a more compassionate, informed response to criminalised women and mothers, there should

---

2. Several CPS Areas have bespoke facilities providing tailored support to help address the particular needs of women and the drivers behind their criminal behaviour, e.g. drug or alcohol abuse; involvement in an abusive relationship. They are provided by both statutory and voluntary agencies. They may be, e.g. dedicated women's community projects or similar 'one-stop-shops.' Where such facilities exist, and a conditional caution may be an appropriate disposal, prosecutors should consider the suitability of the offender for a women specific condition, especially where a referral to a women's community project might lead to breaking their cycle of offending: see https://www.cps.gov.uk/legal-guidance/diverting-women-offenders-and-women-specific-condition-within-national-conditional

be some consideration given to 'women only' courts, where magistrates in those courts have *chosen* to sit. Furthermore, have undergone gender specific, matricentric and trauma-informed training concerning women's pathways into and out of crime and the impact of imprisonment on women. Furthermore, no mother with dependent children should ever be sentenced unexpectedly or without a pre-sentence report (PSR). In the case of *all* mothers, if a custodial sentence is imperative and likely, there must be a period of deferment to allow mothers to make provision for her family and prepare their children. Immediate custody and/remand should cease, and remands in custody should *never* be used if a custodial sentence would not be a *definite* outcome at sentencing on the face of what is known so far, as currently over 60 per cent of women remanded do not go on to receive a custodial sentence (PRT, 2019). This would avoid situations as described by the Mothers whereby they were imprisoned not knowing who would collect her child from school, which had a dangerous and detrimental impact on the Mothers' mental-wellbeing. Pregnant and new Mothers described the additional harm and disproportionate harm caused by their imprisonment. This could be avoided by a cessation of sending pregnant mothers to prison. MBUs should be community-based and modelled on matricentric-feminist principles of support and empowerment.

3. Prison

If we are to continue to send women to prison (and the preferred option is wherever possible that we don't), the additional trauma caused by maternal-imprisonment and the associated disproportionate harms described by the Mothers must be addressed. Large women's prison as we know them should be replaced with smaller, community-based establishments and modelled on matricentric-feminist principles of support and empowerment. In the meantime, the institutional thoughtlessness and uncompassionate policies and practices concerning motherhood evidenced in the text must be acknowledged, challenged and addressed. Following matricentric training for prison staff, compassion and understanding must underpin work with all mothers in prison. Motherhood must be factored into sentence planning in terms of consideration of needs, but also outcomes and preparation for release. Definitions of who is eligible for ROTL and child care leave must be broadened to include grandmothers, who described feeling 'excluded' from such provisions. Consideration must be given for how to improve and maintain contact and relationships with children and caregivers (e.g. improved in-cell and video calling facilities—especially important if Covid-19 restrictions remain in place, and welcoming child friendly visiting spaces, and subsidised telephone contact with children). All of which would positively assist and support maternal identity, role and wellbeing. It is imperative that reception phone calls occur. Delays in facilitating contact with children and caregivers should be avoided at all costs if we are to reduce the trauma, self-harm and suicidal thoughts evidenced by the Mothers. There must be an urgent review of the management of all female prisoners particularly concerning open/closed conditions and the regime restrictions, which the Mothers powerfully described impacted on theirs and sometimes their children's wellbeing. To reduce the additional punishment and harm caused to mothers and their children prison-moves at short notice must be avoided and should never occur when an imminent visit with children is booked. Consideration must be given of how best to support mothers who are involved in proceedings involving their children and 'bridges' facilitated between inside and outside support resources and caregivers, especially in preparation for release. This could be achieved by an expansion of the prison social-work role. Programmes for mothers, over and above parenting programmes must become commonplace in prison, as must 'safe' spaces to facilitate supportive relationships and conversations about motherhood and to prepare for release. Which the Mothers described as so important to their wellbeing. Social workers and permanently funded family engagement workers must have a presence in all female establishments.

4. Family and Caregivers

The Mothers described struggling with the family relationships during and after prison. To better support Mothers and families and improve outcomes, there must be improved support for caregivers and prisoner's families during the period and of incarceration and post-release.

Mothers described how providing formal support for families engaged in caregiving for children of imprisoned parents, especially financial support, would improve the stability of caregiver relationships and reduce the tensions between caregivers and imprisoned mothers. This would result in better co-parenting partnerships and improved outcomes for mothers and their children. Furthermore, as the Mothers stated, positive caregiving relationships would improve their mental health and wellbeing in custody, enabling them to engage more fully in sentence planning and rehabilitation.

5. Post-release Support

The Mothers described a lack of post-release support, regarding their maternal identity and role. Post-release support must be gender-specific and must be mindful of the challenges faced by reintegrating mothers. Motherhood, maternal emotions and maternal identity must be factored into supervision support and release planning. Wherever possible post-release and supervised mothers should be supported by women's centres. In order to provide effective support to criminalised women, women's centres must be centrally and permanently funded in order to deliver good quality, multi-agency effective support. There needs to be some recognition of the enduring impact of maternal imprisonment with the possibility of ongoing support (for mothers no longer subject to licence), or an outreach for post-release support attached to and delivered by women's centres. Probation staff must receive guidance and training in relation to the supervision of mothers and have an increased awareness of the need to work in a trauma-informed and mindful way with post-release mothers and mothers under supervision. All of the above would contribute to improved outcomes and assist mothers. Mitigating some of the challenges described in this book.

6. Multi-agency Working

The Mothers' narratives clearly demonstrated the multiple missed opportunities for support, despite repeated requests by them. There must be a 'joined-up' whole system approach to improving the care and outcomes for criminalised mothers involving all of the agencies that make up the social and criminal justice systems. This would seek to minimise the many missed opportunities to support mothers and divert and support mothers away from criminality. Throughcare, consistency, compassion, understanding and support are key to working positively and effectively with mothers in the CJS. Where it was done well, the Mothers were able to articulate the positive impact it had on their lives, equally where it was not, the consequences were vast. Agencies working together, must seek to empower women and mothers to move forwards with positivity and to pursue opportunities as opposed to focusing only on supervision and compliance.

7. Inclusion, Voice and Valuing Lived Experience
Many of the Mothers expressed a desire to work in the CJS with women in similar situations. Several went on to do so, some in leadership roles where they were able to guide and influence positive practice. In line with matricentric-feminist principles of empowerment and voice, there must be a commitment to involving service users and others with lived experience to inform, shape and lead policy and practice concerning criminalised women. Matricentric feminism and feminist principles provide the scaffold on which future developments can be framed.

8. More Research Around Women who are Racially Minoritised
Whilst writing this book I uncovered several findings worthy of further study, including the experiences of BAME mothers. An examination of the intersectionality of motherhood, race and CJS processes would be an important contribution to the overall understanding of maternal imprisonment. This book confirms and further reveals that there is a relationship between motherhood and desistance — but it is a complicated one and again an area worthy of further study. Investigation concerning motherhood and desistance, particularly combined with maternal experiences of supervision and intersectionality would contribute significantly to making the case for alternatives to custody for most mothers who commit crime

9. Extending Consultation and Training for All Those Working with Mothers in the CJS

Motherhood, maternal identity, role and emotions should be factored into all work with criminalised mothers. All prisons and probation services should consider and be willing to engage with consultation with relevant experts and organizations in how best they could work positively with such mothers. Areas for improvement and the sharing of good practice should be formally pursued, and all staff working with mothers should have profession specific training on how to work effectively, mindfully, compassionately and safely with mothers (all mothers; to include grandmothers and mothers whose children have been removed from their care).[3] Prisons and the Probation Service should appoint a named individual responsible for coordinating policy and practice concerning mothers in prison and under supervision — this is over and above existing policy guidance regarding pregnant and new mothers in prison.

10. Research

Embracing O'Reilly's (2006 2016) ideals of empowered motherhood into criminology, thereby creating a matricentric-feminist criminology, has facilitated the voices of criminalised mothers being heard, and must continue to do so. This would ensure criminalised mothers views and experiences are used to directly inform policy and practice. Motherhood could then contribute to both rehabilitation and desistance by becoming a site of reflection, agency and change in a more constructive and productive way than it has previously been viewed. This would be best achieved by the acceptance and inclusion of matricentric-feminist criminology and MF scholars by wider academic communities in motherhood and criminological schools of thought.

11. Feminist Principles in Research

What I describe in this book can be seen as a call to the research community to truly think about what constitutes feminist research — there are too many examples of 'feminist' studies which do not fully reflect the

---

3. See 9 also

principles of this approach in their design, product or dissemination of findings. Feminist principles and methodology provide a blueprint for how feminist research, in terms of methods, tools and analysis should proceed. As stated by Harding 'the connections between epistemology, methodology and methods are an important aspect of what makes research feminist' (Harding, 2019: 2).

A Few Closing Thoughts

I hope I have demonstrated a need for a genuine commitment to critically examine and challenge failings in policies, institutions and structures. Which currently fail women by individually problematising women and 'intervene harmfully in women's lives' (Clarke and Chadwick 2018: 64). The 'hidden role' and, arguably hidden harms of institutions, like education, the welfare system, police, courts, Social Services, and prisons, must be examined and challenged. This is vital in order to understand how such institutions influence and shape women's lives by exacerbating and reproducing marginalisation and discrimination, making criminalisation more likely. As the book shows, it is rarely simply a matter of 'women making better choices,' which is an oft cited judicial response to female criminality. There have to be real possibilities of other 'choices' to make.

The Mothers described what amounted 'institutional thoughtlessness' (Crawley, 2005), regarding their status and role as criminalised, imprisoned and post-release mothers. This thoughtlessness impacted them in many ways and at every stage of the CJS. The theoretical approach facilitated an understanding of how and why once criminalised the Mothers absorbed society's perception of them as troubled and troublesome. Finding the blame for their imprisonment solely within themselves. However, this self-blame and subsequent self-imposed penance often obscured the root causes of the Mothers' criminality and subsequently left them vulnerable to a broad failure to recognise their pathways into crime and out of crime. Compounded by a lack of informed support.

Furthermore, it had enduring consequences for the Mothers in terms of long-lasting trauma, relationships and outcomes. The challenges to maternal-role and identity from prison as described by the Mothers continued post-release. They felt unsupported, surveilled and mistrusted. Their preoccupation with their re-entry and maternal re-negotiations made it challenging to engage in rehabilitation work or rehabilitative relationships. The failure of custodians and supervisors to take into account their maternal identity and role was a significant factor in the Mothers' inability or reluctance to fully engage.

I hope the book offers new insight, understanding and recommendations on how best to work with mothers affected by the CJS and a greater understanding of why this is important. Furthermore, that it demonstrates how understanding the enduring impact of maternal imprisonment is crucial to the development of compassionate and appropriate support for mothers before, during and after prison. Understanding the social, political and criminal justice context of mothers who break the law will facilitate an appreciation of the discrimination and inequality mothers who have fallen afoul of the law have historically faced, and continue to do so (Clark and Chadwick, 2018; Moore and Wahidin, 2018).

In a few words, what appears here is further proof, if it were needed, of the different ways in which women experience prison to men. This is especially true of mothers, and therefore, without change, women will continue to be damaged by prison, mothers will continue to be separated from their children, and many are destined to remain trapped in the cycles of guilt, trauma and harm.

Furthermore, children will continue to be deeply affected by not only the harm caused to their mothers, but also by their own enduring harm, representing the layered persistent pains of maternal imprisonment. For criminalised women and mothers it is essential to accept the matricentric-feminist position that without social justice there cannot be effective or morally acceptable criminal justice. The pursuit of change must actively facilitate and prioritise the voices of those who have experienced injustice and incarceration in order for 'individuals to speak truth to power' (Scraton 2007 cited in Clarke and Chadwick 2018: 65).

It is fitting to conclude by quoting one of the Mothers, Dee, who provides a timely reminder of the strength and resilience of criminalised women and the need for us all to do better:

'It was awful, it was shit, it hurt, and I'm scarred, my life was chaotic and complicated before prison. My life as a mother in prison was broken. I've experienced more abuse in my life than most people do in a lifetime. I was an addict; I suffer from nightmares and trauma and depression. All of that is true, but don't just call me complex, don't just call me vulnerable. I'm strong but I want to be stronger. I'm free but I want to be freer. I've moved on but I want to go further. I want society and services to support me not just label me, I want people to help me create chances for others not just give one to me, I don't want to be held back I want to be driven forwards.'

References and Bibliography

Abbott, L. (2015) A Pregnant Pause: Expecting in the Prison Estate, in L. Baldwin (auth/ ed.) *Mothering Justice: Working with Mothers in Criminal and Social Justice Settings*, Sherfield on Loddon: Waterside Press.

Abbott, L. (2018) The Incarcerated Pregnancy: An Ethnographic Study of Perinatal Women in English Prisons, Doctoral thesis, University of Hertfordshire.

Abbott, L. and Scott, T. (2019) Reflections on Researcher Departure: Closure of Prison Relationships in Ethnographic Research, *Nursing Ethics*, 26(5), pp. 1424–1441.

Abbott, L., Scott, T., Thomas, H. and Weston, K. (2020) Pregnancy and Childbirth in English Prisons: Institutional Ignominy and the Pains of Imprisonment, *Sociology of Health and Illness*, 42(3), pp. 660–675.

Abrams, L. S. and Curran, L. (2011) Maternal Identity Construction Among Low-income Mothers with Symptoms of Postpartum Depression, *Qualitative Health Research*, 21(3), pp. 373–385.

Agar, M. (1996) *The Professional Stranger: An Informal Introduction to Ethnography*, San Diego, CA: Academic Press.

Aiello, B. and McQueeny, K. (2016) How Can You Live Without Your Kids? Distancing From and Embracing the Stigma of 'Incarcerated Mother,' *Journal of Prison Education and Re-entry*, 3(1), pp. 32–49.

Ainsworth, M.D. (1962) The Effects of Maternal Deprivation: A Review—Findings and Controversy in the Context of Research Strategy, in *Deprivation of Maternal Care: A Reassessment of Effects*, Public Health Papers, 14, Geneva: World Health Organization.

Annison, J., Brayford, J. and Deering, J. (eds.) (2015) *Women and Criminal Justice: From the Corston Report to Transforming Rehabilitation*, Bristol: Policy Press

Arditti, J. A. (2018) Parental Incarceration and Family Inequality in the United States in R. Condry and P. Schaarf-Smith (eds.), *Prison, Punishment and the Family: Towards a New Sociology of Punishment*, New York: Oxford University Press, pp. 41–57.

Arditti, J. and Few, A. (2006) Maternal Distress and Women's Re-entry into Family and Community Life, *Family Process*, 47(3), pp. 303–21.

Arendell, T. (2000) Conceiving and Investigating Motherhood: The Decade's Scholarship, *Journal of Marriage and Family*, 62(4), pp. 1192–1207.

Bachman, R., Kerrison, E. M., Paternoster, R., Smith, L. and O'Connell, D. (2016) The Complex Relationship Between Motherhood and Desistance, *Women and Criminal Justice*, 26(3), pp. 212–231.

Bailey, A. (1995) Mothering, Diversity and Peace: Comments on Sara Ruddick's Feminist Maternal Peace Politics, *Journal of Social Philosophy*, 25(1), pp. 162–82.

Baldwin, L. (auth/ed.) (2015) *Mothering Justice: Working with Mothers in Criminal and Social Justice Settings,* Sherfield on Loddon: Waterside Press.

Baldwin, L. (2017) Tainted Love: The Impact of Prison on Maternal Identity, *Prison Service Journal*, September, 233, pp. 28–34.

Baldwin, L. (2018) Motherhood Disrupted: Reflections of Post-Prison Mothers in Maternal Geographies (Sp edn.) Maternal Geographies (Guest Editor: Catherine Robinson), *Emotion Space and Society*, 26, pp. 49–56.

Baldwin, L. (2019) Excluded from Good Motherhood: Reflections of Mothers After Prison in C. Byvelds and H. Jackson (eds.), *Motherhood and Social Exclusion*, Ontario: Demeter Press.

Baldwin, L. (2021) Motherhood Challenged: A Matricentric Feminist Study Exploring the Impact of Maternal Imprisonment on Maternal Identity and Role, Doctoral thesis, De Montfort University, Leicester: https://dora.dmu.ac.uk/bitstream/handle/2086/20813/Baldwin%20L.%20Final%20Thesis%20published%20%281%29%20%281%29.pdf?sequence=1&isAllowed=y; Executive summary: https://dora.dmu.ac.uk/bitstream/handle/2086/21372/Executive%20Summary%20PhD%20LBaldwin%20PDF.pdf?sequence=3&isAllowed=y

Baldwin, L. and Abbott, L. (2020) Why Do We Still Imprison Pregnant Women? Russell Webster Blog: https://www.Russellwebster.com/Pregnant-Prisoners/

Baldwin, L. and Epstein, R. (2017) *Short but Not Sweet: A Study of the Impact of Short Sentences on Mothers and Their Children,* Oakdale Trust, Leicester: De Montfort University.

Baldwin, L., O'Malley, S. and Galway, K. (2015) Mothers Addicted: Working with Complexity, in L. Baldwin (auth/ed.), *Mothering Justice: Working with Mothers in Criminal and Social Justice Settings*, Sherfield on Loddon: Waterside Press.

Baldwin, L. and O'Malley, S. (2019) Mothering Interrupted: Mother Child Separation via Imprisonment in England and Ireland, in F. Donson and A. Parks (eds.), *Presenting A Children's Rights Approach to Parental Imprisonment,* Hampshire: Palgrave Macmillan.

Baldwin, L. and Quinlan, C. (2018) Within These Walls: Reflections of Women in and After Prison — An Insight into the Experience of Women Imprisoned in Britain and Ireland, *Prison Service Journal*, 240.

Baldwin, M. (ed.) (2000) *The Use of Self in Therapy* (2nd ed.), New York: Hawthorne.

Barnes, C. (2015) Damned If You Do, Damned If You Don't: Frontline Social Worker Perspective in L. Baldwin (auth/ed.) (2015), *Mothering Justice: Working with Mothers in Criminal and Social Justice Settings,* Sherfield on Loddon: Waterside Press.

Barnes, L. and Cunningham-Stringer, E. (2014) Is Motherhood Important? Imprisoned Women's Maternal Experiences Before and During Confinement and their Post-Release Expectations, *Feminist Criminology,* 991, pp. 3–23.

Bassin, D., Honey, M. and Kaplan, M. M. (1994) *Representations of Motherhood*, New Haven: Yale University Press.

Bateman, T., Hazel, N. and Wright, S. (2013) Resettlement of Young People Leaving Custody: Lessons from Literature, London: Beyond Youth http://www. beyondyouthcustody.net/resources/publications/categories/all/

Baunach, P. J. (1985) *Mothers in Prison,* New Brunswick, New Jersey: Transaction Books.

Beresford, S. (2018) 'What About Me?' the Impact on Children When Mothers are involved in the Criminal Justice System, Prison Reform Trust: http://www. prisonreformtrust.org.uk/portals/0/documents/what%20about%20me.pdf

Bloom, B. (1992) Women Offenders: Issues, Concerns and Strategies, Paper Presented to the Western Society of Criminology, San Diego CA, February.

Booth, N. (2017) *Maternal Imprisonment: A Family Sentence*, Bristol: Policy Press/Social Policy Association.

Booth, N. (2017) Prison and the Family: An Exploration of Maternal Imprisonment from A Family-Centred Perspective, Doctoral thesis, University of Bath, Department of Social and Policy Sciences.

Booth, N. (2018) Maintaining Family Ties: The Disparities Between Policy and Practice Following Maternal Imprisonment in England and Wales in L. Gordon (ed.) (2018) *Contemporary Research and Analysis on the Children of Prisoners: Invisible Children*, Cambridge Scholars: Newcastle-upon-Tyne.

Booth, N. (2020) *Maternal Imprisonment and Family Life: From the Caregiver's Perspective*, Bristol: Policy Press.

Bosworth, M. (1996) Resistance and Compliance in Women's Prisons: Towards A Critique of Legitimacy, *Critical Criminology,* 7, pp. 5–19.

Bosworth, M. (1999) *Engendering Resistance: Agency and Power in Women's Prisons*, London: Routledge.

Bosworth, M. (2000) Confining Femininity: A History of Gender, Power and Imprisonment, *Theoretical Criminology*, 4(3), pp. 265–284.

Bowlby, J. (1946) Psychology and Democracy, *Political Quarterly*, 17, pp. 61–75.

Bowlby, J. (1951) *Maternal Care and Mental Health*, Geneva: World Health Organization.

Bowlby, J. (1953) *Child Care and the Growth of Love*, London: Penguin Books.

Bowlby, J. (1957) Symposium on the Contribution of Current Theories to an Understanding of Child Development, *British Journal of Medical Psychology*, 30(4), pp. 230–240.

Bowlby, J. (1958) *The Nature of the Child's Tie to His Mother, International Journal of Psychoanalysis*, 39, pp. 350–373.

Bowlby, J. (1969) *Attachment. Attachment and Loss: Vol. 1. Loss*, New York: Basic Books.

Bowlby, J. (1988) *A Secure Base*, Abingdon: Routledge.

Bradley, A. (2017) Trauma-Informed Practice: Exploring the Role of Adverse Life Experiences on the Behaviour of Offenders and the Effectiveness of Associated Criminal Justice Strategies, Doctoral Dissertation, Northumbria University.

Bradley, A., Day, K. and Mahon, R. (2021) Exploring Shame Love and Healing Within Women's Rehabilitation: An Analysis of Trauma Specific Intervention in I. Masson, L. Baldwin and N. Booth (eds.), *Critical Reflections from the Women, Families, Crime and Justice Research Network*, Bristol: Policy Press.

Bradley, R. and Davino, K. (2002) Women's Perception of the Prison Environment: When 'Prison Is the Safest Place I've Ever Been,' *Psychology of Women Quarterly*, 26(4), pp. 351–359.

Breheny, M. and Stephens, C. (2010) Youth or Disadvantage? The Construction of Teenage Mothers in Medical Journals, *Culture, Health and Sexuality*, 12(3), pp. 307–322.

Brown, M. and Bloom, B. (2009) Re-Entry and Renegotiating Motherhood: Maternal Identity and Success on Parole, *Crime and Delinquency*, 55, pp. 313–36.

Buncy, S. and Ahmed, I. (2019) Sisters in Desistance: Community-based Solutions for Muslim Women Post-Prison: https://www.studocu.com/en-gb/document/university-of-east-london/theoretical-criminology/sisters-in-desistance-final/15355015

Burgess-Procter, A. (2014) Methodological and Ethical Issues in Feminist Research with Abused Women: Reflections on Participants Vulnerability, *Women's Studies International Forum*, 124–134.

Caddle, D. and Crisp, D. (1997) Imprisoned Women and Mothers, Home Office Research Study 162, London: Home Office.

Canton, R. (2015) Crime Punishment and the Moral Emotions: Righteous Minds and their Attitudes Towards Punishment, *Punishment and Society*, 17(1) pp. 54–72.

Canton, R. and Dominey, J. (2020) Punishment and Care Reappraised in L. Gelsthorpe, P. Mody and B. Sloan (eds.), *Spaces of Care*, Oxford: Hart.

Carlen, P. (1983) *Women's Imprisonment: A Study in Social Control*, London: Routledge and Kegan Paul.

Carlen, P. (ed.) (1985) *Criminal Women*, Cambridge: Polity Press.

Carlen, P. (1994) Why Study Women's Imprisonment? Or Anyone Else's? An indefinite Article in R. D. King and M. Maguire (eds.), *Prisons in Context*, Clarendon Press, pp. 131–40.

Carlen, P. (1998) *Sledgehammer: Women's Imprisonment at the Millennium*, Hampshire: Palgrave Macmillan.

Carlen, P. (2002) *Women and Punishment: The Struggle for Justice*, Cullompton: Willan.

Carlen, P. (2004) Risk and Responsibility in Women's Prisons, *Current Issues in Criminal Justice*, 5(3) pp. 258–266.

Carlen, P. and Worrall, A. (1987) *Gender, Crime and Justice*, Milton Keynes, Open University Press.

Carlen, P. and Worrall, A. (2004) *Analysing Women's Imprisonment*, Cullompton: Willan.

Carlton, B. and Seagrove, M. (eds.) (2013) *Women Exiting Prison: Critical Essays on Gender, Post-Release Support and Survival*, Oxford: Routledge.

Casey-Acedevedo, K., Bakken, T. and Karle, A. (2003) Children Visiting Mothers in Prison: The Effects on Mothers' Behaviour and Disciplinary Maladjustment, *Australian and New Zealand Journal of Criminology*, 37(3), pp. 418–430.

Chesney-Lind, M. and Eliason, M. (2006) From Invisible to Incorrigible: The Demonisation of Marginalised Women and Girls, *Crime, Media, Culture*, 2(1), pp. 29–47.

Chesney-Lind, M., and Pasko, L. (2004) *The Female Offender: Girls, Women, and Crime*, London: Sage.

Chesney-Lind, M. and Pasko, L. (eds.) (2013) *Girls, Women, and Crime: Selected Readings*, Thousand Oaks, CA: Sage.

Clarke, B. and Chadwick, K. (2018) From Troubled Women to Failing Institutions: The Necessary Narrative Shift for the Decarceration of Women Post Corston in L.

Moore, P. Scraton and A. Wahidin (2018) *Women's Imprisonment and the Case for Abolition: Critical Reflections of Corston Ten Years On*, London: Routledge.

Codd, H. (2004) Prisoners' Families: Issues in Law and Policy, Institute of Advanced Legal Studies, Guest Lecture, 7 June, London.

Codd, H. (2008) (2013) *In the Shadow of Prison: Families, Imprisonment and Criminal Justice*, Devon and Portland: Willan Publishing.

Collins, C. (2020) Is Maternal Guilt a Cross-National Experience? *Qualitative Sociology*, pp. 1–29.

Collins, P. H. (1994) *Motherwork. Mothering: Ideology, Experience and Agency*, New York: Routledge.

Collins, P. H. (2005) Black Women and Motherhood in *Motherhood and Space* (pp. 149–159), New York: Palgrave Macmillan.

Comfort, M. (2008) *Doing Time Together*, Chicago: University of Chicago Press.

Cooper, L. and Rogers, C. (2015) Mothering and 'Insider' Dilemmas: Feminist Sociologists in the Research Process. Sociological Research online: http://www.socresearchonline.org.uk/20/2/5.html

Corston, J. (2007) The Corston Report: A Report By Baroness Jean Corston of A Review of Women With Particular Vulnerabilities in the Criminal Justice System, London: Home Office http://www.justice.gov.uk/publications/docs/corston-report-march-2007.pdf

Corston, J. (2011) Women in the Penal System: Second Report on Women with Particular Vulnerabilities in the Criminal Justice System, London: Howard League for Penal Reform.

Couvrette, A., Brochu, S., and Plourde, C. (2016), The 'Deviant Good Mother,' *Journal of Drug Issues*, 46(4), pp. 292–307.

Covington, S. (2007) Working With Substance Abusing Mothers: A Trauma-informed, Gender-responsive Approach, *The Source*, 16(1), pp. 1–11.

Covington, S. and Bloom, E. (2003) Gendered Justice: Women in the Criminal Justice System in E. Bloom (2003) *Gendered Justice: Addressing Female Offenders*, Carolina Academic Press.

Crawley, E. (2004) Emotion and Performance: Prison Officers and the Presentations of Self in Prisons, *Punishment and Society*, 6(4), pp. 411–427.

Crawley, E. (2005) Institutional Thoughtlessness in Prisons and Its Impacts on the Day-to-Day Prison Lives of Elderly Men, *Journal of Contemporary Criminal Justice*, 21(4), pp. 350–363.

Crenshaw, K. W. (2017) *On Intersectionality: Essential Writings*, New Press.

Crewe, B. (2011) Soft Power in Prison: Implications for Staff—Prisoner Relationships, Liberty and Legitimacy, *European Journal of Criminology*, 8(6), pp. 455–468.

Crewe, B., Hulley, S. and Wright, S. (2017), The Gendered Pains of Life Imprisonment, *British Journal of Criminology*, 57(6), pp. 1359–1378.

Crewe, B., Bennett, P., Smith, A. and Warr, J. (2014) The Emotional Geography of Prison Life, *Theoretical Criminology*, 18(1), pp. 56–74.

Daly, K., and Bordt, R. L. (1995) Sex Effects and Sentencing: An Analysis of the Statistical Literature, *Justice Quarterly*, 12, pp. 141–175.

Davies, S. E., Cook, S. and Davies, S. (eds.) (1999) *Harsh Punishment: International Experiences of Women's Imprisonment*, University Press of New England.

De Beauvoir, S. (2009) [1949] *The Second Sex*, Translated by Constance Borde and Sheila Malovany-Chevallier, Random House: Alfred A. Knopf.

Devlin, A. (1998) *Invisible Women*, Winchester: Waterside Press.

Dhami, M. K., Ayton, P. and Loewenstein, G. (2007) Adaptation to Imprisonment: Indigenous or Imported? *Criminal Justice and Behavior*, 34(8), pp. 1085–1100.

Di Quinzio, P. (1999) *The Impossibility of Motherhood: Feminism, Individualism, and the Problem of Mothering*, London: Routledge.

Dolan, R. (2016) Pregnant Women, Mothers, Mother and Baby Units and Mental Health in Prison, *Psypag Quarterly*, 100, pp. 32–35.

Dominey, J. and Gelsthorpe, L. (2020) Resettlement and the Case for Women, *Probation Journal*, 67(4), pp. 393–409.

Doucet, A. (1998) Interpreting Mother-Work: Linking Ontology, Theory, Methodology and Personal Biography, *Canadian Woman Studies* (18), pp. 52–58.

Doucet, A. and Mauthner N. (2006) Feminist Methodologies and Epistemologies in C. D. Bryant and D. L. Peck (eds.), *Handbook of 21st Century Sociology*, pp. 26–32, Thousand Oaks, CA.

Duncombe, J. and Jessop, J. (2002) Doing Rapport and the Ethics of 'Faking Friendship' in T. Miller, M. Birch, and M Mauthner (eds.), *Ethics in Qualitative Research*, London: Sage, pp. 108–121.

Dwyer, S. C. and Buckle, J. L. (2009) The Space Between: On Being an Insider-Outsider in Qualitative Research, *International Journal of Qualitative Methods*, 8(1), pp. 54–63.

Easterling, B. A., Feldmeyer, B. and Presser, L. (2019) Narrating Mother Identities from Prison, *Feminist Criminology*, 14(5), pp. 519–539.

Eaton, M. (1986) *Justice for Women? Family, Court, and Social Control*, Milton Keynes: Open University Press.

Eaton, M. (1993) *Women After Prison*, Milton Keynes: Open University Press.

Edwards, S. (1984) *Women on Trial: A Study of the Female Suspect, Defendant, and Offender in the Criminal Law and Criminal Justice System*, Dover, New Hampshire; Manchester University Press.

Ellison, L. and Munro, V. E. (2017) Taking Trauma Seriously: Critical Reflections on the Criminal Justice Process, *International Journal of Evidence and Proof*, 21(3), pp. 183–208.

Enos, S. (2001) *Mothering From the Inside: Parenting in A Women's Prison*, New York: State University of New York Press.

Epstein, R. (2012) Mothers in Prison: The Sentencing of Mothers and the Rights of the Child, *Coventry Law Journal*, December 2012, Special Issue: Research Report.

Farmer, M. (2017) *The Importance of Strengthening Prisoner's Family Ties to Reduce Reoffending and Prevent Intergenerational Crime*, London: Ministry of Justice.

Farmer, M. (2019) *The Importance of Strengthening Female Offenders' Family and Other Relationships to Prevent Reoffending and Reduce Intergenerational Crime*, Ministry of Justice: London.

Fawcett Society (2004) *A Report of the Fawcett Society's Commission on Women and the Criminal Justice System*, London: Fawcett Society.

Feinman, C. (1994) *Women in the Criminal Justice System* (3rd edn.), USA: Preager.

Finch, J. (1993) *'It's great to have someone to talk to': Ethics and Politics of Interviewing Women*, Milton Keynes: Open University Press.

Flynn, C. (2014) Getting There and Being There, Visits to Prisons in Victoria: The Experiences of Women Prisoners and their Children, *Probation Journal*, 61(2), pp. 176–191.

Foucault, M. (1977) *Discipline and Punish*, New York: Vintage Books.

Freud, S. (1941) Splitting of the Ego in the Defensive Process, *International Journal of Psychoanalysis*.

Friedan, B. (1963) *The Feminine Mystique*, London: Penguin Books.

Garcia-Hallett, J. (2019) Maternal Identities and Narratives of Motherhood: A Qualitative Exploration of Women's Pathways Into and Out of Offending, *Feminist Criminology*, 14(2), pp. 214–240.

Garey, A. I. (1995) Constructing Motherhood on the Night Shift: 'Working Mothers' as 'Stay at home Moms,' *Qualitative Sociology*, 18, pp. 415–317.

Garland, D. (2012) *The Culture of Control: Crime and Social Order in Contemporary Society,* Chicago: University of Chicago Press.

Gelsthorpe, L (2004) Back to Basics in Crime Control: Weaving in Women, *Critical Review of International Social and Political Philosophy,* 7(2), pp. 76–103.

Gelsthorpe, L. (2007) Sentencing and Gender in R. Sheehan, G. McIvor and C. Trotter (eds.), *What Works with Female Offenders,* Cullompton: Willan Publishing.

Gelsthorpe, L. and Hedderman, C. (2012) Providing for Women Offenders: The Risks of Adopting A Payment by Results Approach, *Probation Journal,* 59(4), pp. 374–390.

Gelsthorpe, L. and Morris, A. (1988) Feminism and Criminology in Britain, *British Journal of Criminology,* 28(2), pp. 93–110.

Gelsthorpe, L. and Morris, A. (1990) *Feminist Perspectives in Criminology,* New York: Open University Press.

Gelsthorpe, L. and Morris, A. (2002) Women's Imprisonment in England and Wales: A Penal Paradox, *Criminal Justice,* 2(3), pp. 277–301.

Genders, E. and Player, E. (1990) Women Lifers: Assessing the Experience, *Prison Journal,* 70(1), pp. 46–57.

Gilbert, P. (2000) The Relationship of Shame, Social Anxiety and Depression: The Role of the Evaluation of Social Rank, *Clinical Psychology and Psychotherapy,* 7, pp. 174–189.

Gillies, V. (2006) *Marginalised Mothers: Exploring Working Class Experiences of Parenting,* London: Routledge.

Giordano, P. C., Cernkovich, S. A., and Rudolph, J. L. (2002) Gender, Crime, and Desistance: Toward A Theory of Cognitive Transformation, *American Journal of Sociology,* 107, pp. 990–1064.

Goffman, E. (1959) *The Presentation of Self in Everyday Life,* Garden City, NY: Doubleday Anchor.

Goffman, E. (1961) *Asylums,* London: Penguin.

Goffman, E. (1961) On the Characteristics of Total Institutions, Paper Presented at a Symposium on Preventive and Social Psychiatry.

Goffman, E. (1963) *Stigma: Notes on the Management of Spoiled Identity,* London: Prentice Hall.

Goffman, E. (1977) The Arrangement Between the Sexes, *Theory and Society,* 4(3), pp. 301–331.

Gomm, R. (2013) What Will 'Count' and Be Transformed for Women in the Criminal Justice System? *British Journal of Community Justice,* 11(2–3), pp. 153–157.

Grabe, M. E., Trager, K. D., Lear, M. and Rauch, J. (2006) Gender in Crime News: A Case Study Test of the Chivalry Hypothesis, *Mass Communication and Society,* 9(2), pp. 137–163.

Gunn, A. and Samuels, G. (2020) Promoting Recovery Identities Among Mothers with Histories of Addiction: Strategies of Family Engagement, *Family Process*, 59, pp. 94–110.

Hackett, L. (2015) Working with Women and Mothers Experiencing Mental Distress—Creating A Safe Place for Constructive Conversations in L. Baldwin (auth/ed.) (2015), *Mothering Justice: Working with Mothers in Criminal and Social Justice Settings,* Sherfield on Loddon: Waterside Press.

Haidt, J. (2003) The Moral Emotions in R. J. Davidson, K. R. Scherer and H. Hill Goldsmith (eds.) *Handbook of Affective Sciences*, Oxford: Oxford University Press, pp. 852–70.

Hairston, C. F. (1991) Family Ties During Imprisonment: Important to Whom and For What? *Journal of Sociology and Social Welfare*, 18, pp. 87–104.

Hairston, C. F. (2003) Prisoners and Their Families: Parenting Issues During incarceration in J. Travis, and M. Waul (eds.), *Prisoners Once Removed: The Impact of Incarceration and Re-entry on Children, Families, and Communities*, pp. 259–282, Washington, DC: Urban institute Press.

Hammersley, M. and Atkinson, P. (2007) *Ethnography: Principles in Practice* (3rd edn.), London: Tavistock.

Harding, N. A. (2020) Co-Constructing Feminist Research: Ensuring Meaningful Participation While Researching the Experiences of Criminalised Women, *Methodological Innovations*, 13(2).

Harding, S. (1987) Is there A Feminist Method? in S. Harding (ed.), *Feminism and Methodology: Social Science Issues,* Bloomington: Indiana University Press, pp. 1–14.

Hayes, M. O. (2009) The Lived Experience of Mothering After Prison, *Journal of Forensic Nursing*, 5(4), pp. 228–236.

Hays, S. (1996) *The Cultural Contradictions of Motherhood,* New Haven, CT: Yale University Press.

Hedderman, C. (2012) *Empty Cells or Empty Words: Government Policy on Reducing the Number of Women Going to Prison*, London: Criminal Justice Alliance.

Hedderman, C. and Hough, M. (1994) *Does the Criminal Justice System Treat Men and Women Differently?* London: Home Office.

Hedderman, C. and Jolliffe, D. (2015) The Impact of Prison for Women on the Edge: Paying the Price for Wrong Decisions, *Victims and Offenders*, 10(2): 24.

Heidensohn, F. (1996) *Women and Crime*, London: Macmillan International.

Held, V. (1995) The Meshing of Care and Justice, *Hypatia*, 10(2), pp. 128–132.

Henley, N. M. (1977) *Body Politics: Power, Sex and Nonverbal Communication*, Englewood Cliffs, NJ: Prentice-Hall.

Hochschild, A. (1983) *The Presentation of Emotion*, Thousand Oaks, CA: Sage.

Hogg, M., Terry, D. and White, K. (1995) A Tale of Two Theories: A Critical Comparison of Identity Theory with Social Identity Theory, *Social Psychology Quarterly*, 58(10) pp. 2307–2787.

Hornsey, M. J. (2008) Social Identity Theory and Self Categorization Theory: A Historical Review, *Social and Personality Psychology Compass*, 2, pp. 204–22.

Houck, K. D. F. and Loper, A. B. (2002) The Relationship of Parenting Stress to Adjustment Among Mothers in Prison, *American Journal of Orthopsychiatry*, 72, pp. 548–558.

Howard League (2018) *Voice of A Child*, London: Howard League for Penal Reform.

Huebner, B., Dwyer, S. and Hauser, M. (2009) The Role of Emotion in Moral Psychology, *Trends in Cognitive Sciences*, 13(1), pp. 1–6.

Hughes, E. C. (1945) Dilemmas and Contradictions of Status, *American Journal of Sociology*, 50, pp. 353–359.

Jackson, D. and Mannix, J. (2004) Giving Voice to the Burden of Blame: A Feminist Study of Mothers' Experience of Mother Blaming, *International Journal of Nursing Practice*, 10, 150–158.

Jeffries, S. (2002) Does Gender Really Matter? Criminal Court Decision Making in New Zealand, *New Zealand Sociology*, 17(1), pp. 135–149.

Jewkes, Y., Jordan, M., Wright, S. and Bendelow, G. (2019) Designing 'Healthy' Prisons for Women: Incorporating Trauma-informed Care and Practice (TICP) into Prison Planning and Design, *International Journal of Environmental Research and Public Health*, 16(20), 3818.

Jewkes, Y. and Laws, B. (2020) Liminality Revisited: Mapping the Emotional Adaptations of Women in Carceral Space, *Punishment and Society*, pp. 1–19.

Johnston, H. (2019) Imprisoned Mothers in Victorian England, 1853–1900: Motherhood, Identity and the Convict Prison, *Criminology & Criminal Justice*, 19(2), 215–231.

Jordan, S. (2013) *Missing Voices: Why Women Engage With, or Withdraw From, Community Sentences*, London: Griffins Society.

Kaplan, E. A. (1992) *Motherhood and Representation: The Mother in Popular Culture and Melodrama,* Oxford: Routledge.

Keller, J. (2010) Rethinking Ruddick and the Ethnocentrism Critique of Maternal Thinking, *Hypatia,* 25, pp. 834–851.

Kelly, G. A. (1955) *The Psychology of Personal Constructs,* New York: Norton.

Kerrison, E. M. and Bachman, R. (2016) Second-Chance Grandparenting: How A New and Renewed Identity Impacts the Desistance Process, *Across the Spectrum of Women and Crime: Theories, Offending, and the Criminal Justice System,* pp. 225–242.

Kiernan, K., Land, H. and Lewis, J. E. (1998) *Lone Motherhood in Twentieth Century Britain: From Footnote to Front Page,* Oxford: Oxford University Press.

Kincaid, S., Roberts, M. and Kane, E. (2019) *Children of Prisoners: Fixing A Broken System,* Crest Advisory.

Kitzinger S. (1992) *Ourselves as Mothers: The Universal Experience of Motherhood,* New York: Addison-Wesley.

Kitzinger, J. (1994) The Methodology of Focus Groups: The Importance of Interaction Between Research Participants, *Sociology of Health and Illness,* 16(1), pp. 103–121.

Knight, V. (2012) A Study of In-cell Television in A Closed Adult Male Prison: Governing Souls With In-cell Television, Unpublished doctoral thesis, Leicester: De Montfort University.

Knight, V. (2016) Personal Control: Television, Emotion and Prison Life in *Remote Control,* London: Palgrave Macmillan, pp. 121–152.

Knight, V. (2017) *Remote Control: Television in Prison,* Springer.

Lapierre, S. (2008) Mothering in the Context of Domestic Violence: The Pervasiveness of a Deficit Model of Mothering, *Child and Family Social Work,* 13(4), pp. 454–463.

Layder, D. (2004) *Emotion in Social Life: The Lost Heart of Society,* London: Sage.

Layder, D. (2006) *Understanding Social Theory,* London: Sage.

Layder, D. (2012) *Doing Excellent Small-Scale Research,* London: Sage.

Letherby, G. (1994) Mother or Not, Mother or What: Problems of Definition and Identity, *Women's Studies: International Forum,* 17(6), 525–532.

Letherby, G. (1997) Interfertility and Involuntary Childlessness: Definition and Self-Identity, Unpublished doctoral thesis, Staffordshire University.

Letherby, G. (2003) *Feminist Research in Theory and Practice,* Buckingham: Open University Press.

Letherby, G. (2004) Quoting and Counting: An Autobiographical Response to Oakley, *Sociology,* 38(1), pp. 175–189.

Letherby, G. and Zdrodowski, D. (1995) 'Dear Researcher': The Use of Correspondence as a Method within Feminist Qualitative Research, *Gender and Society,* 9(5), pp. 576–593.

Leverentz, A. (2006) The Love of a Good Man? Romantic Relationships As a Source of Support or Hindrance for Female Ex-offenders, *Journal of Research in Crime and Delinquency,* 43, pp. 459–488.

Leverentz, A. (2013) People, Places, and Things: How Female Ex-Prisoners Negotiate their Neighborhood Context in M. Chesney-Lind and L. Pasko (eds.), *Girls, Women, and Crime: Selected Readings,* Thousand Oaks, CA: Sage, pp. 229–250.

Leverentz, A. (2014) *The Ex-Prisoner's Dilemma, How Women Negotiate Competing Narratives of Re-Entry and Desistance,* New Jersey: Rutgers University Press.

Liebling, A. (1999) Doing Prison Research: Breaking the Silence, *Theoretical Criminology,* 3(2), pp. 147–173.

Liebling, A. (2009) Identifying and Measuring Prison Moral Climates in The Correctional Psychologist, *IACFP Quarterly Newsletter,* International Association for Correctional and Forensic Psychology.

Liss, M., Schiffrin, H. and Rizzo, K. (2012) Maternal Guilt and Shame: The Role of Self-Discrepancy and Fear of Negative Evaluation, *Psychological Science,* 5: https://scholar.umw.edu/psychological_science/5

Lockwood, K. (2013) Mothering From the Inside: Narratives of Motherhood and Imprisonment, Doctoral thesis, University of Huddersfield.

Lockwood, K. (2017) Listening to Mum: Narratives of Mothers in Prison in J. Woodiwiss, K. Smith and K. Lockwood (eds.), *Feminist Narrative Research: Opportunities and Challenges,* Hampshire: Palgrave Macmillan.

Lockwood, K. (2018) Disrupted Mothering: Narratives of Mothers in Prison in T. Taylor and K. Bloch (eds.), *Marginalised Mothers, Mothering from the Margins,* Bingley: Emerald Publishing.

Lockwood, K. A. (2020) The Ties That Bind: Stories of Women in Prison Who Are Mothers to Older Adult Children in *Mothering From the Inside: Research on Motherhood and Imprisonment,* Emerald Publishing, pp. 105–125.

Lombroso, C. and Ferrero, G. (1895) *The Female Offender* (Vol. 1), D. Appleton.

Loper, A. B. (2006) How Do Mothers in Prison Differ from Non-Mothers? *Journal of Child and Family Studies,* 15, 82.

Loper, A. B. and Tuerk, E. H. (2006) Parenting Programs for incarcerated Parents: Current Research and Future Directions, *Criminal Justice Policy Review*, 17(4), pp. 407–427.

Loper, A. B. and Tuerk, E. H. (2011) Improving the Emotional Adjustment and Communication Patters of Incarcerated Mothers: Effectiveness of a Prison Parenting Intervention, *Journal of Child and Family Studies*, 20, pp. 89–101.

Maruna, S. and Mann, R. (2019) Reconciling 'Desistance' and 'What Works,' HM Inspectorate of Probation Academic Insights: 1.

Masson, I. (2019) *Incarcerating Motherhood: The Enduring Harms of First Short Periods of Imprisonment on Mothers*, Oxon: Routledge.

Maynard, M. and Purvis, J. (1994) *Researching Women's Lives from a Feminist Perspective*, London: Taylor and Francis.

McCann, C. and Kim, S. Y. (2016) *Feminist Theory Reader: Local and Global Perspectives*, London: Taylor and Francis.

McMahon, M. (2019) No Bail, More Jail? Breaking the Nexus Between Community Protection and Escalating Pre-Trial Detention, Research Paper No. 3, Victoria: Parliamentary Library and Information Service.

McNay, L. (2013) *Gender and Agency: Reconfiguring the Subject in Feminist and Social Theory*, New Jersey: John Wiley and Sons.

McIvor, G. (2004) *Women Who Offend*, London: Jessica Kingsley Publishers.

McIvor, G., Trotter, C. and Sheehan, R. (2009) Women, Resettlement and Desistance, *Probation Journal*, 56(4), 347–361.

Mead, M. (1935) Sex and Temperament in Three Primitive Societies in M. Kimmel (ed.), *The Gendered Reader*, Oxford: Oxford University Press.

Middleton, A. (2006) Mothering Under Duress Examining the Inclusiveness of Feminist Mothering Theory, *Journal of the Association for Research on Mothering*, 8(1, 2), pp. 72–82.

Miller, T. (2008) *Making Sense of Motherhood: A Narrative Approach*, Cambridge: Cambridge University Press.

Miller, J. (2011) Presidential Address, Social Justice Work: Purpose-Driven Social Science, *Social Problems*, 58(1), pp. 1–20.

Ministry of Justice (2018) Female Offender Strategy, London: Ministry of Justice.

Minnaker, J. and Hogeveen, B. (eds.) (2015) *Criminalised Mothers, Criminalised Mothering*, Ontario, Canada: Demeter Press.

Minson, S. (2014) *Mitigating Motherhood: A Study of the Impact on Sentencing Decisions in England and Wales,* Howard League for Penal Reform.

Minson, S. (2018) Evidence on the Sentencing of Mothers, Provided to the All-Party Parliamentary Group Inquiry into the Sentencing of Women, London.

Minson, S. (2018) The Sins and Traumas of Fathers and Mothers should not be Visited on their Children: The Rights of Children when a Primary Carer is Sentenced to Imprisonment in the Criminal Courts in R. Condry and P. S. Smith (eds.), *Prisons, Punishment and the Family: Towards a New Sociology of Punishment?* Oxford: Oxford University Press.

Minson, S. (2019) Direct Harms and Social Consequences: An Analysis of the Impact of Maternal Imprisonment on Dependent Children in England and Wales, *Criminology and Criminal Justice,* 19(5), pp. 519–536.

Minson, S. (2020) *Maternal Sentencing and the Rights of the Child,* Springer Nature.

Minson, S., Nadin, R. and Earle, J. (2015) Sentencing of Mothers: Improving the Sentencing Process and Outcomes for Women with Dependent Children, Discussion Paper, Prison Reform Trust.

Mireault, G. C., Thomas, T. and Brown, B. A. (2002) Maternal Identity Among Motherless Mothers and Psychological Symptoms in their Firstborn Children, *Journal of Child and Family Studies,* 11(3), pp. 287–297.

Moore, L. and Scraton, P. (2014) *The Incarceration of Women; Punishing Bodies, Breaking Spirits,* Hampshire: Palgrave Macmillan.

Moore, L. and Wahidin, A (2018) The Post-Corston Women's Penal Crisis in England and Wales in L. Moore, P. Scraton and A. Wahidin (eds.) (2018) *Women's Imprisonment and the Case for Abolition: Critical Reflections on Corston Ten Years On,* London: Routledge.

Moore, L., Scraton, P., and Wahidin, A. (2018) *Women's Imprisonment and the Case for Abolition: Critical Reflections on Corston Ten Years On,* London: Routledge.

Moran, D., (2013) Between Outside and Inside? Prison Visiting Rooms as Liminal Carceral Spaces, *Geojournal,* 78(2), pp. 339–351.

Morris, A. (1987) *Women, Crime and Criminal Justice,* Oxford: Blackwell.

Morriss, L. (2018) Haunted Futures: The Stigma of Being a Mother Living Apart From Her Child(ren) As A Result of State-ordered Court Removal, *The Sociological Review,* 66 (4), 816–831.

Motz, A., Dennis, M. and Aiyegbusi, A. (2020) *Invisible Trauma: Women, Difference and the Criminal Justice System,* London: Routledge.

Munro, V. (2018) Domestic Violence, Trauma and Vulnerability: Critical Reflections in J. Child and A. Duff (eds.), *Criminal Law Reform Now*, Oxford: Hart.

Murray, J. (2007) The Cycle of Punishment: Social Exclusion of Prisoners and Their Children, *Criminology and Criminal Justice*, 7(1), pp. 55–81.

Murray, J. and Farrington, D. (2005) Parental Imprisonment: Effects on Boys' Antisocial Behaviour and Delinquency Through the Life-Course, *Journal of Child Psychology and Psychiatry*, 46(12), pp. 1269–1278.

Naffine, N. (1997) *Feminism and Criminology*, New Jersey: John Wiley and Sons.

Neyer, G. and Bernardi, L. (2011) Feminist Perspectives on Motherhood and Reproduction, *Historical Social Research/Historische Sozialforschung*, pp. 162–176.

Noakes, L., and Wincup, E. (2004) *Criminological Research: Understanding Qualitative Methods*, London: Sage.

Oakley, A. (1974) *Woman's Work: The Housewife, Past and Present*, USA: Vintage Books.

Oakley, A. (1979) *Becoming a Mother*, Oxford: Martin Robertson.

Oakley, A. (1981) *From Here to Maternity: Becoming a Mother*, Harmondsworth: Penguin.

Oakley, A. (1981) Interviewing Women: A Contradiction in Terms? in H. Roberts (ed.), *Doing Feminist Research*, London: Routledge and Kegan Paul, pp. 30–61.

Oakley, A. (1993) *Essays on Women, Medicine and Health*, Edinburgh: Edinburgh University Press.

Oakley, A. (2016) Interviewing Women Again: Power, Time and the Gift, *Sociology*, 50(1).

Odum, T. C. (2017) Our Journey, Our Voice: Understanding Motherhood and Reproductive Agency in African American Communities Submitted to University of Cincinnati, Unpublished thesis.

O'Malley, S. (2018) The Experience of Imprisonment For incarcerated Mothers and Their Children in Ireland, Doctoral thesis, National University of Ireland: Galway.

O'Malley, S. (2018) *Motherhood, Mothering and the Irish Prison System*, National University of Ireland, Galway.

O'Malley, S. (2019) Matricentric Feminist Criminology in O'Reilly, A. (ed.) (2020) *The Routledge Companion to Motherhood*, Routledge.

O'Malley, S. and Devaney, C. (2016) Maintaining the Mother-Child Relationship Within the Irish Prison System: The Practitioner Perspective, *Child Care in Practice*, 22(1), pp. 20–34.

O'Malley, S. and Devaney, C. (2016) Supporting incarcerated Mothers in Ireland with their Familial Relationships: A Case For the Revival of the Social Work Role, *Probation Journal*, 63(3), pp. 293–309.

O'Neill, J. (2015) Time After Time: A Study of Women's Transition from Custody, Research Paper, 2015/04, The Griffins Society.

Opsal, T. D. (2009) Women on Parole: Understanding the Impact of Surveillance, *Women and Criminal Justice*,19(4), pp. 306- 328.

Opsal, T. D. (2011) Women Disrupting a Marginalised Identity: Subverting the Parolee Identity Through Narrative, *Journal of Contemporary Ethnography*, 40(2), pp. 135–167.

Opsal, T. (2015) It's their World, So You've Just Got to Get Through: Women's Experiences of Parole Governance, *Feminist Criminology*, 10(2), pp. 188–207.

O'Reilly, A. (2004) Introduction in A. O'Reilly, *From Motherhood to Mothering: The Legacy of Adrienne Rich's of Woman Born,* Albany: State University of New York Press.

O'Reilly, A. (2006) *Rocking the Cradle: Thoughts on Motherhood, Feminism and the Possibility of Empowered Mothering Canada,* Demeter Press.

O'Reilly, A. (2010) (Ed) 21st Century Motherhood: Experience, Identity, Policy, Agency, New York: Columbia University Press.

O'Reilly, A. (ed.) (2012) *From Motherhood to Mothering: The Legacy of Adrienne Rich's of Woman Born*, Albany: State University of New York Press.

O'Reilly, A. (2016) *Matricentric Feminism, Theory, Activism and Practice,* Ontario: Demeter Press.

Padel, U. and Stevenson, P. (1988) *Insiders: Women's Experiences of Prison,* London: Virago.

Parker, R. (1995) *Mother Love/Mother Hate: The Power of Maternal Ambivalence*, Basic Books.

Parliamentary Joint Committee on Human Rights (2019) Inquiry Report Published on Children Whose Mothers Are in Prison.

Parsons, T. (1937) *The Structure of Social Action*, New York: McGraw Hill.

Parsons, T. (1955) *Family Structure and the Socialisation of the Child, Family: Socialisation and Interaction Process,* pp. 35–131.

Phillips, A. (1994) Feminism, Equality and Difference in L. McDowell and R. Pringle (eds.) *Defining Women: Social Institutions and Gender Divisions,* Milton Keynes: Open University Press, pp. 197–205.

Piper, A. and Berle, D. (2019) The Association Between Trauma Experienced During Incarceration and PTSD Outcomes: A Systematic Review and Meta-Analysis, *Journal of Forensic Psychiatry and Psychology,* 30(5), pp. 854–875.

Pithouse-Morgan, K., Khau, M., Masinga, L. and Van De Ruit, C. (2012) Letters to Those Who Dare Feel: Using Reflective Letter-Writing to Explore the Emotionality of Research, *International Journal of Qualitative Methods*, 11(1), 40–56.

Pollock, J. M. (1998) *Counselling Women in Prison,* Thousand Oaks, CA: Sage.

Pollak, O. (1950) *The Criminality of Women,* Philadelphia, University of Pennsylvania Press.

Powell, C., Marzano, L. and Ciclitira, K. (2016) Mother—Infant Separations in Prison: A Systematic Attachment-Focussed Policy Review, *Journal of Forensic Psychiatry and Psychology*, pp. 1–16.

Priestley, P. (1999) *Victorian Prison Lives,* London: Pimlico Press.

Prison Reform Trust Bromley Briefings (2019) Prison Fact File Winter Edition: http://www.prisonreformtrust.org.uk/Publications/Factfile

Quinlan, C. (2011) *Inside Ireland's Women's Prisons Past and Present,* Dublin: Ireland Academic Press.

Raikes, B. (2016) Unsung Heroines: Celebrating the Care Provided by Grandmothers for Children with Parents in Prison, *Probation Journal*, 63(3), pp. 320–330.

Raikes, B. and Lockwood, K. (2011) Mothering From the Inside: A Small-Scale Evaluation of Acorn House, An Overnight Child Contact Facility at HMP Askham Grange, *Prison Service Journal*, 3(194), pp. 19–26.

Rees, A., Staples, E. and Maxwell, N. (2017) Evaluation of Visiting Mum Scheme: Final Report, Cardiff: CASCADE.

Reid, M. (1983) Review Article: A Feminist Sociological Imagination. Reading Ann Oakley, *Sociology of Health and Illness,* 5, pp. 83–94.

Reimer, V. and Sahagaian, S. (2015) *The Mother-Blame Game*, Ontario, Canada: Demeter Press.

Renzetti, C. M. (2013) *Feminist Criminology,* Abingdon: Routledge.

Rich, A. (1976) (1995) *Of Woman Born: Motherhood as Experience and Institution,* London: Virago.

Richie, B. E. (2001) Challenges Incarcerated Women Face as they Return to their Communities: Findings from Life History Interviews, *Crime and Delinquency*, 47(3), pp. 368–389.

Rittenour, C. and Colaner, C. (2012) Finding Female Fulfilment: Intersecting Role-based and Morality-based Identities of Motherhood, Feminism, and Generativity as Predictors of Women's Self Satisfaction and Life Satisfaction, *Sex Roles*, 67.

Roberts, D. E. (1993) Motherhood and Crime, *Iowa Law Review*, 79, p. 95.

Rose, N. (1989, 1999) *Governing the Soul: The Shaping of the Private Self*, London: Free Association Books.

Rotkirch, A. (2009) Maternal Guilt, *Evolutionary Psychology*, 8, 90–106.

Rowe, A. (2011) Narratives of Self and Identity in Women's Prisons: Stigma and the Struggle for Self-Definition in Penal Regimes, *Punishment and Society*, 13, pp. 571–591.

Rubin R. (1984) *Maternal Identity and Maternal Experience*, New York: Springer.

Ruddick, S. (1983) Maternal Thinking in J. Trebilcott (ed.) *Mothering: Essays in Feminist Theory*, New Jersey: Rowman and Littlefield.

Ruddick, S. (1989) *Maternal Thinking: Toward a Politics of Peace*, Boston: Beacon Press (Reprinted in 1995).

Ruddick, S. (2002) An Appreciation of Loves Labor, *Hypatia*, 17, pp. 214–224.

Rutter, M. (1972) *Maternal Deprivation Reassessed*, Harmondsworth: Penguin.

Schultz, A. (1972) Choice and the Social Sciences in Lester Embree (ed.) *Life World and Consciousness*, Evanston: North-western University Press, pp. 565–596.

Shammas, V. L. (2017) Pains of Imprisonment in K. R. Kerley (ed.) *The Encyclopaedia of Corrections*, Wiley-Blackwell.

Sharpe, G. (2015) Precarious Identities: 'Young' Motherhood, Desistance and Stigma, *Criminology and Criminal Justice*, 5(4), pp. 407–422.

Sheehan, R. (2014) Women Exiting Prison: Supporting Successful Reintegration in a Changing Penal Climate, *British Journal of Community Justice*, 12(2), pp. 57–66.

Sheehan, R. and Flynn, C. (2007) Women Prisoners and their Children in R. Sheehan, G. McIvor and C. Trotter (eds.) *What Works With Women Offenders?* Devon: Willan.

Sim, J. (2009) *Punishment and Prisons: Power and the Carceral State*, London: Sage.

Sikand, M. (2017), *Lost Spaces: Is the Current Provision for Women Prisoners to Gain a Place in a Prison Mother and Baby Unit Fair and Accessible?* The Griffins Society, University of Cambridge Institute of Criminology.

Slaughter, A. M. (2015) *Why Women Still Can't Have It All* (pp. 84–102), Oneworld.

Smart, C. (1976) *Women, Crime and Criminology: A Feminist Critique*, London: Routledge and Kegan Paul.

Smart, C. (1996) *Deconstructing Motherhood. Good Enough Mothering? Feminist Perspectives on Lone Motherhood*, pp. 37–57.

Snider, L. (2003) Constituting the Punishable Woman: Atavistic Man incarcerates Postmodern Woman, *British Journal of Criminology*, 43, pp. 354–378.

Soffer, M. and Ajzenstadt, M. (2010) The Multidimensionality of 'Pains of Imprisonment' Among Incarcerated Women in Israel, *Women and Health*, 50(6), pp. 491–505.

Sparks, R. (1994) Can Prisons be Legitimate? Penal Politics, Privatization, and the Timeliness of an Old Idea, *British Journal of Criminology*, 34, pp. 14–28.

Stanley, L., and Wise, S. (1983, 1993) *Breaking Out Again: Feminist Epistemology and Ontology*, London: Routledge.

Stewart, P. (2015) A Psychodynamic Understanding of Mothers and Babies in Prison in L. Baldwin (auth/ed.) (2015), *Mothering Justice: Working with Mothers in Criminal and Social Justice Settings,* Sherfield on Loddon: Waterside Press.

Stone, R. (2016) Desistance and Identity Repair: Redemption Narratives as Resistance to Stigma, *British Journal of Criminology*, 56(5), pp. 956–975.

Strozier, A. L., Armstrong, M., Skuza, S., Cecil, D. and Mchale, J. (2011) Co-Parenting in Kinship Families with Incarcerated Mothers: A Qualitative Study, *Families in Society*, 92(1), pp. 55–61.

Stryker, S. and Burke, P. J. (2000) The Past, Present, and Future of An Identity Theory, *Social Psychology Quarterly*, 63, pp. 284–297.

Sutherland, J. (2010) Mothering, Guilt and Shame, *Sociology Compass*, 4(5), pp. 310–321.

Swigart, J. (1991) *The Myth of the Perfect Mother: Parenting Without Guilt*, Chicago: Contemporary Books.

Sykes, G. M. (1958, 2007) *The Society of Captives: A Study of a Maximum-Security Prison*, Princeton University Press.

Takševa, T. (2018) Motherhood Studies and Feminist Theory: Elisions and Intersections, *Journal of the Motherhood Initiative for Research and Community Involvement*, 9(1), pp. 177–194.

Thomsen, T. U. and Sørensen, E. B. (2006) The First Four-Wheeled Status Symbol: Pram Consumption as a Vehicle for the Construction of Motherhood Identity, *Journal of Marketing Management*, 22(9–10), pp. 907–927.

Thurer, S. (1994) *Myths of Motherhood: How Culture Reinvents the Good Mother*, Middlesex: Penguin Books.

Tiger, L. and Fox, R. (1972) Primate Pilgrimage-From Bananas to Ballots, *Psychology Today*, 5(9), P. 23.

Tyler, I. and Slater, T. (2018) Rethinking the Sociology of Stigma, *Sociological Review*, 66(4), pp. 721–743.

Valentine, G. (1998) Sticks and Stones May Break My Bones: A Personal Geography of Harassment, *Antipode*, 30, 303–332. Republished in the *Journal of Lesbian Issues* (2000), 4, 81–113.

Wahidin, A. (2004) *Older Women in the Criminal Justice System: Running Out of Time*, London: Jessica Kingsley.

Walker, T. and Towl, G. (2016) *Preventing Self-injury and Suicide in Women's Prisons*, Sherfield on Loddon: Waterside Press.

Walker, S. and Worrall, A. (2000) Life as A Woman: The Gendered Pains of Indeterminate Imprisonment, *Prison Service Journal*, 132.

Walklate, S. (2001) *Gender, Crime and Criminal Justice*, Devon: Willan.

Warr, J. (2016) The Deprivation of Certitude, Legitimacy and Hope: Foreign National Prisoners and the Pains of Imprisonment, *Criminology and Criminal Justice*, 16(3), pp. 301–318.

Weitzman, N., Birns, B. and Friend, R. (1985) Traditional and Non-traditional Mothers' Communication With their Daughters and Sons, *Child Development*, 56, pp. 894–898.

Wells, J. (2019) This Video Call May Be Monitored and Recorded: Video Visitation as A Form of Surveillance Technology and Its Effect on Incarcerated Motherhood, *Screen Bodies*, 4 (2), pp. 76–92.

West, C. (1996) Goffman in Feminist Perspective, *Sociological Perspectives*, 39(3), pp. 353–369.

Winnicott, D. W. (1987) *Babies and Their Mothers*, Da Capo Press (a collection of Winnicott's essays and presentations between 1957–1970 are presented posthumously).

Wolf, N. (2003) *Misconceptions: Truth, Lies and the Journey to Motherhood*, New York: Doubleday.

Women in Prison (2017) Corston + 10: The Corston Report 10 Years on. How Far Have We Come on the Road to Reform for Women Affected by the Criminal Justice System? Women in Prison and Barrow Cadbury Trust.

Worrall, A. (1990) *Offending Women*, London: Routledge.

Wright, S. (2017) Narratives of Punishment and Frustrated Desistance in the Lives of Repeatedly Criminalised Women in *New Perspectives on Desistance*, pp. 11–35, Hampshire: Palgrave Macmillan.

Zedner, L. (1991) Women, Crime and Penal Responses: A Historical Account, *Crime and Justice*, 14, 307–362.

Zedner, L. (1995), Wayward Sisters: The Prison for Women, *The Oxford History of the Prison*, pp. 328–361.

Zedner, L. (2010) Pre-Crime and Pre-Punishment: A Health Warning: Lucia Zedner Calls for Restraint, *Criminal Justice Matters*, 81(1), pp. 24–25.

Index

Seen & Heard

100 Poems by Parents & Children Affected by Imprisonment

Edited by Lucy Baldwin & Ben Raikes, Foreword by Diane Curry OBE

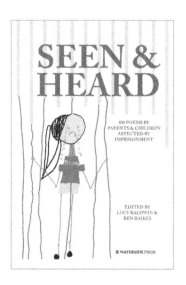

A collection of poems and drawings by parents and children affected by imprisonment in the UK and abroad. They address the thoughts, feelings and beliefs of the authors as they express themselves concerning their emotions and experiences. Over a million children and family members are affected by imprisonment in the UK alone and the poems seek to emphasise the sense of loss, deprivation and isolation involved. They also show resilience—and how enforced separation impacts each and every day of the writer's life.

'These are frank and unsentimental poems as well as skilled and effective ones. Many tell a story briefly and powerfully and if there were a hallmark or collective strength of the anthology it might be authenticity of voice' *Probation Journal.*

Paperback & ebook | ISBN 978-1-909976-42-9 | 172 pages | 2019

Mothering Justice
Working with Mothers in Criminal and Social Justice Settings
Edited by Lucy Baldwin

Written by experts with first-hand experience, *Mothering Justice* was the first whole book to take motherhood as a focus for criminal and social justice interventions. It makes a powerful case that in particular the imprisonment of mothers and its effect on their children is unnecessary, unjust, devastating and wasteful.

'I cannot help but jump around punching the air at this book. It has dared to expose the barriers both in Criminal and Social Justice Areas. Lucy Baldwin et al have delivered a stunning panoramic view of Motherhood ... an eye-opening publication bringing the forces of Mother Nature to the Judiciary and Social Justice'
Criminal Law & Justice Weekly

Paperback & ebook | ISBN 978-1-909976-23-8 | 320 pages | 2015

www.WatersidePress.co.uk